DATE DUE

JE 10 '90			

DEMCO 38-296

Advance praise for *PROSPERITY:*

"Is the United States on the verge of a new golden economic age in which living standards for middle class American families rise more rapidly than they did during the last quarter century and in which family income inequality narrows rather than expands? Bob Davis and David Wessel, two astute, tough-minded observers of the American economy who write for the *Wall Street Journal,* think the answer to this question is yes. In this book they defend their daring and sure to be controversial predictions with both compelling analytical arguments and detailed anecdotal accounts of how individual American families, companies, and communities are already benefiting from the information technology revolution, better educational opportunities, and global competition and growth. *Prosperity* provides a fascinating and thoughtful case for optimism about the effects of the new economy on America's middle class. I hope—and I think—that their case will prove to be right."

> —*Laura D'Andrea Tyson, former chair, President Clinton's Council of Economic Advisers, Class of 1939 Chair in Economics and Business Administration, Haas School of Business, University of California at Berkeley*

"As no one has done before, Davis and Wessel have brilliantly documented how technology, education, and globalization have prepared the ground for middle class prosperity for the next twenty years. This is one of the most important books of the 1990's."

> —*John Naisbitt, author of* Megatrends

"This is an amazing book—it manages to humanize economics without dumbing it down. You may not agree with all of Davis and Wessel's predictions, but this is the best book I've ever seen about how a changing economy affects the lives and work of real people."

> —*Paul Krugman, author of* Peddling Prosperity,
> *professor of economics, MIT*

"Davis and Wessel make a clear and compelling case that it's now possible for America to achieve a broadly-shared prosperity. The jury is still out on whether we will choose to do so."

> —*Robert B. Reich, author of* Locked in the Cabinet,
> *former secretary of labor*

"A refreshingly optimistic view of our economic future based on a highly-readable range of factors, including technology, trade, and education."

—*Frank M. Newman, chairman and CEO, Bankers Trust,*
former deputy secretary of treasury

"Eras of great economic upheaval often carry within themselves the seeds of enhanced opportunity and widespread economic progress. At times of such rapid change, contemporaneous commentary often is shallow and backward looking. *Prosperity* defiantly breaks out of that mold. Whether I agreed or disagreed with the authors, it was well worth digesting their analysis and predictions."

—*Michael J. Boskin, T.M. Friedman Professor of Economics and*
Hoover Institution Senior Fellow, Stanford University;
former chairman, President's Council of Economic Advisors

"This lively, easy read gives us hope for the future. At last, a dose of optimism. This book holds out the exciting prospect of a more just and equal society."

—*Douglas Fraser, former president, United Auto Workers*

"Davis and Wessel have written a cogent, highly readable, and important book. They argue eloquently that all the pieces are in place to ensure America's continued prosperity—particularly for the middle-class. This is an important book for anyone who cares about America's future. I highly recommend it!"

—*David T. Kearns, former chairman and CEO, Xerox Corp.*

"*Prosperity* is a beautifully balanced, grounded exploration of one of the most important topics I can imagine. A must read for those wanting to understand the economic and social fabric of our technological society as we enter the twenty-first century."

—*John Seely Brown, director, Xerox Palo Alto Research Center (PARC)*

PROSPERITY

Prosperity

The Coming Twenty-Year Boom and What It Means to You

BOB DAVIS AND DAVID WESSEL

TIMES BUSINESS

RANDOM HOUSE

Copyright © 1998 by Bob Davis and David Wessel

All rights reserved under International and Pan-American Copyright
Conventions. Published in the United States by Times Books, a
division of Random House, Inc., New York, and simultaneously in
Canada by Random House of Canada Limited, Toronto.

Davis, Bob
    Prosperity : the coming twenty-year boom and what it means to you /
Bob Davis and David Wessel.
      p.   cm.
    Includes bibliographical references and index.
    ISBN 0-8129-2819-9 (alk. paper)
    1. Economic forecasting—United States. 2. United States—
Economic conditions—1981–   I. Wessel, David.
II. Title.
HC 106.82.D38   1998
330.973'001'12—dc21   97-44858
                                           CIP

Random House website address: www.randomhouse.com
Printed in the United States of America on acid-free paper

9 8 7 6 5 4 3 2

To Debbie and Naomi,
for their love and inspiration

Contents

PROSPERITY

1

Broadly Shared Prosperity

Why the middle class will do better in the decades ahead.

Sometimes a careful observer can see something big happening in the economy before it shows up in the official statistics. This is one of those times. The seeds of prosperity are sprouting. The next ten to twenty years will see the flowering of an era of broadly shared prosperity for the American middle class, a contrast to the economic disappointments of the past twenty-five years.

What makes us so sure?

We are newspaper reporters, and this is a book of reporting. We see technology, education, and globalization already shaping our economic future for the better. We have been to factories in Milwaukee, Wisconsin, and offices in Columbus, Ohio, to see workers benefiting as their efficiency improves. We have been to Greenville, South Carolina, and Bangalore, India, to see the gains, and the pains, of international trade. We have been to a community college in Cleveland to see education equipping people for technology-driven jobs, and to the U.S. Army's Fort Knox to see technology simplifying computer-powered tanks so that average high school graduates can use them. We have looked into the past in Newton, Iowa, where Maytag Corporation makes washing machines; examined the present through the eyes of middle-class families in Chattanooga, Tennessee, and explored the future of technology in Silicon Valley and Boston.

Not so long ago, the prognosis for the American middle class seemed bleak. According to popular wisdom, repeated in the press and by politicians, factory workers and middle managers would be downsized out of their middle-class jobs and relegated to flipping burgers at McDonald's or cleaning toilets as outsourced janitors. The top tier—investment bankers, corporate lawyers, heart surgeons, and software geniuses—would enjoy the bounty of the American economy, and everyone else would scrape and claw for what was left over. That isn't going to be America's future. The future is to be welcomed, not feared. Government numbers don't fully show it yet, but the economy is beginning to deliver a better life for middle-class Americans.

Randy Kohrs gives reason to hope. After the video store he had been managing in Cedar Rapids, Iowa, shut in June 1991, he was jobless— again. With only a high school diploma, the 37-year-old Kohrs couldn't find work that paid more than minimum wage, much less a job that offered his family health insurance. He remembers pondering his life insurance policy and thinking, "If I died, all the bills would be paid."

His wife pushed him to check out classes at the local community college. Three years later, he graduated with a degree in respiratory therapy and quickly landed a job at an Iowa City hospital. The job paid twice what his old job had, and came with health insurance. He now has a new car, a new three-bedroom mobile home, and enough money to celebrate his son's twenty-first birthday with a trip to Las Vegas.

Teresa Wooten also shows the opportunities of the coming era. When she was growing up in the dreary milltown of Clinton, South Carolina, she figured the best she could hope for was to be a secretary. For years, she worked at one of the clothing factories that dot South Carolina's Piedmont Mountain region, until the factory started downsizing and threatening to move to Mexico. Teresa didn't become a poster image for those who demonize foreign trade and globalization. The 37-year-old Wooten now supervises brake installers at a German-owned factory that makes BMW Z3 roadsters for customers in the United States and abroad—a tangible reminder that Americans prosper as our economy becomes more international. Wooten makes around $40,000 a year, drives a BMW model 328, and has started saving for retirement and her teenager's education.

The American middle class has been squeezed since 1973, a watershed that divides the years after World War II into two economic epochs. In the

Golden Age, which stretched from 1950 to 1973, the incomes of husbands and wives living at the middle of the middle class doubled, after the effects of inflation are eliminated. In the Age of Anxiety, which stretched from 1973 through 1996, their incomes grew only 15%.

In other words, the income of the typical American married couple rose as much, in percentage terms, in the first *three* years of Lyndon Johnson's presidency as in *twenty* years of Presidents Ford, Carter, Reagan, Bush, and Clinton.

The new American pessimists say that the 60 million or so families in the American middle class don't appreciate how good their lives are, and should accept the painfully slow economic progress of the past ten or twenty years. A spate of books with such baleful titles as *America: Who Stole the Dream?*, *The End of Affluence*, and *The Good Life and Its Discontents* delivered a message to Americans that the economy's best days are over and they should stop whining about it. "We cannot, or at least should not, blame ourselves for the impermanence of a Golden Age. We have to get over it," British-born journalist Michael Elliott writes, in one of the cheerier books on America's economy, *The Day Before Yesterday: Reconsidering America's Past, Rediscovering the Present.*

Elliott and his ilk are wrong. The three big forces of future prosperity—technology, education, and globalization—will make the next twenty years better for American middle-class families. Here's why:

- The pace of economic progress will quicken. The $2 trillion invested in computer and communications technology since 1973 will finally produce faster economic growth and more rapidly rising living standards. For the past twenty years, American businesses and workers have stumbled as they tried to use successive generations of computers to improve efficiency; in the next two decades, they will master the new networked computers and unleash a surge in productivity.

- This new prosperity will be widely shared, helping millions of Americans who thus far have been pushed to the sidelines in the high-tech economy. The forces that have widened the chasm between more educated and less educated workers will be reversed. Community colleges, the unheralded aid stations of American education, will help millions move from $7-an-hour jobs to $17-an-hour jobs. And technology will become easier to use, opening to many more Americans jobs now reserved for educated elites.

• Globalization, seen as a threat to middle-class prosperity by many workers and by politicians as different as Richard Gephardt and Pat Buchanan, will prove to be a boon. The pain caused when imports put Americans out of work will be offset by bigger gains from trade. New and better jobs will be created by U.S. companies that export to developing countries that were once too poor to buy anything made in America, and by foreign companies that build plants and offices in the United States. American consumers will benefit from cheaper and better imported goods. The United States will prosper alongside India and China as their huge populations climb into the ranks of global middle-class consumers.

Middle class is an elastic concept in American discourse. It is used to describe everyone who earns more than a McDonald's cashier but less than Microsoft's Bill Gates. In Washington, middle class seems to describe everyone who makes as much as a congressman, even though the current $136,700 salary puts a Representative's family among the best-paid 5% of Americans. Statistically, the typical middle-class American family is a married couple living at the median income—$49,700 in 1996. Half of all American couples have higher incomes, and half live below the median. This book primarily focuses on the future of American families whose incomes are between $35,000 and $75,000 a year—roughly, four of every ten families. This book isn't about the poor or the rich, but about the bulk of Americans who live in between.

We have in mind people like Jim and Ann Marie Blentlinger, a hardworking, churchgoing young couple in Chattanooga, Tennessee. Jim and Ann Marie have two children, two jobs, two cars, two televisions, and a three-bedroom house. Jim, a graduate of the local community college, has had four jobs in three years, and is now using a computer to design the interiors of buildings for a local engineering firm. Ann Marie is a public-school teacher, though she sometimes thinks she would rather be staying home with her kids. Working two jobs, Jim and Ann Marie wonder why they aren't living twice as well as couples were a generation ago, when only the husband brought home a paycheck. They wonder why other young Chattanoogans living in mountaintop houses overlooking the city are doing so much better. They quietly hope that Ann Marie's parents will be willing to help them with their mounting bills.

Despite their worries, people like the Blentlingers and their children will be winners in the economy of the next twenty years as technology, education, and globalization combine to improve their income and standard of living. We concentrate on married couples like the Blentlingers because they still represent the dominant, even if shrinking, share of the American population. The Census Bureau says 56% of all Americans over 18 are now living with their spouses, and 69% of children under 18 are living with both parents. We also focus on married couples because if the American economy can't deliver a rising standard of living for them, it won't do so for the single mom, the young man who can't read, or the child who is trapped in the violence and despair of an inner city. A rising standard of living for the middle class won't eliminate drugs, crime, fear, rotting inner cities, or children mired in poverty. This book isn't about those problems, as severe as they are. But America will have neither the will nor the wallet to eradicate social blight unless its middle class lives better.

In this book, we try to unravel a number of mysteries, especially why living standards have grown so slowly during an era of revolutionary technological change. We have looked at the past to see what we could learn about the future. A century ago, electricity was America's great technological hope. Enthusiasts predicted electricity would revolutionize factories and homes, and would lift the living standards of everyone. Eventually, it did just that, but it took decades longer than experts predicted. Technology changes at dizzying speeds, but people and organizations don't—a lesson that is relevant to today's computer industry.

Dusty factory records at Maytag Corporation, and interviews with veterans of Maytag's first decades as a washing-machine maker tell the story. For years, manufacturers built factories that now seem laughably inefficient. Machine tools were powered by leather belts connected to a central shaft that ran the length of a factory ceiling. To turn on a single machine, a foreman literally had to turn on an entire factory. By 1900, engineers had invented a better way: equipping machine tools with small electric motors. Workers could proceed at their own pace, and energy was conserved. But it took until 1925—decades after the birth of electric technology—before Maytag and many other manufacturers understood how best to use the new power source and reorganized their workplaces. "It all takes time to change people's ideas and attitudes," says Thomas Smith, Maytag's former chief of research and development, who started work at Maytag in 1926.

The same goes for computers. In the mid-1970s, industry analysts predicted that the personal computer would soon lead to paperless offices and robotic workplaces. Billions of dollars were invested in making those visions come true—and billions were wasted. Just as with electric technology, managers needed decades to learn how best to use computer technology and reorganize workplaces for efficient production.

This frustrating period of education is nearing completion. Companies are learning how to use technology not simply to automate old ways of doing business, but to find new ways that make their workers more productive. In Atlanta, insurance broker Mark Swank taps into a global computer network to find information gathered by thousands of other brokers who work for the insurance firm of Johnson & Higgins. Using the network, Swank queries brokers around the world and digs into reports once hoarded by the firm's New York headquarters. When Swank was drafting a proposal to restructure insurance for the international operations of bottler Coca-Cola Enterprises Inc., the best advice came, via computer, from a broker in France—someone Swank had never met.

Figuring out how to use computers more wisely will help boost productivity and living standards, but that isn't the only reason to be optimistic. Figuring out how to use people more wisely will contribute as well. Beneath all the management fads and buzzwords that are so easy to ridicule, successful American businesses and workers are changing the organization of the workplace—and improving efficiency in the process. Miller Brewing Company's brewery in Trenton, Ohio, a small town in southern Ohio's factory belt, makes 50% more beer per worker than Miller's next most productive brewery, which has essentially the same equipment. The trick—easier to describe than to achieve—is to rely heavily on teams of well-trained workers to run the brewery without supervisors constantly looking over their shoulders. This is more than the latest management fad; this reorganization of the workplace is a major avenue to faster growth in productivity.

Productivity—the goods and services produced from each hour's work—is crucial to improving the lot of the middle class. Increasing productivity means making more stuff for less effort. Growth in productivity is the reason we have more and better things than our grandparents did. Disappointing growth in productivity is a major reason the middle class has fared so poorly over the past quarter-century. And faster growth in productivity is a big reason the middle class will do better. "Productivity isn't everything, but in the long run, it's almost everything," economist Paul Krugman of the Massachusetts Institute of Technology has said. "To a pretty close approximation, the rate of growth of our living standard equals the rate of growth of our domestic productivity. Period."

From World War II to 1973, productivity grew at a brisk 2.7% a year, doubling living standards in twenty-five years. But, for reasons that remain unclear, productivity has grown by only 1.0% a year since 1973; at that rate, it will take nearly 70 years to double living standards.

These days, productivity has a bad reputation. Corporate executives boast of "productivity gains" when they fire people, battle unions, and downsize. But, for the economy as a whole, a gain in productivity is terrific news. Improved productivity may reduce employment at a particular company, but it boosts employment and living standards economy-wide. Unemployment was much lower in the 1950s and 1960s, when productivity was rising faster than at any other time in the post-World War II years.

Agriculture is a good example of how greater productivity benefits America overall, despite the pain and dislocation that can accompany it. In 1800, it took an American farmer 344 hours to produce 100 bushels of corn. A century later, it took 147 hours. By 1980, it took only *three* hours of work. Richer land was farmed, better machinery was used, and labor-saving techniques were adopted. Fewer workers were needed to feed a larger population. The percentage of Americans working on farms, which was about 75% of the labor force in 1800 and about 40% in 1900, has fallen to less than 3% today.

This transformation staggered farmers from the 1880s through the Great Depression. Many could no longer make a living cultivating the land their parents had left them. Many didn't live as well as they once had. Many were forced to sell their homesteads, move to the city, and take up dirty and dangerous factory work. "There is something radically wrong," a leading farm journal's editor wrote in the 1890s, an era when the pace of change was as frightening as it is today. "There is a screw loose. Manufacturing enterprises never made more money and were in a more flourishing condition, and yet agriculture languishes."

Collectively, today's Americans are better off. We have food to spare, which we trade with other nations to get VCRs and oil. With fewer people on farms, we have freed workers to do things unimagined by our nineteenth-century ancestors, from etching semiconductors to teaching toddlers in nursery schools. We consume as many or more calories and as much protein as Americans did in 1900, yet we spend far less time working to buy food. We would have more farm jobs if we turned back the clock and undid two centuries of improved farm productivity. But few of us would choose living conditions circa 1800 over today's.

The same logic applies to manufacturing. In 1950, an average factory worker turned out $19 worth of goods, measured in today's dollars, for each hour on the job. In 1996, an average hour's factory work produced $61 worth of goods. This threefold increase in productivity has made possible higher wages, better health benefits, bigger profits, and higher stock prices. Had productivity remained at 1950 levels, we might have three times as many factory jobs as we do today, but, for three times as much work, we wouldn't have one more thing to consume or sell. It would be as if every worker in every U.S. factory worked three shifts instead of one, but didn't produce any more goods and didn't take home any more money.

When economy-wide productivity rises, wages rise too. Sometimes, it takes a while for wages to catch up with productivity gains, but they do eventually. All workers benefit, even those whose individual productivity hasn't improved. Think about barbers. A barber cuts, perhaps, three heads of hair an hour—no more than a barber did in 1898. Barbers' productivity hasn't increased at all, but their wages have increased. Why? If barbers were still being paid what they were paid in 1898, no one would work as a barber. People will stay in the hair-cutting trade only if they make roughly as much as they would make in some other job. So, as the overall level of wages in the economy rises, barbers' wages rise, too.

We expect productivity to grow at least a half-percentage point faster over the next two decades than the approximate annual increase of 1% a year during the past two decades. That rate of growth will lift the living standards of American families across the board. What will push productivity into high gear? Computer technology, the reorganization of work, and the improved education of workers will, as we elaborate later in this book. A half-percentage gain won't return the United States to the pace of productivity gains in the Golden Age, but it would be the biggest economic story in a generation. It would make a huge difference.

Here's one way to look at it. If the economy chugs along as it has been doing, with 1% annual growth in productivity, the income of the typical married couple would grow from around $49,700 in 1996 to around $60,650 in 2016. Add another half-percentage point of productivity growth, and the couple would make an additional $6,000 in 2016. That's $6,000 more—measured in today's dollars so that the comparisons aren't distorted by inflation—for every American family without a minute's more work. To middle-class families, $6,000 a year is eight months' worth of mortgage payments on the typical newly purchased single-family home.

Or think, as many Americans do, about the prospects that Social Security will go bust when the baby boomers start retiring. If productivity and wages grow a half-percentage point faster than Social Security's experts have assumed, the fifty-year price tag for fixing Social Security will be cut by more than a third—without any change in tax rates, benefit formulas, or the retirement age.

"Yes," comes the frequent rejoinder to promises about faster economic growth, "but Alan Greenspan and other officials at the inflation-obsessed Federal Reserve will never let the economy grow that fast." Not so. The Fed will welcome and nourish a productivity-led growth spurt.

To a degree unappreciated by the public, the Fed's powerful chairman is convinced that productivity will quicken in the years ahead. Although Greenspan's every comment on the current state of the economy is scrutinized for clues to the next jiggle in interest rates, his emphatic optimism about the future of the U.S. economy gets less attention than it deserves. Greenspan is scanning the horizon for hints of inflation, but he is looking almost as intently for the rise in productivity trends that he forecasts with increasing confidence.

Faster productivity growth by itself would be a big boost to the middle class. But we see another development that will have equally profound consequences: a narrowing of the gap between well-heeled Americans and those in the middle of the middle class.

The wage gap between the top earners and the rest of America's workers has grown steadily wider since the 1970s. Some predict it will get wider still, and a small platoon of workers with choice jobs will retreat into guarded, gated communities while the rest of America stagnates. In that view, the middle class will wither. But we expect a far different and better outcome as the supply of educated workers increases and the appetite of employers for ever-more-skilled workers diminishes. The widening income inequality that has distinguished the past twenty years comes in many forms and has many causes. Divorce and unwed motherhood have created a growing number of single-parent, single-paycheck families at the bottom of the economy. Marriages of well-paid professional men and well-paid professional women have created a growing number of well-off families at the top. A new willingness to pay extraordinary salaries to superstars—in music, sports, television, investment banking, law, medicine—has created a small but highly visible super-rich elite.

Ultimately, though, most Americans live on their paychecks, and the root of discomforting inequality can be found in wage disparities. Among the most important factors driving inequality has been employers' growing demand for educated workers, at a time when there is a glut of unskilled workers. That drives up the wages of the educated, and drives down the wages of the less educated.

This won't persist. Now that wages for workers with a college education have risen far above those of workers who finish only high school, more Americans are deciding to go to college—and many others are going to community colleges. The two-year schools often are derided as destinations for people not smart enough, motivated enough, or rich enough to go to four-year colleges. That's an outdated image. The nation's 1,100 community colleges have evolved into institutions that successfully give workers the skills that employers need.

Sue LaPorati was 24 years old, divorced, raising two preschool children, and working in a checkout line of a Cleveland supermarket when her union threatened to call a strike. "I went home that night and said, 'This is ridiculous. I can't survive like this.' Like Mom always told me: I should go to college." The union didn't strike, but in the fall of 1988 she enrolled anyway at Cuyahoga Community College, known locally as Tri-C. Living on a $6-an-hour part-time job at the supermarket, child-support payments, and food stamps, LaPorati spent six years as a part-time student, shored up along the way by a Tri-C program for "displaced homemakers"—women who are divorced, widowed, or separated.

LaPorati tapped the program for books, and got federal grants to cover most of her tuition. Her children went to a federally funded Head Start preschool, and often spent weekends with their father while she worked at the supermarket. At Tri-C, LaPorati stumbled into an introductory computer course and was hooked. She completed an associate degree in computer studies in 1994, and two years later finished a bachelor's degree in business at a local private college. Even before graduating from Tri-C, she got a part-time computer job at Allied Signal Corporation. She now works there full-time, monitoring on her desktop computer the prices her company charges for its truck brakes. She earns $30,000 a year. "I'm not complaining," she says with more than a little understatement. "Tri-C was a very good stepping stone for me."

Community colleges will help increase the pool of well-trained workers over the next decade, by offering graduates a way to prosper and by easing the shortage of trained workers that has pushed their wages far above those of high school graduates. Education promotes equality by increasing the supply of the most desired workers. College and high school graduates alike will enjoy rising wages; improving productivity will see to that. But wages of high school graduates will rise more rapidly than wages of their college-educated counterparts because employers won't have to pay quite as much of a premium for education as they do today. The wage gap will narrow, and prosperity will be more widely shared.

Think of two teams of mountain climbers scaling a peak. The first team, already high up on the mountain, represents college-educated workers. The second team, stumbling at the base of the mountain, represents workers with high school diplomas. In the era of broadly shared prosperity, the college team will continue to climb higher, but the high school trekkers will finally head upward too, and will reduce the distance between them and their college-educated peers.

Another reason to expect a narrower wage gap is that the appetite of employers for highly skilled workers won't continue to grow as voraciously as it has in recent years. For the past quarter-century, computers have undermined the wages of low-skilled workers and enhanced the wages of those who can master the machines. Technology has led employers to demand better-trained workers who are agile at solving problems. Americans who use computers at work earn close to 20%

more than those who don't, according to an influential analysis by Princeton University labor economist Alan Krueger.

But computers also have the potential to make less skilled workers more productive and more desirable. That's happening already. Grocery clerks once had to be able to add and subtract in their heads. Later, they had to have nimble fingers to punch the cash register keys. With modern scanners, they simply have to position bar codes on packages over a red laser light.

Today, much of the push to simplify technology comes from those working with the handicapped and from the military, whose machinery must be designed so that it can be used by ordinary young Americans. Simplified technologies designed for these special users then spread throughout the economy. Text scanners, for instance, were created so that books could be entered into computer databanks and read to the blind; now, they make it possible for people who can't type to enter data into a computer. Voice-recognition technology was designed, in part, as a way for those without the use of their hands or eyes to run computers; by eliminating the keyboard, the technology will make computers easier for others to use, too. Army tank designers are pioneering ways to simplify software so high school graduates can operate increasingly sophisticated computer-controlled devices; civilian computer designers are sure to catch on soon.

Faster economic growth in the 1990s offers tantalizing evidence that growth itself will help reduce inequality, even though it didn't do so during the 1980s. To the rule that economic expansions boost wages and job prospects for the worst-paid Americans, and foster equality, the 1980s may have been an unhappy exception.

In Davidson Plyforms Inc.'s cavernous factory in a modern industrial park on the outskirts of Grand Rapids, Michigan, a hearty economy and a very low unemployment rate are paying off for men and women with few skills. With high-powered vacuums sucking up the sawdust, woodworkers, many of them Hispanic, feed sheets of plywood veneer into presses, and shape the plywood into chair seats for office furniture. In 1995, Davidson lost a remarkable 43% of its workers to turnover, mostly because workers found it so easy to get jobs elsewhere. Turnover in a factory is expensive; recruiting and screening applicants is costly, and new workers don't work as efficiently as experienced ones.

With business booming among Grand Rapids manufacturers and with fierce competition for workers, Davidson raised the $7-per-hour starting wage to $8 an hour in the summer of 1997, and improved the company's performance-bonus plan. Just as important, it stepped up its effort to groom supervisors and "leadmen" from the production ranks, and it methodically improved worker training—steps that will brighten the future earnings prospects for the company's low-wage workers. If sustained, this recipe—robust economic growth, a low unemployment rate, higher wages for the worst paid, more training for the least skilled—holds enormous promise for workers who have been left behind for the past twenty-five years.

Along with technology and education, a third big factor affects the well-being of the American middle class: globalization. Foreign trade is blamed for everything that has gone wrong for the U.S. economy over the past quarter-century, especially for destroying jobs in American factories. Trade often is accused of widening the gap between the wages of those at the top and those at the bottom, but technology has done far more than trade to worsen wage inequality. Overall, the United States greatly benefits from global trade and investment, which bring Americans jobs, better and cheaper goods, and a higher standard of living than they otherwise would enjoy.

If any place in the United States should be complaining about globalization, it would seem to be Greenville, South Carolina, a long-time garment and textile center, in a state where imports have eliminated about one-third of apparel jobs since 1986. But Greenville is prospering precisely *because of* the growth of the global economy. Tiny South Carolina attracts as much foreign investment as all of the giant nation of India does, and much of that investment ends up in Greenville and nearby Spartanburg. German, Japanese, and Swiss-owned factories are now welcome in an area once known for its hostility toward outsiders. To meet the foreign firms' exacting demands, local suppliers are increasing productivity and expanding exports. As a result, wages have risen throughout the region. At Spartanburg Steel Products Inc., a local firm that stamps out auto body parts for BMW and Toyota, workers get productivity bonuses averaging about $1 an hour, on top of the $11-an-hour base pay, when they exceed production and quality standards.

Americans who fear international trade look at places like Bangalore, a burgeoning center for software programming in southern India, and fret that the low wages paid to programmers there will undercut wages paid in America. Some American programmers will surely lose out to competition from Bangalore, but the threat of low-wage foreign competition is greatly overstated. American wages and technological panache lure the best of Bangalore's talent to move to the United States, and Bangalore's software houses are largely left doing the dull work Americans don't want to bother with anyway.

At the same time, as Bangalore and other third world boomtowns prosper, they become better markets for American wares. In Milwaukee, about 100 General Electric Company factory workers, each earning about $45,000 a year, are building ultrasound machines to ship to Indian village hospitals and to other markets in developing nations.

For all the reasons we've mentioned, we are confident that living standards for the middle class will improve. But we aren't cocky; predicting the economic future is a hazardous vocation, and experts often get it wrong. Many social scientists predicted that World War II would be followed in America by a depression instead of a boom. Few economists anticipated in the mid-1960s that the civil rights movement would produce significant gains for African Americans.

Forecasting the impact of technology isn't any easier. Thirteen years before their flight at Kitty Hawk, Wilbur Wright told his brother Orville that humans wouldn't fly for fifty years. In 1941, Simon Kuznets, a Nobel laureate in economics, argued that "the cumulative effect of technical progress in a number of important industries has brought about a situation where further progress of similar scope cannot be reasonably expected" and that "economic effects of further [technological] improvements will necessarily be more limited than in the past." The invention of the transistor, the personal computer, genetically engineered drugs, lasers, space satellites, and nuclear power made hash of that prediction.

Many gloomy predictions are simply extrapolations of the recent past, a technique that never captures the historic moments when an economy changes direction. We go beyond extrapolation to predict a turn in the economy that will have long-lasting benefits for the majority of Americans. The United States inevitably will suffer again from recession. The stock market will not rise inexorably every day for the next twenty years. But that's not what matters. The trajectory of the American middle class, at long last, has turned upward.

We take a hardheaded attitude toward future-gazing. It has taken decades for the forces of technology, education, and globalization to begin to improve living standards for middle-class Americans. If we're right, evidence of the changes that will dominate the economy of the next two decades should be visible today, not just in the nation's technology centers, but in quieter places around the nation. That principle has guided our travels, and has taken us to steamy Southern cities and frosty Midwestern towns far from the coastal centers of innovation. We're heartened by what we have found. The forces we're writing about already are transforming even small cities in the heartland of America. "The future is out there in small pieces that you can see right now," says Ramana Rao, chief technologist at InXight Software Inc., a Silicon Valley company developing ways to simplify computers.

This book is divided into three sections. In the first section, The Past, we describe the reassuring parallels with the early years of the twentieth century, a time of slow economic growth and widening inequality that was followed by a burst of innovation and prosperity. In the second section, The Present, we trace the rise of the American middle class after World War II, the strains of the Age of Anxiety, and the puzzling failure of computer technology to produce more prosperity in recent years. In the third section, The Future, we look ahead to show how the combined effect of computers, education, and globalization already are beginning to create an Age of Broadly Shared Prosperity.

PAST

2

Looking Back to Look Ahead

Lessons from the beginning of the twentieth century.

The world marked the opening of the twentieth century with a spectacular fair, The International Universal Exposition in Paris, an extravaganza unrivaled in scope or ambition by any other that followed. The exposition drew more than 50 million admissions in 1900—an extraordinary number, considering that the population of France at the time was only 40 million. Into 350 acres along the Seine, the organizers packed pavilions with exhibits ranging from a champagne bottle as tall as a house to an opportunity to look at the moon through the world's biggest telescope. It was an occasion for national boosterism as well as the promotion of technological innovation. The fair was the first to display large numbers of automobiles—the French auto industry being advanced for the time—and it showcased the latest breakthroughs in "wireless telegraphy" and X rays.

Back then, a world's fair was a way for the farsighted and the bold to look into the distant future; it was the equivalent of Walt Disney World's Epcot, Carl Sagan's television specials, futuristic science-fiction movies, and computer simulations all rolled into one grand event. For a farsighted perspective, nothing matched the prescience of the Paris exposition's organizers when they put so much emphasis on electricity, a technology that would transform the world economy and the way people lived.

The Paris exposition later would be remembered for its celebration of the potential uses of electricity, in no small part because of the florid writings of historian Henry Adams, a descendant of two U.S. presidents. "It is a new century, and what we used to call electricity is its God," he wrote, overwhelmed and terrified by what he saw in Paris. On display were switches and meters, transformers and rheostats, arc lamps and desk lamps, an electrically powered moving sidewalk, an electric cigar lighter, electric hair curlers, and an "electro-magnet for extracting metallic substances from the human eye." Electric spotlights cast beams across the Paris sky at night, a novelty when electric lighting was almost exclusively used indoors.

The organizers didn't emphasize it, but careful visitors to Paris in 1900 might also have discovered a second key to the prosperity of the twentieth century: education. Overlooked by subsequent recollections, and not nearly as captivating to fair-goers as the moving sidewalk, was the celebration of the ambitious American school system. "Everyone who is familiar with the education system of the United States refers to it as more practical than any other national system," the French director of primary education wrote to the Americans who planned the exhibit. "We hope that you will send to Paris an exhibit containing an explanation of this word 'practical.'" So, in nine-foot-high cabinets of highly finished oak, dozens of local school boards posted photographs, report cards, and samples of students' work, from kindergarten—still a curiosity—to elite universities. New York City sent three-minute movies showing fire drills, morning assemblies, lab work, and kindergarten classes. Each was accompanied by a phonograph that played the appropriate soundtrack.

New York City, Albany, Newark, Chicago, Denver, and several towns in Massachusetts sent descriptions of their high schools, a distinctly American institution. Somerville, Massachusetts, displayed photos of its Latin High School and an 1899 yearbook describing English High School "in all its cosmopolitan branches from art to science, from study to laboratory." English High was a forerunner of high schools that were later to spread throughout America. Hailed by the local school committee when it opened in 1895 as the "college of the people," the school offered what was seen as a practical education for teenagers who would go to work, not to college, after graduating. English High students studied modern languages, instead of Latin or

Greek, and were offered courses such as mechanical drawing, cooking, and bookkeeping.

The displays at the Paris exposition of 1900 offer some profoundly encouraging lessons. The painfully slow evolution of electricity from a curiosity to an engine of economic growth foreshadowed the evolution of computers. Similarly, the development of high schools into educational institutions for children of the working class foreshadowed the evolution of today's community colleges, which are improving the fortunes of lesser-skilled workers. The parallels aren't perfect, but they are heartening. "It isn't as though we are going through a change that is unprecedented," says Claudia Goldin, an economic historian at Harvard University who has studied the period and its modern implications.

In ways that echo today, America was both a successful and a troubled nation at the beginning of the twentieth century. For the wealthy, the economy was thriving. American industrial might was embodied in the oil, steel, and rail empires ruled by men like John D. Rockefeller, Andrew Carnegie, and J. P. Morgan. American warships and trading vessels steamed into Asian ports. Around 1890, the United States passed Britain as the world's most productive economy, a position it still maintains.

But the changes were so great, the pace so quick, that many Americans were unnerved. The 1890s were marked by violent labor strikes and a surge of populism. An episode of speculative pressure on the U.S. dollar forced the President of the United States to turn to J. P. Morgan to rescue the currency—because the world had more confidence in Morgan than in the U.S. government. And the flow of immigrants from the poorest corners of Europe increased substantially, adding to the nation's vitality, but depressing wages for workers who competed with the new arrivals.

American intellectuals saw worrisome signs. Historian Frederick Jackson Turner warned that the closing of the frontier ended the source of all that made America great. Henry Adams grieved over the crumbling of the nineteenth-century order: "I can already see that the fellow who gets to 1950 will wish he hadn't," he wrote to his son from Paris in 1900.

Upton Sinclair, in his 1906 novel *The Jungle*, stripped the facade from Chicago's food-processing plants, not to campaign for food safety but to expose the stomach-churning reality of working people's lives. "There are learned people who can tell you out of the statistics that beef boners make forty cents an hour," he wrote, "but, perhaps these people have never looked into a beef boner's hands. . . . Your hands are slippery, and your knife is slippery, and you are toiling like mad, when somebody happens to speak to you, or you strike a bone. Then your hand slips up on the blade, and there is a fearful gash. And that would not be so bad, only for the deadly contagion. The cut may heal, but you never can tell." The only solution, according to Sinclair, was socialism.

The doomsayers of 1900 were wrong, of course, and Upton Sinclair's prescription was especially wrong. Over the next 30 years, the American people prospered as changes in technology and education spread and living standards rose. In 1900, only 3% of American homes had electric lights and 15% had flush toilets. Washing machines, radios, and automobiles were rare. By 1930, two-thirds of American homes had electric lights and half had flush toilets. One of every four households owned a washing machine, four in ten had radios, and six in ten owned a car. Life improved in other ways too. The percentage of babies who died before their first birthday was halved in the first three decades of the century. Baby boys born in 1931 grew to be 2.2 inches taller than boys born in 1900, a simple way to gauge the quality of life and adequacy of diet. "Big business in America," muckraking journalist Lincoln Steffens wrote in 1929, in what might be seen as a response to Upton Sinclair, "is producing what the Socialists held up as their goal: food, shelter and clothing for all."

The period ended, of course, with the worst crisis in American capitalism. The Great Depression is an awesome reminder of the damage that misguided government economic policies can do. But that isn't the only lesson to learn from the "prosperity decade" of the 1920s, a time of impressive economic growth, improving productivity, rising wages, and better living standards.

In retracing the history of that time—the gradual but far-reaching impact of electricity and the remarkable impact of high schools—we see encouraging parallels to our own time. We see hope for the American middle class.

In 1900, Newton, Iowa, was a town of about 3,500. The pioneers who settled it were joined later by German and Dutch immigrants, and by freed and runaway slaves. Looking around turn-of-the century Newton, you would have seen life changing in ways that mirrored changes around the country. In 1897, irked by mud so deep that it took six horses to pull an empty wagon, the town leaders proposed paving the main roads, and used the improbable slogan, "Eat, drink and be merry for tomorrow we pave." There are differing accounts, but the first automobile was spotted in Newton on either the Fourth of July 1899 or the Fourth of July 1902. Residential electric-light service was inaugurated around 1896. Frederick L. Maytag, a prosperous and politically powerful Newton manufacturer of farm equipment, noticed that a competitor had just begun to make hand-operated washing machines in the slack season. Newton's three-year high school awarded its first three diplomas in 1875; by 1900, it was a four-year school with about 90 students, nearly all of whom were preparing for college.

Then, as now, Newton was a medium-size town, not even a major population center in Iowa, let alone a dark urban circle on a map of America. What was happening in Newton was happening elsewhere in America, though. As the next two chapters detail, Newton's past is a way to see how electricity and high schools changed the American economy and the way Americans lived.

3

Plugged In

What the evolution of electricity says about the computer age.

To understand the power of personal computers to speed economic growth at the start of the twenty-first century, it is critical to understand how electricity lifted the economy at the start of the twentieth century. Two lessons are clear. New technology enhances productivity and growth, and it takes decades for powerful innovations, like electricity or computers, to fulfill their potential. The good news: After thirty years of experimentation, America is on the cusp of a computer-powered productivity surge, just as America was on the cusp of an electricity-powered growth spurt a century ago. To learn what's ahead, let's first look back.

The electric age was young in 1876, when two small electric generators were used to power a bright lamp in the corner of an exhibit hall at the Centennial Exposition in Philadelphia. "What curiosities," spectators remarked. Six years later, Thomas Edison built the first electric utility, which lit up Wall Street using generators so huge they were nicknamed "Jumbo," after a circus elephant. Around the same time, an Edison protégé invented electric motors.

Electric lingo quickly became part of American culture. People were "plugged in" to the changes, which they found "electrifying"; they "made the connection" between new technology and their futures. Electric generators were dubbed "dynamos," a shortened version of "dynamoelectric machine," and became synonymous with verve and energy. Stock traders in London bid up the shares of new electric companies, prompting the *Economist,* in 1882, to warn against speculative fever. In 1901, the Sears, Roebuck catalog promoted an electric belt that wrapped around the waist and scrotum to revive sexual powers through "vitalizing, soothing current." Scads of inventors tried to patent electric-powered perpetual-motion machines—until 1911, when the U.S. Patent Office required that patent applications had to be accompanied by working models. Theodore Dreiser summed up the hopes of the era in his 1900 novel *Sister Carrie,* when his protagonist arrives in electrified Chicago, brilliant in the night. "The streets, the lamps, the lighted chamber set for dining are for me," wrote Dreiser, speaking for a generation of rural youth coming to the city.

But the enthusiasm for electricity didn't translate quickly into broad economic gain, nor did it rapidly change the way most people worked. Not until the 1920s did many American factories learn how to use electricity effectively. When they did, electricity released a productivity surge that lifted the economy and increased workers' incomes. That's evident in Newton, Iowa, which established itself as a manufacturing center early in the new century.

In 1900, Maytag Corporation opened two factories in Newton to build farm equipment. Both were two stories high and electric-powered. Precise descriptions of the buildings don't survive, but if they were typical of the time, big electric motors turned a steel shaft, three inches or so in diameter, that was suspended from the ceiling and ran the length of the building. Leather belts, mounted on pulleys, connected the rotating shaft to a variety of jigs, lathes, grinders, and other machine tools. Oil cans, perched high above, continuously dripped lubrication on the shaft and into the factory air. The place was hellishly hot, jet-engine noisy, and Marx Brothers inefficient. To turn on any single machine, the giant shaft had to be powered up. Machines had to be regularly shut down when their leather belts snapped. Production was intermittent; work was dangerous.

"One fellow was machining on one of these huge lathes," recalls Ed McCardell, who worked in the 1920s at a Newton factory that used shafts and belts. "The poor devil got his clothes caught [in the belt system]. It was whirling this guy around. Fortunately, it didn't kill him, but it broke him all up. He was no good from then on."

A 46-year Maytag veteran, Harry Vance, remembers the shaft-and-belt layout. Machines were "lined up from one end of the shop to the other, with a big belt line in the ceiling," he says. "And for most of the small drill presses, there was just one main drive that ran the whole line." As a prank, he says, drill-press operators would twist the belts so they would run backward and catch some machinist unaware.

Newton's manufacturers didn't make big productivity gains until they ripped out the shafts and retooled their factories to use new-age machinery, powered by individual electric motors. The new tools let owners step up production, reduce waste, and pay workers according to their ability. But the change didn't occur until midway through the 1920s. It took electricity thirty years to begin to transform the American workplace and home, and another twenty years to complete the job. Computers are on a similar trajectory; they will start noticeably boosting productivity soon, and will lift economic growth over the next decade or two.

Over the first thirty years of the electric age, the technology accomplished mighty tasks: lighting up cities, running electric trolleys, and making steam engines obsolete. But in economic terms, the technology's most important years were still ahead of it, as inventors and entrepreneurs learned how to use electricity to revolutionize production. Paul David, a Stanford University economic historian who has drawn elaborate parallels between electricity and computers, says that technology buffs often suffer from "telescopic vision." To them, he says, the possible future appears closer and more vivid than it really is. Like today's computer gurus, electricity's promoters underestimated how long it would take for technological change to work its way through the economy. In 1849, when electricity was merely a scientific curiosity, the U.S. Patent Commissioner already was noting that "the belief is a growing one that electricity in one or more of its manifestations is ordained to effect the mightiest of revolutions in human affairs."

Paul David argues that computers will follow a path similar to electric motors, making the electric age a metaphor for the computer age. Today, we stand roughly as far into the microcomputer revolution as Americans stood in the electric revolution in 1900. By this analogy, the invention in 1969 of computer memory chips and, a year later, of microprocessors, will have the same historic significance as the invention of the dynamo a century earlier. Microprocessors pack the essentials of a computer engine on a single chip, and memory chips permit cheap storage of libraries of information. Together, they spawned the personal computer industry, improved products ranging from machine tools to automobiles, and forced many businesses to revamp their management structure. But microcomputing's most important economic contribution will come over the next ten or twenty years, as more companies learn how to use the technology to improve their productivity, and fewer companies waste time and money. Only now, for example, are companies beginning to understand the changes wrought by the Internet and other computer networks, which allow workers to share information instantaneously around the world and to work together on projects while remaining on premises on different continents.

Why should productivity gains take so long to appear? Partly, because new technologies require generations of improvement—and because old technologies battle back. (During the electric age, lighting companies sold chandeliers outfitted with gas jets *and* electric bulbs, for customers who didn't fully trust the new technology or who preferred muted gaslight.) Partly, because factories and offices are reluctant to ditch expensive equipment for an unproven technology. But mostly it has taken so long because people have a hard time understanding new technologies well enough to become comfortable with them, and then to understand how best to use them. "There's a naïve view of technology and organizations that says that technology can change rapidly," says Thomas Hughes, a University of Pennsylvania technology historian. "There's a great deal of inertia built into many technologies because of the commitment of people, institutions, and money."

Mark Twain understood. In *A Connecticut Yankee in King Arthur's Court,* a New England machinist is magically transported back to sixth-century England. He brings with him the miracles of nineteenth-century engineering, which so impress the nobility that he is dubbed "Sir Boss." But the knights eventually rebel, destroying telephones, phonographs, and typewriters. Twain's style is satiric, but his point is serious: New technology won't change people's lives permanently unless the culture and mindset are ready for change. "Old habit of mind is one of the toughest things to get away from in the world," Sir Boss says ruefully. "It transmits itself like physical form and feature."

Factory owners first used electricity to replace the waterwheels and central steam engines that powered elaborate belt-and-shaft systems. That's the usual progression in technology: New machines that are vastly more flexible than their forerunners modestly improve old systems. The first office computers, for instance, were used as expensive typewriters, and some still are. Radio was initially considered only a fancy telephone that let two people communicate long-distance, not a new form of mass communication.

Nevertheless, some industries benefited early from electric power. Textile and saw mills, historically built adjacent to rivers or canals, were no longer at the mercy of droughts that dried up their power source. New England textile makers, freed from their dependence on local waterways, could move their factories south, closer to the cotton fields. For workers, electric lights brightened the factory floor, and electric fire alarms warned of danger.

As early as 1898, *Cassier's,* an engineering magazine, published articles pointing out the inefficiencies of factories rigged with shafts and belts. "The whole plant must be run if a single man in the farthest end of the shop wishes to drill a half-inch hole," complained one *Cassier's* article. About two-thirds of the power generated was wasted by the friction between the belts and shafts, according to estimates at the time.

Technologically, the solution was already in hand. Rather than run a factory as if it were one immense machine looped and belted together, a number of inventors proposed to power machine tools individually. Lathe-workers could then machine metal parts while the sanders were silent. Energy would be conserved rather than wasted. The forest of factory leather belts could be felled. The workplace would be airier and safer; workers, more productive. In 1884, Frank Sprague, a former Edison employee, exhibited his first electric motor; two years later, he used one to run an elevator in Boston. "His is the only true motor," said a suitably impressed Edison. Sprague's early motors were too large to run machine tools, but other inventors soon developed miniaturized versions to power dental machines, sewing machines, and fans. "It has proven better to discard shafting and belts altogether and supply a special motor to each tool," a manufacturing magazine proclaimed in 1893.

But few companies were ready to make such bold moves; electric-motor technology advanced slowly. In the late 1890s, a number of factories replaced their single, central shafts with several smaller ones. Each of the minishafts was powered by its own big electric motor, making it easier for companies to set up specialized machine shops or woodworking departments. The Keating Wheel Company built a factory in Middletown, Connecticut, in 1897, with shops in six wings perpendicular to the plant's main building, a compact arrangement that required less real estate and would have been impossible with a central shaft. The factory decentralization, during the 1890s, hints at the kind of change that roiled the computer industry in the 1970s. That's when Fortune 500 firms began to buy minicomputers to run their accounting and engineering systems rather than rely on centralized mainframe computers, which were the shaft-and-belt technology of the computer age.

Despite the promise of huge boosts in productivity, factory owners often waited decades before they pulled down the shafts and replaced them with machines powered by individual motors. In 1899, only 3% of factories used motor-driven machinery. Many factories, especially new ones, added the machines over the following two decades. Still, by 1919, only one-third of all U.S. factories had shifted to the new technology. But then, suddenly, there was a giant leap. By 1929, a majority of American factories, 56%, had motorized as factory managers raced to get ahead of their competitors.

Why did factories wait so long to use the new technology? Lack of publicity certainly wasn't to blame. Newspapers and magazines back then were about as fast as today's at trumpeting change. If anything, the famous inventors of the nineteenth century were bigger hypsters than Bill Gates, Steve Jobs, and other computer wizards. Without government grants or universities to sustain them, Thomas Edison, George Westinghouse, and their competitors relied on newspapers and magazine articles to make their pitches for financial backing.

Before interviews, Edison would transform himself into the Great Inventor. "Suddenly gone were his natural boyishness of manner, his happy hooliganism," *Harper's* magazine reported. "His features froze into immobility, he became statuesque in the armchair, and his unblinking eyes assumed a faraway look." Edison told the *New York Sun* that he had solved the problem of electric lighting systems at least a year before he had actually managed to do it—the sort of ploy that software companies now use to keep their competitors off-guard and their customers loyally waiting.

Advertising fed the new technology craze, as computer ads do today, touting the latest gadgets as chic. In 1915, General Electric released a short silent film, *The Home Electrical,* that ran before feature films at local movie houses. In it, a buoyant couple, Mr. and Mrs. Wise, show off their new electric appliances to an intrigued visitor, Mr. Newhouse. In the bathroom, there's an electric heater to warm water for shaving—assuming the device didn't fall in the sink first and electrocute its owner. The kitchen sports an electric waffle maker, electric water heater, electric skillet, electric percolator, electric toaster, and electric range. "If you pardon me, while you gentlemen are enjoying your electric lighted cigars, I'll go see the baby," says Mrs. Wise, in the panel of type explaining her soundless words. The film pans to the two men lighting cigars with a contraption as big as an ice cream cone. "I certainly owe these wonderful conveniences and labor savers to my wife," declares Mr. Newhouse as he leaves. Their good deed done, Mr. and Mrs. Wise walk arm-and-arm into the parlor. She nods toward the fireplace. He shakes his head and turns on the electric heater instead. The lights fade as their faces are illumined by the glow of a GE logo.

But if consumers were smitten, factory owners remained wary of installing the new, electric-motor-driven machinery. They made the same investment calculations that managers make today before springing for expensive new computer networks. They had sunk millions of dollars into belt-driven machinery, made of durable steel and wood, which still worked reasonably well. Why scrap it all for some engineers' vision of new technology? Besides, other experts calculated that the new machinery would actually increase costs. Plant managers would need to buy individual motors with a total power capacity as much as seven times greater than a centralized shaft-and-belt system. Each individual motor had to be powerful enough to handle the maximum demand, while the centralized system ran at middling capacity. To pay for that new equipment, productivity would have to surge. Who wanted to take the risk?

In 1926, F. H. Penney, a GE executive touring the New Haven, Connecticut, Machine Tool Exhibition, confessed that he was confused about whether it made sense to fully replace shafts and belts with individually powered tools. "It is difficult to decide which would be the better of the two methods," he said.

The electric age also was torn by time-consuming battles between competing systems, which are mirrored in the computer age's struggles between Intel microprocessors versus Motorola; Apple personal computers versus IBM; Lotus software versus Microsoft. Back then, the biggest fight was between direct current (DC) and alternating current (AC). Both had technical advantages. DC, invented first, had the advantage of proving its practicality. It was also cheap for local transmission. The problem with DC was in long-distance transmission. Engineers would have had to tie together grids of hundreds of local DC generating stations to cover a state, which would have driven up costs. AC's advantage was long distances. Using AC, engineers could envision building huge power stations capable of transmitting current hundreds of miles.

As with any standards battle, the fight was as much about personality and corporate power as technology. DC was backed by Thomas Edison; AC, by George Westinghouse. Edison, the master publicist, worked with a self-styled electrician who toured the country electrocuting calves, horses, and other animals larger than people, to "prove" that AC was the more deadly current. New York State, home to many of Edison's enterprises, adopted the "electric chair" to execute murderers—and chose a Westinghouse AC generator to execute the first prisoner in 1890. Thus was born a ghoulish public relations campaign: Do you want the executioner's current coursing through your home and streets? Edison eventually failed; he couldn't get laws passed in New York and Virginia to outlaw AC. Meanwhile, powerful industrialists were pressing utilities to build power plants, which could handle distant customers only through AC transmission. By 1900, it was clear that AC would became the electric standard, even though the fight continued for many years after.

The standards battle slowed for many years the pace at which the technology advanced. Thomas Hughes, the technology historian, provides this account of early twentieth-century London, then the world's largest city: "Greater London had sixty-five electrical utilities, seventy generating stations averaging only 5,285 KW [kilowatts] in capacity, forty-nine different types of supply systems, ten different frequencies, thirty-two voltage levels for transmission and twenty-four for distribution and about seventy different methods of charging and pricing. Londoners who could afford electricity toasted bread in the morning with one kind, lit their offices with another, visited associates in nearby office buildings using still another variety and walked home along streets that were illumined by yet another kind."

Echoes of these standards battles reverberated in Newton, Iowa, where Maytag's progress was hindered by its failure to use electricity more effectively. The rate at which Maytag modernized its factories reflected the nation's overall progress, and shows how the new technology finally transformed the bulk of American workplaces and homes. Maytag exemplifies how a powerful new technology—whether electricity or computers—ultimately benefits manufacturers, workers, and consumers. After decades of dithering, Maytag finally used the latest in electric-motor technology to boost production, keep costs low, and make washing machines affordable for many American families.

Before Maytag, washday was known as "Blue Monday"—for good reason. In the early part of the century, fewer than one-third of homes had running water. It took hours merely to cart water from a well or tenement faucet, boil it on a stove, and dump it into a bathtub. Hours more were devoted to scrubbing shirts and pants on a washboard, and wringing them out. In 1907, Maytag introduced its first washer, the Pastime, which had to be cranked by hand, and offered scant help to housewives who could wash only about four shirts per load. In 1911, Maytag brought out an electric-powered washer, which it touted in ads as "wonderfully simple."

But it wasn't until 1914 that the company made a splash nationally. Recognizing that most homes—especially farm homes—weren't yet wired for electricity, Maytag produced the "Multi-Motor washer," which had a built-in gasoline motor and an exhaust hose to snake through an open window. The Multi-Motor became a fad of personal-computer-like proportions, as tinkerers figured out ways to run butter churns, milking machines, ice-cream makers, and even printing presses off the washer's motor.

Although Maytag's future depended on the spread of electricity, electrifying Newton, Maytag's hometown, was delayed for reasons of personality and politics. It took the imperious Frederick L. Maytag to clear away the obstacles. F. L., as he was known, was the kind of man who would line up his employees on his birthday and have them march through town in celebration. He used a combination of business pressure and political connections that might have gotten him indicted today. Maytag served eight years as state senator in the early 1900s, and chaired the Iowa senate's appropriations committee, which approved highways, railroads, telephones, and other projects dear to his company.

In 1919, local business leaders drafted the 61-year-old Republican to run for mayor, on the platform of solving the city's electricity problems. Thirty years earlier, as a Newton city council member, Maytag had convinced the city to build its own DC electric plant, putting Newton at the cutting edge of the era's technology. But the municipal utility's service had deteriorated, forcing Maytag Corporation and other Newton manufacturers to search elsewhere for power hookups or to install their own generators. After winning the election, Mayor Maytag introduced Newton, in 1920, to A. H. Rich, a shadowy businessman who said he had long experience in the electric industry. He proposed to buy Newton's power station for $41,000 and transform it to AC, by then the national standard.

Many townspeople suspected a sweetheart deal between the mayor and Rich. A rival washer-maker, Harry L. Ogg, defended Maytag in a letter to the *Newton Daily News*. "Criticism was made of Mr. Rich because he expects to come here and make money. I wonder why else he should come?" Ogg wrote. Newton voters approved the plan, and, true to his word, Rich quickly modernized the aging plant. The new private utility also helped consumers replace old DC washing-machine motors with new AC ones. But the skeptics may have been right to suspect a payoff, although it isn't clear whether the mayor profited. Rich was a front man for an electricity entrepreneur who gained control of the new Newton utility within two years and sold it to Iowa Southern Utilities Company for $375,000—nearly ten times the price Rich had paid Newton.

Maytag's political triumph handsomely benefited his company, which at last had a reliable source of electricity to power factory expansion. Demand for Maytag washers soared. In 1919, the company introduced a cast-aluminum washer—a big improvement over wooden washers, which cracked and leaked, and copper washers, which stained clothes. But washers still cleaned clothes inefficiently. Under the washer's lid, an apparatus that looked like a three-legged stool snagged clothes and dragged them through the water. In 1922, Maytag addressed that problem with "Gyrofoam" agitators. Installed in the bottom of washing tubs, the agitators churned the hot soapy water, which circulated through the clothes. Modern washers use the same principle.

In 1924, Maytag manufactured 105,000 washers, twice as many as it had produced just four years earlier, making it the world's largest washing-machine company. But F. L. Maytag wasn't as quick to recognize the need to further modernize his factory as he was to improve Newton's electric power supply. Remarkably, his company resisted using the latest electric technology in its factories. A Maytag aluminum foundry, built in 1920, used electric-motor-driven conveyor belts to carry parts. Other Maytag buildings used conveyors to transport new washing machines from the factory to railway freight cars. But, by and large, the company continued to rely on shaft-and-belt technology.

Production supervisors simply didn't believe that the new ways could boost output. When one of Maytag's Newton competitors, Automatic Washer Company, ordered some motor-driven machine tools, few were impressed. "People said: 'They won't last, they won't last, belt-driven was better,'" recalls John Wert, who worked at Automatic in 1919, before joining Maytag two years later. "Everybody was wrong on that."

Before Maytag would join Automatic Washer and other companies in a shift to the new manufacturing technology, F. L. Maytag had to sign on. But he was indifferent to the technology debate; his love was selling washing machines, not making them. According to Maytag Corporation lore, his salesmanship saved the Gyrofoam washer, which was considered so radical for its time that few dealers were at first willing to order it. Undaunted, Maytag headed west by railroad with a crated Gyrofoam to show retailers. Rejected in Denver, Salt Lake City, and Los Angeles, he finally made a sale to an Oakland dealer, who later grew rich ordering trainloads of Gyrofoams. Maytag was welcomed back to Newton as a hero.

Nevertheless, the company would have stagnated if it hadn't found ways to boost production. With dozens of competitors, one of them surely would have found a way to leapfrog Maytag. One history of Maytag credits F. L. Maytag's son Elmer, then the company's treasurer, for recognizing the problem. He prevailed on his father, "who didn't want to turn his cash into brick and mortar," to make the necessary investment. Thomas Smith, Maytag's research and development chief, who started working at the company in 1926, says the entire Maytag family resisted change. "They held on to technology until they were convinced there was something more advanced," he says. "Everybody resists change, especially if they're a part of what's going on."

In 1925, decades after the dawn of the electric age, Maytag finally plunged deeply into electric motor technology. In February, the company opened another new aluminum foundry, which it planned to run three shifts a day. "It is equipped with the latest type of machinery, including complete automatic conveying and handling machinery for sand [used to mold aluminum parts]," boasted a 1925 Maytag stock prospectus. In May, the *Newton Daily News* carried banner headlines of Maytag's plan to double production to 1,300 washers a day by building a six-story factory and outfitting it "with the latest in labor-saving machinery." "Sales Force of Maytag Company Has Been Stepping Ahead of Daily Factory Production by More Than 200 Washing Machines per Day for the Last Ninety Days—Expansion of Plant Could Not be Delayed Longer," explained one headline. The Chicago architect hired to design the factory paid detailed attention to the electrical wiring, particularly in the machine shop, where electrical outlets were spread throughout to power the new, motor-driven equipment.

Ever frugal, Maytag Corporation installed several shafts on the first floor of the new building, which opened in 1926, to run the company's remaining belt-driven machines. But Maytag didn't need shafts elsewhere. With lighter ceilings, Maytag could use less expensive building materials, build the plant taller than past buildings, and save money on real estate. Maytag was especially proud of its modern machine shop, located on the second floor. "Behold the finest equipped tool room in the middle west," trumpeted a Maytag photo-brochure describing the factory. "A living room could be no cleaner." There wasn't a belt-driven machine in the shop, which made tools, dies, gauges, and fixtures used elsewhere in the factory.

The *Newton Daily News,* in 1926, lauded the machine shop's "automatic machines," which bored holes in castings and shaped them "without the human element entering any of the operations." In other parts of the factory, Maytag used electric cranes to move buckets of pig iron and scrap, electric trucks to transport parts from operation to operation, and electric-powered conveyor belts to speed final assembly. A photo of the new grinding and polishing department shows a bright, airy room with compact grinding machines. A Maytag photo of an earlier polishing department, taken perhaps five years before, shows a grim Dickensian scene where tangles of belts block windows and sun-light. With Maytag's needs for electricity growing, the local utility built a substation at the factory in late 1926. Machines powered by individ-ual motors "probably pushed the world ahead fifteen, twenty, thirty years," says John Wert, who started working at Maytag in 1921. "They opened the industrial world."

Maytag's production records bear that out. In 1920, after Maytag in-troduced the aluminum washer, the company produced an average of 189 machines per worker per year. Then, sales and productivity slumped during a deep nationwide recession. By 1923, production was back to 1920 levels, but productivity lagged at 149 machines per worker. The next year, worker output wasn't much better. By that rough gauge, worker productivity actually declined in the early 1920s. However, in 1926, after Maytag started using its new factory, production jumped to an average of 221 machines per worker. Wages rose as productivity improved. A Maytag worker in 1926 produced 48% more washers than a 1923 counterpart and made 32% more money, after adjusting for inflation.

Corporate sales followed an even steeper trajectory. In 1922, Maytag earned $300,000 on sales of $2.5 million. In 1926, the company's earn-ings skyrocketed to $6.8 million on sales of $28.7 million. That's a net profit margin of 24%, roughly the same as Microsoft's today. Maytag marked its fabulous growth by erecting a huge electric sign overlooking New York's Broadway in 1926. A Maytag Gyrofoam was outlined in white lighting.

Maytag's productivity gains were replicated elsewhere. Between 1922 and 1926, in Detroit, Henry Ford built a massive automobile production complex based on the electric-motor technology and known as River Rouge. Ford eschewed blueprints, preferring to plan the factories and power plants using scale models of machine tools, conveyors, pillars, and other parts. "Ford said, 'The essence of what I'm doing is flow, flow, flow,'" Thomas Hughes, the technology histo-rian, says. "The old belts limited where you could place machine tools. Electric motors allowed him to redesign the factory." With the new factory technology, Ford productivity climbed. By 1925, the au-tomaker was pushing Model Ts out the factory door every thirty sec-onds. Nationwide, the pace of productivity improvement in manufacturing quickened by five percentage points in the 1920s; Paul

David, the economic historian, attributes close to half that rise to the cumulative effects of electric technology.

The success of Ford, Maytag, and other manufacturers spread throughout the country, partly through the talents of Frederick Winslow Taylor, one of the first and most influential management consultants. A skilled machinist and inventor, Taylor dissected factory work to figure out the most a worker could do, and then created pay schemes to prod the worker to deliver. "Production went to his head and thrilled his sleepless nerves like liquor or women on a Saturday night," wrote novelist John Dos Passos. Taylor "never loafed and he'd be damned if anybody else would. Production was the itch under his skin."

Taylorism has long since fallen out of fashion; "efficiency experts" are lampooned as know-it-alls with stopwatches. Taylor was able to achieve some impressive gains in the old belt-driven factories, but electric-motor technology gave him new flexibility. When factory owners scrapped their belts and shafts, they unharnessed worker productivity. No longer was the pace of production controlled by a centralized machine. Faster workers could produce more than slower ones. With the technological changes, companies were able to expand the practice of tying wages to productivity—"piecework," as it was known then. (Today, that trend is reappearing, although it usually is gussied up as "pay for productivity.") Piecework is often associated with worker abuse. But, in the 1920s at least, it paid better than straight salary, enhanced productivity, and was sought by many workers.

Electric technology had finally transformed society at large. Wages were improving, appliances were making housework easier, and America was advancing economically. In 1929, Eugene O'Neill wrote a play called *Dynamo* that echoed the ruminations of Henry Adams at the Paris exhibition of 1900. Electricity, the symbol of modern technology, had triumphed; the material world was prospering at the expense of the spiritual. "It all comes down to electricity in the end," says a character named Reuben, who has lost the religious faith of his youth. "What fool preachers call God is in electricity somewhere."

There is a "take-off" point for technology—a time when a technology builds sufficient momentum that it spreads throughout the economy at an accelerating pace. If the technology is powerful enough, the take-off can lift national productivity. With electric technology, take-off occurred around 1920, when half of all factories were electrified. At that point, a majority of the nation's factories were committed to using electric technology and replacing shaft-and-belt systems with electric motors. The trend began to feed on itself. As factory after factory installed individually powered machines in the 1920s, word spread through a web of industry contacts—employees changing jobs, machine-tool salesmen making the rounds, and trade shows featuring new technologies. "The full transformation of industrial processes by the new power technology was a drawn out and by no means certain affair," writes Paul David. "When it finally came, however, the delayed payoff was very palpable."

The United States is now at a similar take-off point—this time, powered by microcomputers. Census Bureau surveys show that about half of American workers today use computers on the job—a fair analogy to the percentage of factories using electricity in 1920. And as with electricity, productivity will start to increase dramatically. Massachusetts Institute of Technology economist Erik Brynjolfsson expects a productivity boost of half a percentage point a year from computers and sees evidence that the surge is occurring already. After surveying the nation's largest firms, he has found that computer investments pay a higher return than other kinds of investment—the kind of payoff that would be expected in a computer-led surge. Economist Daniel E. Sichel, a Brookings Institution economist who studied the parallels between computers and electricity before he joined the Federal Reserve Board as a senior researcher, puts the maximum potential increase in productivity at 0.3%. As Chapter 1 explains, half a percentage point of added growth, when compounded over two or three decades, would greatly improve the lives of most Americans.

Critics of the electricity metaphor say it offers little insight into today's productivity paradox. But they interpret history in an overly literal fashion and they suffer from technological hubris. Changing technology profoundly enough to move society requires changing the mindset of a generation of Americans. There's little reason to expect that process to move more rapidly in the computer era than it did in the electric age.

Some skeptics point out that computers have been around since the end of World War II—well before the invention of the microprocessor.

So why haven't they already produced the vaunted productivity gain? By the late 1950s, insurance companies and other big firms were already using mainframe computers to handle vast amounts of data. By 1970, there were 125,000 computer operators trained to handle the machines. And there was a payoff: Mainframes boosted the productivity of big, centralized firms that could use them to track personnel, sales, and inventory worldwide.

But personal computers and small electric motors are different from the technologies from which they sprang. They decentralize power to individual users. Electric motors let machinists run jigs and sanders as rapidly as they could manage. Their pace of work wasn't determined by a centralized shaft-and-belt system. Personal computers let workers at many different levels of a corporation call up and use information that was once centrally stored in refrigerator-sized computers and controlled by lab-coated managers. Now, companies everywhere are linking personal computers into global networks, and trying to figure out how workers can use the networks effectively. Learning how best to use this new technology and wring productivity gains from radical decentralization takes years, but the payoff is worth it. For instance, Schneider National Corporation, one of the nation's largest truckers, tracks its vehicles through networks of computers and satellites, and moves them seamlessly from deliveries to pickups. Factories can count on inventory when they need it; truckers can save on fuel and manpower—the very essence of productivity.

The critics are right in one regard: Computer hardware changes more rapidly than electric hardware did years ago. But that doesn't mean that people change as rapidly. Companies must learn how to use the machinery effectively and change organizational structures, across the nation, in ways that take advantage of the new technology. That's why the pace of innovation frequently spans decades. While computer hardware innovation hums along, human and corporate adaptability slogs at a much slower pace. "The mere fact that technological change is faster doesn't imply productivity growth is faster," says Paul David. "To introduce technologies, you have to disrupt organizations. You don't want to do that on a continual basis."

Take an example from the more recent past. After World War II, the U.S. Air Force pressed aircraft manufacturers to buy automated machine tools. An older generation of skilled machinists was retiring, and the Air Force was worried because the new jets the generals wanted to buy required precision parts. Given the success of American technology during the war, the Pentagon figured it could get U.S. industry to replace fallible workers with machines. Conditions couldn't have been better for the new technology. The Air Force recruited the nation's top engineering school, MIT, to develop the machines, and paid for the research. Then it bought many of the early machines for the aircraft manufacturers. "Whatever the problems, whatever the cost, the public would pay the bill," David K. Noble writes in a history of the effort.

In 1973, twenty-five years after the technology was introduced, hardly any industrial manufacturing was carried out on automated machine tools. Companies outside the Pentagon's orbit derided the new technology, and only 5% of small machine shops even owned one of the machines. The machinery proved more expensive, less reliable, and harder to use than expected. Strikes and worker slowdowns were commonplace as managers wrestled with workers for decades over how the new technology should be used, and whether workers running the new machines deserved pay increases or pay cuts. Eventually, the machines were outfitted with personal computer controls, which made them more productive for factories. But it took at least forty years before the technology transformed the workplace. Success involved resolving questions of learning, politics, and organization as much as it did questions of machinery. Those are the same questions that today's companies have been grappling with for years. The result will be the same: productivity gains.

Says Stanford University economic historian Nathan Rosenberg: "Ultimately, what is often called for is not just technical expertise but an exercise of the imagination."

4

"A People's College"

How high schools made broadly shared prosperity possible.

Technology, for all its potential, isn't enough to ensure a better life for the middle class; education is the second element in the prosperity equation. Education fosters improved productivity, and then spreads the added wealth throughout society. At the same time that electricity was working its way through the American economy in the early decades of the twentieth century, American high schools were expanding and changing their ways in order to educate the children of unschooled farmers and factory hands.

The new high school, no longer reserved for the wealthy, produced workers prepared for the new technology of that era. In this way, it counteracted the forces of inequality that had pushed wages for the educated elite far above the wages of others. In our own time, the rise of the community college parallels the transformation of the high school. The result will be the same: broadly shared prosperity.

In 1910, a high school diploma was a rarity. Only about one in ten of the seventeen-year-olds in Iowa and other Midwestern states was a high school graduate. High school existed "to prepare for the duties of life that small proportion of all the children in the country—a proportion small in number, but very important to the welfare of the nation . . . whose parents are able to support them while they remain so long at school," declared ten prominent educators convened by the National Education Association at the end of the nineteenth century.

By the early 1930s—just two decades later—the typical Midwestern seventeen-year-old had a high school diploma. The high school had been transformed from an academy preparing the elite for college to "a people's college," as advocates dubbed it. High school changed the way Americans lived, and counteracted the inequality of that era. Its largely forgotten history is a reminder of the potency of education to lift the standard of living for people at the middle of the middle class. It is a lesson we are learning anew today with community colleges and worker training programs.

Then, as now, the gap between wages of winners and losers in the economy was large. Then, it was between office and factory workers, and between skilled production workers at high-tech companies such as Maytag, and less skilled workers in textile mills and shoe factories. The surging supply of high school graduates filled the growing need for educated workers and helped reduce that wage gap.

Today's wage gap is between workers who go to college and those who lack such education or equivalent skills. Unless this widening inequality is arrested, the benefits of a more rapidly growing economy will continue to go primarily to the best educated. Just as high schools introduced more wage equality in the 1920s, community colleges will help do the same in the decades to come by producing more skilled workers.

In turn-of-the-century Newton, Iowa, high school was an intimate but serious affair reserved for the children of the most fortunate families. It was conducted in just one of the twelve classrooms in a turreted brick building erected after the Civil War to replace the town's one-room schools; other classrooms were filled with students from lower grades. When the high school roll was called each morning, each pupil responded with a quotation from an author, ancient or modern. E. J. H. Beard, an exemplar of the nineteenth-century "school man," as educators of the time were known, was firmly in control by 1900, serving both as superintendent of schools and principal of the high school.

Beard arrived in Newton in 1892, at age 50, with two of his daughters. Vesta taught Latin at Newton High School until 1940; Gertrude gave piano lessons. Beard was one of the old guard who saw high school exclusively as a way to educate the elite. He was a committed conservative academic with rimless glasses, a thick mustache, and an

Old Testament demeanor. "Just what his three initials stood for I never knew, but we used to call him 'old Ezramiah, Jeremiah, Hezikiah Beard,'" one 1912 alumnus said. Change came to Newton High School only after Beard was gone.

Just as college was only for the elite and lucky before the G.I. Bill, federally subsidized loans, and community colleges, high school in the early twentieth century was for the few—for boys like F. L. Maytag's son, Lewis, Class of 1905. High schools weren't free. One unenlightened Massachusetts paper manufacturer argued that subsidizing high school education would be a waste of money. He objected to proposals for tuition-free public high schools because they offered to "boys and girls wholly unfit for secondary education, a temptation to exchange the actual benefit of remunerative work . . . for the doubtful advantage of a training that can have no direct bearing upon their life work."

It wasn't until 1912 that the Iowa legislature required taxpayers, rather than parents, in communities without high schools to cover the tuition tab for teenagers who wanted to attend classes in nearby towns. In the era before the school bus, just getting to high school was often difficult and expensive. Lawrence Hammerly, who graduated from Newton High in 1915, paid 25 cents a week to stable his horse while he was in class, a substantial sum when a factory worker typically earned $2 a day.

Although prominent national educators already were debating the appropriate mission for high schools, there appears to have been no debate at E. J. H. Beard's high school in the early 1900s. Beard's students were prepared for college, business school, nursing school, or a teaching post in one of the small "country schools" elsewhere in the county. Beard required each student to take four years of Latin, a requirement questioned elsewhere at the time. The reading list emphasized Shakespeare, Tennyson, and Burke. The only subjects beyond core academics were music, debate, and athletics.

Beard's graduates, in his mind, were headed for more education, not the workplace. In a turn-of-the-century report to the state, he claimed that 82 of his 90 high school students were "fitting for college or other higher institutions." That was a bit of puffery: Some of those who were listed as "fitting," or preparing, for college didn't go. But in 1915, at least 13 of the 21 boys—nearly two-thirds—in the graduating class at Newton High began college or other higher education, evidence of the narrow purpose of Beard's high school. Nationally, roughly half the high school graduates were planning to go on for further education, according to principals' reports.

Over the first quarter of the twentieth century, a crusade to expand and redefine the high school unfolded, and the institution was transformed into a way to educate the many rather than the few. Titans of education such as Harvard President Charles Eliot, and teachers in small towns such as Newton, struggled to reconcile the competing demands of college entrance requirements and changing industrial technology; of Yankee factory owners and Italian immigrants; of those who wanted to read Plato and those who wanted to learn to type; of those who valued knowledge for its own sake and those who simply wanted a decent job. In a view that foreshadowed changes to come, the Iowa State Teachers Association declared in 1901 that high school ought to provide education "for its own sake or as a training for practical life, rather than simply a preparation for study in the colleges and universities." By the end of the 1920s, the high school more closely resembled today's high school than it resembled the high school of 1900.

Nearly a century later, community colleges are trying to resolve similar internal tensions about their purpose. Academic-minded professors long to teach sonnets, not remedial English, and they celebrate each transfer to a four-year college as proof that their schools are successful. Their practical-minded colleagues preach the wisdom of teaching software, and celebrate each time a former student gets a $17-an-hour paycheck. The particulars of the debate aren't as important as the outcome. As with the early twentieth-century high schools, today's community colleges do both: They prepare some students for further education, but give most students what they need to get good-paying jobs.

Outside the South, high schools expanded with amazing speed, enrolling students whose parents had never dreamed of getting a high school diploma. California and New England led the way, followed by the prosperous agricultural states of the Midwest. Between 1899 and 1930, Newton's population tripled, but the high school graduating class increased eightfold. In 1898, the graduating class had been so small that the ceremony included a Saturday night reception at Beard's house for the families of the graduates—all 16 of them. By the 1920s, high school graduations everywhere were no longer intimate. A 1924 ceremony in Pasadena, California, drew an audience of 50,000 to the

Rose Bowl, which was decorated "as a corner of old Holland where a winding canal curved its way through a flower-covered meadow and . . . a Dutch windmill turned its great vanes in the breeze."

High schools drew the children of farmers, factory workers, and unschooled immigrants—kids who a generation earlier would have ended their education no higher than eighth grade. "To quote a Salvation Army phrase, we are 'getting deeper down' in the masses," a Philadelphia high school teacher said in 1904. In Providence, Rhode Island, roughly one in every twenty teenage boys from blue-collar families was in high school in 1880, compared to one in ten in 1900, more than one in four in 1915, and nearly one in two in 1925. In 1910, fewer than one in five children of Irish immigrants in Providence went to high school; in 1925, three-quarters did. In the same way, many of today's community colleges draw heavily from African American, Hispanic, and immigrant communities. Roughly half of all African American and Hispanic college students are enrolled in community colleges.

Newton High School moved into a new building of its own in 1907. The new high school was described at the time as "the pride of the city, built on the most modern and approved plans for schools even to items of sanitary fountains." The fountain and the large mirror that hung above it proved such a distraction that they eventually were removed. Newton High had about 200 pupils at the time the new building was opened, but the school board was planning for growth. Room 27, which served as an assembly hall where the entire student body would gather for weekly lectures by local preachers and businessmen, was built with 384 oak and iron desks bolted to the polished hardwood floor.

Newton High was one of thousands of high schools built in a national construction boom. On average, more than one new high school building was completed every day between 1890 and 1918. These buildings were celebrated as shrines to progress. In the 1922 Sinclair Lewis novel *Babbitt,* George Babbitt boasts about the virtues of Zenith, his hometown, starting with "the facts about our high schools, characterized by their complete plants and finest school-ventilating systems in the country, bar none," and only then turning to Zenith's hotels, banks, office towers, paved streets, and art museum.

As high school enrollments broadened, curricula did too. Shop classes were added for boys; cooking, for girls. Typing was taught. Cities created separate "Latin" high schools for the traditional academics and "English" high schools for teaching modern languages, science, and commerce. None of this change was smooth, much was controversial, and nothing was permanent. In some places, strictly vocational high schools were established. In others, English and Latin high schools were combined in a single "comprehensive high school." Debates over the purpose of high schools were constant: Were they training able young workers or worldly young thinkers? The same debates recur today in community colleges, which offer one degree to students interested in transferring to a four-year college, and another to those who simply want the skills needed to get a good job.

The high schools' response to these conflicting demands left many, including President Theodore Roosevelt, dissatisfied. Commissions were formed to study the effects of secondary schools on American competitiveness. Then, as now, they concluded the schools were failing. In his annual message to Congress in 1907, President Roosevelt said, "Our school system is gravely defective in so far as it puts a premium upon mere literacy training and tends therefore to train the boy away from the farm and the workshop. Nothing is more needed than the best type of industrial school, the school for mechanical industries in the city, the school for practically teaching agriculture in the country."

In Newton, change followed—and was hastened by—Beard's retirement at age 70 in 1912. "Those who followed Dr. Beard retained the central academic emphasis, but bit by bit it was tempered by the technical," Charity Brom, a Class of 1915 graduate, recalled in a reminiscence published decades later. The longtime Newton teacher said that, as Iowa became industrialized during and after World War I, "schools . . . built curriculums to train skilled workers, supervisors, office employees and administrative personnel. The workers and management who came to man these industries changed the earlier homogenous society of each community, and this changed the school curriculum needs."

A room in the basement of Newton's new high school building was designated for "manual training," later known as "shop," though it wasn't equipped until three years after the school was finished. Within a few years, the instructor was requiring each boy (girls took "domestic science" in the cooking room) to fill out a form at the end of the day that listed the time spent at woodworking, and the kind and amount of work done. "In this way," the 1915 yearbook reported, "it is easy to tell approximately how much each individual would be worth to an employer." Mechanical drawing was soon added. For a time, the high school offered evening manual-training classes twice a week for working men, and Saturday morning "continuation classes" for the ambitious who worked during the week.

By the early 1920s, the yearbook reported enthusiastically that "manual training is playing a big part in high-school education these days. . . . The industrial class is for the class of boys who do not intend to go to college and is better to fit them for earning a livelihood by teaching them the rudiments of some trade." A parallel track in farm mechanics, an obvious draw in eastern Iowa, was developed about the same time.

Taking advantage of a 1917 federal law that offered federal funds to local school systems for vocational education, Newton High was among the first Iowa high schools to initiate a "trade and industries" program in which boys spent mornings in school and afternoons in factory jobs. Within a few years, participants had a choice of drafting, radio, machine shop, plumbing, battery repair, and printing—and were taking correspondence courses because they had exhausted their teachers' knowledge.

Employers were enthusiastic, particularly F. L. Maytag. In 1934, Robert L. Smith, later a successful Newton businessman and the town's mayor, studied mechanical drawing at the high school in the morning and worked as an apprentice toolmaker at Maytag in the afternoon for 10 cents an hour—and got a 10% bonus if he made all As in school. By the time a participant finished high school, according to a glowing article in Maytag's in-house magazine, he was "an experienced student workman with the fundamental facts and the industrial viewpoint well established in his mind. The 'industrial viewpoint' is one which in many cases is not evident in the student completing his school work without having had the benefit of association with men actually engaged in the line of work he has selected."

Maytag's support for local high schools was typical. "Although this age [the 1920s] was not the first to proclaim the interdependence of business and education," Edward Krug, a historian of high schools, has written, "it cherished the idea with loving care and proclaimed it as a perfect marriage."

More than 60 years later, community colleges boast of their success with what they call "co-op jobs" or "internships," rediscovering old ways to integrate classroom learning with on-the-job experience. And modern Maytag is as enthusiastic about the modern community college as its ancestor was about the high school. As its price for remaining in Newton, the company persuaded the state, in 1992, to open a branch of Des Moines Area Community College in an abandoned warehouse next to the Maytag complex. Every year, about 300 Maytag employees take courses there, such as a six-session course in reading sophisticated blueprints. In the works is a forty-hour course on safety, arithmetic, and other basic skills for would-be assembly-line workers.

The high-tech industries of the early twentieth century soaked up high school graduates, just as high-tech companies today absorb community college graduates. In the 1920s and 1930s, high school grads went to work, in disproportionate numbers, in leading-edge factories. They ended up at plants that, like Maytag, were making new products, and at petroleum-refining and chemical plants that were using new production methods. The more an industry relied on electricity, a measure of its technological sophistication, the greater the proportion of high school graduates in its workforce. Electricity increased the demand for skilled workers who could run the new machinery, and diminished the demand for unschooled laborers who hauled parts by wheelbarrow. "High school graduates were sought because they could read manuals and blueprints, knew about chemistry and electricity, could do algebra and solve formulas, and, we surmise, could more effectively converse with nonproduction workers in high-technology industries," according to Harvard economic historian Claudia Goldin, who, with her Harvard colleague, labor economist Lawrence Katz, has painstakingly documented the effects of the expansion of high schools on workers' wages. Similar patterns emerged outside manufacturing. Workers selling or servicing radios and other new goods were more likely to have had a high school education; even gas station attendants were far more educated than the typical blue-collar worker.

Despite the success of high schools at preparing students for relatively well-paying jobs, the move toward vocational education didn't meet with universal acclaim. Traditional "school men" grew suspicious of the motives of businessmen who were promoting industrial education. The education establishment worried that it would lose control of substantial amounts of government money to specialized vocational education bureaucracies. John Dewey, a critic of what he called "narrow trade education," asked pointedly, in 1917, whether the true purpose of vocational schooling was to increase profits for business or to increase the "intelligence and power of the worker for his own personal advancement." He left no doubt that, to his dismay, he thought it was the former. In much of the country, because of resistance from teachers, tension between companies and unions, and public suspicion that tax dollars were supporting particular companies and industries, the separate industrial track was abandoned in favor of comprehensive high schools that combined academic and vocational courses. Very similar issues arise today as community colleges offer training to employees of local businesses.

The high school movement occurred just as the industrial revolution arrived in business offices, much as community colleges' expansion has coincided with the widespread use of computers. Typewriters had been around for years, but they weren't used extensively until the early 1900s. They were later joined by adding machines, calculators, address machines, dictaphones, mimeo machines, and the precursors of computers, keypunch machines. Just as the assembly line replaced the nineteenth-century artisan who made a product from start to finish, the office changed, too. Machines replaced workers, made some chores easier, and permitted work to be divided into a set of discrete tasks, each of which was performed by a different worker. High schools supplied the workers who could use the new technology of the time, just as community colleges train workers to use computers today.

Young people flocked to high schools, partly because graduates were landing the white-collar clerical jobs that were lucrative and prestigious. Then, as now, when wages for educated workers rise, more people go to school. At the time, stenographers, dictating-machine operators, bookkeepers, cashiers, and typists earned more than production workers. In 1922, a clerk or bookkeeper in a Newton manufacturing company or local government office earned about $33 a week, or about 50% more than the average factory worker. In case young people didn't notice, the education establishment pointed it out. The National Education Association (NEA) publicized figures showing that high school graduates earned twice as much as less-educated laborers. The NEA said that *every day* a child stayed in school added $9.02 to his or her lifetime earnings—no small sum at a time when laborers earned $500 a year. Today, in much the same fashion, the American Association of Community Colleges boasts that someone with an associate degree has lifetime earnings of about $250,000 more than someone with only a high school diploma.

High schools responded to the changing market for their graduates. Commercial courses appear to have taken off at Newton High School around 1915. With furnishings made by the woodworking class, the high school set up four teller windows—real estate and insurance, wholesale, central agency, and banks—behind which students stood as they learned the rudiments of each type of office. "This . . . equips the students so that they may immediately enter a business office upon completing their study and be able to do justice to the work," the 1918 yearbook said. When the school acquired an adding machine, it was big enough news to merit a mention in the yearbook, in the same way that today's schools boast of Internet connections. Remington Typewriter offered pennants to anyone who could type twenty-five words a minute, and a certificate and card case to those who could maintain a speed of forty words a minute for ten minutes. In 1922, almost a third of Newton High's students were enrolled in the typing course, a reflection of a national trend. Economic historian Claudia Goldin notes that, by 1934, as many U.S. high school students were taking typing as were taking Latin or algebra, which had been mainstays of the old curriculum.

The new technology of the office allowed ordinary high-school-educated workers to replace the gifted bookkeepers who could do sums in their heads. For the first time, large numbers of women got office jobs. Anxiety about the impact of automation rose, particularly among the men whose jobs were at risk. The same sort of unease is showing up today.

The hero of Elmer Rice's 1923 play, *The Adding Machine,* is a veteran department-store bookkeeper named Zero. He expects to be promoted, but instead is startled to learn that he is to be replaced by an adding machine:

ZERO: Addin' machines?

BOSS: Yes, you've probably seen them. A mechanical device that adds automatically.

ZERO: Sure, I've seen them. Keys—and a handle you can pull.

BOSS: That's it. They do the work in half the time and a high school girl can operate them.

Zero promptly kills the boss.

But even as office machinery eliminated some jobs, it lowered the cost of gathering and analyzing information, as computers do today, and thereby sharply increased demand for workers who could use the machines. The fraction of workers in higher-paying clerical jobs nearly doubled between 1920 and 1930, from 5% of the workforce to 9%. In the 1920s, landing a white-collar job meant you were making it, and a high school education helped you get there. Just as today's clerical workers are expected to know word-processing software before they are hired, those who wanted office jobs needed to have office skills. O. Henry's short story, "Springtime à la Carte," centers on a woman in New York who "could not enter that bright galaxy of office talent" because she doesn't know stenography. Instead, she tries to make a living as a free-lance typist. In exchange for three meals a day, she types 21 copies of the daily bill-of-fare for a neighborhood restaurant.

Breaking into an office job was often difficult, particularly for children from blue-collar and immigrant families. Here too, high school made it possible. "The experience . . . could hardly be clearer regarding the advantages associated with schooling: Those who entered high school were able to attain higher-status occupations," historian Joel Perlmann concluded after matching records from public and Catholic high schools with handwritten census forms and city directories for 12,000 residents of Providence, Rhode Island.

This change came so quickly that it could be seen in a single generation. In Somerville, Massachusetts, where high school caught on early, Irish immigrant James Kenney, a carpenter, and his wife had seven children. The oldest five didn't go to high school. Thanks to their income and domestic help—the oldest daughter stayed home to help her mother—the Kenneys were able to both pay a mortgage and send their youngest two boys to Somerville's English High School around the turn of the century. One of the two, Charles, landed a desirable job as a clerk. (The eldest of the seven became a local Democratic politician and champion of public education.)

A high school education offset many of the disadvantages of being the child of a blue-collar immigrant. "The high school . . . served as a small window of opportunity for those farther down the social pyramid," sociologist Reed Ueda concluded in his book on the impact of high school on the people of Somerville. "In adulthood, the children of immigrant workers who went to high school rose to the vanguard of a pluralistic middle class," he found. Among boys from blue-collar families who attended Somerville's English High School in the years immediately before and after 1900, 86% of the Yankees and 66% of the Irish ended up in white-collar jobs.

This increase in the number of high-school-educated workers had an enormous effect on wages. The 1920s were a period of sharply increasing demand for educated workers, much as the 1980s and early 1990s were. But, in the 1920s, unlike recent times, employers didn't have to pay a premium to hire the educated. Why the greater wage equality in the 1920s? Largely because so many more people, lured by the prospect of higher wages, went to school and were equipped for jobs in the expanding, increasingly high-tech office. The fraction of the total labor force with high school diplomas, though still small, more than doubled between 1910 and 1930. And the gap between office wages and factory wages, which seemed as daunting then as the wage gap between high school graduates and college graduates does today, narrowed substantially. As community colleges turn out more workers prepared for the modern workplace, a similar narrowing of today's wage gap will occur.

Using data from old government surveys to track movements in wages of clerical and production workers, Harvard's Goldin and Katz showed that the premium for working in the office began to evaporate around the time of World War I. Wars often cause big changes in wages and benefit the poorly paid, but this phenomenon persisted in peacetime. From 1914 to 1929, blue-collar workers' wages rose more rapidly than wages of their white-collar counterparts; high schools were beginning to solve the shortage of office workers, so they weren't as scarce. The premium that employers had to pay to hire clerks fell by 31% for women and by 41% for men. The changes in wages were remarkably rapid. In 1914, a female clerk earned twice the amount a female production worker was paid. By 1924, the clerk was earning only 40% more, though the difference widened a bit, later in the 1920s.

Nevertheless, both sets of workers were winners. If wages converge because the wages of skilled workers fall to the level of unskilled workers, or if both sets of workers do poorly, there's little cause for celebration. In the first two decades of the twentieth century, white-collar workers did poorly and blue-collar workers did well, helped by the surge in industrial production generated by World War I. Those years were marked by greater wage equality, but not by widespread prosperity.

In the peacetime prosperity of the 1920s, however, wages of both white-collar and blue-collar workers rose. Wages of male urban clerks climbed 14% between 1919 and 1929. Wages of male production workers climbed 21%. Education paid off for the office workers, but the economy-wide increase in productivity pushed wages up for blue-collar workers as well. It is precisely this pattern—more productivity, more wage equality, more broadly shared prosperity—that lies ahead for America today.

The very rich still got richer during the 1920s. A booming stock market lifted the fortunes of those who had money to invest, and the wealthy benefited from deep tax cuts engineered by Treasury Secretary Andrew Mellon, who served three Republican presidents from 1921 to 1932. But in labor markets that determined whether the vast majority of Americans did well or not, there was more equality, and the expansion and evolution of the high school deserves much of the credit.

The equality trend persisted through the World War I boom and the subsequent bust. It persisted through a period of rapid inflation and the painful deflation that followed. It may have been helped by the strength of unions in the 1910s, but it continued even when union clout waned during the 1920s. It certainly was reinforced by the curtailing of immigration of unskilled workers in the 1920s. But, even if the borders had remained open, the added number of high school graduates was so large that it would have overwhelmed the effects of immigration on wages.

The trend toward more wage equality was a distinctly American phenomenon, another reason to credit education. In Britain, by comparison, wages of office workers remained well above those of blue-collar workers until after a high school boom hit there, after World War II.

Economist Jan Tinbergen once described the path of wages as a "race between technological development and access to education." The 1920s demonstrated that a period of rapid and pervasive technological change can also be a period of more widely shared prosperity. The key, then and now, is schooling.

PRESENT

5

The Golden Age

The rise of the American middle class, 1950–1973.

No one knew it at the time, but 1973, the Watergate year, was a watershed for the American middle class. It marked the end of a quarter century of unprecedented and broadly shared prosperity, and the beginning of a quarter century of living standards that improved so slowly that many people believed they weren't improving at all. For the middle class, it was the end of the Golden Age and the beginning of the Age of Anxiety.

The contrast between the two periods has been particularly disheartening for many Americans. Today's middle class knows how remarkably living standards improved for their parents' and grandparents' generations—the move from a cramped city apartment to a suburban house, from one to two cars, from beach-bungalow vacations to flights to Europe or Walt Disney World. For decades, Americans measured their economic progress while turning the pages of the family photo album and hearing again the stories of the hardships of their parents' youth. In past times of temporary economic distress, Americans drew reassurance from the certainty that at least they had much more than their parents had had at a similar stage of life. With considerable reason, today's middle-class Americans wonder why they haven't made a similar leap forward. Many worry that the next generation may not make any economic progress at all.

Growing, but more slowly

Median income of married couples (1996 dollars)

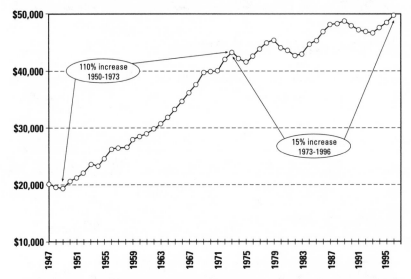

Growth in the income of the typical married couple, adjusted for inflation, rose rapidly during the Golden Age, but slowed significantly around 1973. Half of all couples had income above the median level; half had incomes below it. Source: Census Bureau.

To appreciate why there has been so much anxiety and so little confidence in the American economy, at least until very recently, it's useful to recall how well the American economy performed during the twenty-five years leading up to 1973. Productivity soared, and the benefits were so widely distributed that almost every tier of society enjoyed rising living standards. Not everyone participated equally: many women were relegated to the kitchen; many blacks were forced to live with much less than whites had. But, during the Golden Age, the American economy delivered the goods to the growing American middle class, in ways that it failed to do after 1973.

In this chapter and the next, we tell the story of the American middle class, largely through the eyes of two couples in Chattanooga, Tennessee. One family, the Kerleys, was smack in the middle of the middle in 1973; the other, the Blentlingers, is in the middle of the middle class today. This chapter traces the powerful rise in living standards that lifted the Kerleys well above their parents. Chapter 6 describes the Age of Anxiety, in which life for the Blentlingers and the rest of the middle class hasn't improved nearly as rapidly as it did during the Golden Age. The final chapter in this section explains why the much-celebrated computer revolution has failed—so far—to produce a new Golden Age of economic growth and productivity.

Chattanooga, a city of about 150,000 people that sits astride the Tennessee River on the Tennessee–Georgia border, is a good place to see how life has changed for a middle class that was created in the unanticipated burst of prosperity that followed World War II. For a quarter century after the war, economic progress was tangible and obvious. In 1950, 25% of Chattanooga's homes didn't have access to a flush toilet. A decade later, only 7% lacked flush toilets. In 1950, hardly any American homes were air-conditioned; by 1970, more than half the homes in Tennessee were. In 1950, fewer than one in ten American homes had a television. By 1973, nearly every home in Chattanooga (and elsewhere in America) had at least one TV, and many had more.

Chattanooga's economy resembles that of many other places in America. Although very much a Southern city that still celebrates its role in pivotal Civil War battles fought along its mountain ridges, Chattanooga, for 150 years, has been more industrial than the rest of the South and therefore more resembles the rest of the country than some other Southern cities do. Chattanooga enjoyed a post-World War II manufacturing boom, and then suffered through the wrenching factory downsizing that plagued so much of the country. Once a bulwark of Southern unionism, Chattanooga's unions are quiescent today. "Union decline seen as area selling point," a *Chattanooga Times* headline announced in 1994. Like other cities, it has struggled with rising crime, troubled public schools, recurrent racial tension, and the economic costs of enjoying cleaner air and water.

A wave of downsizing and layoffs swept over Chattanooga in the 1980s and early 1990s, as it did elsewhere, leaving behind a widespread feeling of economic insecurity and betrayal. The Tennessee Valley Authority, the giant government agency created in the New Deal years to electrify the region's farms and small towns, downsized in 1988 and again in 1994. Between 1990 and 1996, it cut its local workforce by 900 people, or nearly 20%. And a new chief executive at the Provident Company, owned by the local McClelland family, took over the troubled insurance company in 1993 and eliminated an entire layer of managers. The bitterness was intense. "A lot of people believe that the McClellands were such strong Christians and, now that the company has lost sight of that, God will not bless the company," said Janet Jobe, who lost a management job after fourteen years at Provident. In a community where layoffs were expected at factories but never at rock-solid white-collar employers, the Provident dismissals unsettled even those who weren't directly affected.

Reflecting a national trend, Chattanooga has moved away from manufacturing to a service economy; that has stranded some people and lifted the fortunes of others. Fewer than one in five workers in Chattanooga is in manufacturing today, down from about one in three in 1970. About 7,500 jobs were lost in manufacturing, most during the 1980s. But, in all, the Census Bureau counted 33,000 more jobs in Chattanooga's Hamilton County in the 1990 census, an increase of 25% from 1970. Some 9,000 jobs were added in retailing, plus 7,500 in health care, and 5,000 in finance, insurance, and real estate.

In 1973, Dennis Kerley, then twenty-five years old, tended machines that wound nylon onto 1,500-pound spools at DuPont & Co., one of the mainstays of the Chattanooga economy. His wife, Ann, stayed home with their two—soon to be three—boys. Each morning, in those pre-cholesterol-scare days, she rose around six o'clock to make him fried eggs, bacon, and grits, and to pack his lunch. Then he drove across town in a gas-guzzling '71 Ford Galaxie. He remembers that the pollution hanging over the Tennessee River valley was sometimes so thick he'd have to turn on his headlights.

The work at DuPont was so dull that Kerley daydreamed about rolling a bowling ball down the plant's vast hallways to see whether he could hit the back wall hundreds of yards away. His supervisor made all the decisions. "You were a body or a number to fill a position," he recalls. But the pay was good and, despite occasional layoffs, the job was secure. On his earnings alone, the high school graduate and his 27-year-old stay-at-home wife came close to the median income for American married couples, an achievement that few one-earner couples accomplish today. During one ten-month layoff in 1970, Kerley was so sure he would eventually be called back that he didn't bother looking for work. Chattanooga employers, familiar with DuPont's habit of layoff and recall, weren't much interested in workers like Kerley anyhow. "At that time," he says, "if you got a job at a good company, you felt you'd be there until you retired." In July 1973, DuPont employed 4,100 people in Chattanooga and was on its way to 5,000.

In 1973, Dennis and Ann Kerley didn't feel affluent. They budgeted with extraordinary care and, to save money, drank iced tea instead of Coca-Cola. But they knew they were living a lot better than their parents had, and they had little doubt that their children's generation would do better still. Like other middle-class Americans, they could measure economic progress with their memories; they didn't need to be convinced.

Dennis remembered that his mother, Mary Kerley, and her seven siblings lived in a four-room house as narrow as a one-car garage—and rented out the living room to a boarder. As a child, Mary went barefoot in the summer to save her shoes for the winter. When she married, she vowed she would do better by her children, and she did. Her folks didn't have enough money to buy Christmas presents every year; Mary always had gifts for her children. Mary had to drop out of junior high school; she made sure her children finished high school. But, as Dennis puts it, "It didn't take that much to make her feel that she was a whole lot better off. When Mom looks back [to the 1950s], she thinks she was doing pretty well; I say, 'No.'"

Dennis's father, an outgoing man, tried repeatedly to make it as a salesman, but never did. He finally landed a secure job at a Chattanooga flour mill in 1957, and steadily climbed the ranks there for twenty-eight years. He didn't make enough to support the family on his salary, though. Dennis's mother worked first at a deli and later at the plant that baked Little Debbie snack cakes.

Until Dennis was seven, in 1955, his family lived in rented houses that sometimes lacked hot running water. That wasn't uncommon. In Chattanooga's Hamilton County, four of every ten houses lacked hot and cold running water in 1950. Though no official tally was kept, an estimated one-third of all Americans lived in poverty at the beginning of the 1950s. "I can remember when they couldn't buy me a pair of shoes, even when I had holes in my shoes. I can remember when we didn't have quite enough of everything. Those were tight times," Dennis says today from the comfort of his 1990s well-clothed, well-fed middle-class life. His wife, Ann, one of seven children, remembers sleeping two, sometimes three, to a bed.

By today's standards, Americans didn't have much in the early 1950s, when Dennis and Ann Kerley were growing up. The typical family did not live in houses like those on *Leave It to Beaver* or *Ozzie and Harriet.* But the standard of living of American families improved faster in the 1950s and 1960s than at any other time in American history. In 1949, the typical American lived in a family with income only about 25% greater than the poverty line. In 1969, the typical American family's income was 2 ½ times the poverty level. This rapid improvement in living standards for the bulk of American families sharply distinguishes the Golden Age from the decades that followed.

One good way to measure the living standard of Americans is to tally the goods and services produced per person. The U.S. economy made available 2.5% more goods and services per person in each year between 1950 and 1973. Each year since 1973, the economy has produced only 1.5% more goods and services per person. That may sound like a small difference, but, in automobile terms, it's as if the economy sped at 80 mph during the Golden Age, then slowed to 50 mph and has been stuck at that speed ever since.

What accounted for this unique Golden Age? First, labor productivity, or the goods and services produced for every hour of work, rose sharply. From 1870 to 1950, productivity increased an average of about 2.0% each year. Then, in the Golden Age from 1950 to 1973, it increased at a brisk 2.7% each year. Wages rose with productivity. Earnings of men who worked year-round, full time, nearly doubled. But since 1973, labor productivity has improved at only about 1% each year. By Census Bureau reckoning, earnings of the typical man working year-round, full time, actually have *fallen* since 1973, after adjusting for inflation. Women's earnings have risen.

The middle class did well during the Golden Age because prosperity was broadly shared. That accomplishment wasn't celebrated at the time, but seems remarkable in light of today's widespread inequality. The rich had a lot more than the poor, of course, but the gap between them didn't widen significantly from the end of World War II to the end of the 1960s.

During the wartime economy of the 1940s, the difference between the wages of well-paid and poorly paid workers shrank significantly, partly because of government controls. In the prosperous decades that followed, the wage gap remained stable. At the bottom, muscular unions, a rising minimum wage, and a strong demand for lesser-skilled factory workers helped lift wages. With help from the G.I. Bill, colleges produced enough graduates to satisfy employer demand. Wages of college grads rose at roughly the same pace as those of less-educated workers. And when a glut of college graduates flooded the labor market in the early 1970s, wages for high school graduates rose even faster than those of their more-educated peers.

Workers at DuPont's Chattanooga plant voted to end union representation in 1958, but the company operated under union-style practices anyhow, partly to fend off new union organizing drives. The distance between rank-and-file earnings and managers' earnings was so slim that workers routinely rejected promotions. "Sometimes we'd offer operators the opportunity to be a supervisor," recalls Ray Childers, then a supervisor at a DuPont plant in Old Hickory, Tennessee. "They'd turn it down because the flat-time earnings of a supervisor didn't compare very well to an operator who could work overtime. He could make more money than the boss."

The Golden Age versus The Age of Anxiety
Annual percentage change, 1950-1973 vs. 1973-1996

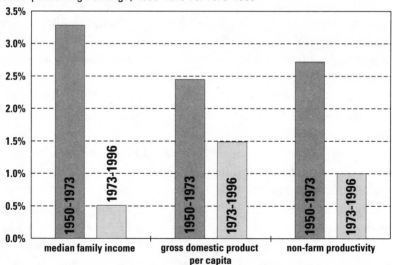

By almost every measure—including median family income, gross domestic product per capita, and output for an hour of work—American living standards rose much more slowly during the Age of Anxiety (1973-1996) than during the Golden Age (1950-1973). All data are adjusted to remove the effects of inflation. Source: Census Bureau, Bureau of Economic Analysis, Bureau of Labor Statistics.

The physical monuments to the shared prosperity of the Golden Age are everywhere today: housing developments like Levittown on Long Island; the network of interstate highways that stretches from coast to coast and border to border; and the state colleges that still educate millions of ambitious young Americans.

In the 1950s, William Levitt brought Henry Ford's techniques of mass production to home construction. As *New York Times* architecture critic Paul Goldberger described it, Levitt turned the single-family, detached house "from a distant dream to a real possibility for thousands of middle-class American families." There was no down payment, no closing fee, no haggling. The houses weren't lavish compared to today's designs. Each owner got a kitchen, a living room, two bedrooms, one bathroom, a washing machine, an outdoor barbecue, and an attic, but no basement. Each house came with an eight-inch television set. Across the country, an increasing percentage of American families bought their own homes in the late 1940s and the 1950s, a tangible realization of the American dream. By 1960, 61% of all the homes in Chattanooga were owned by their occupants, an increase of nearly ten percentage points in a single decade.

Car ownership was another mark of the unaccustomed affluence of the American middle class, and with cars came better vacations. Disneyland opened in California in 1955. Dennis Kerley's mother took her first-ever vacations (invariably, camping trips), and Florida impressed her. "I saw that ocean," she recalls. "It was like nothing I'd ever seen." The number of cars on the road increased by 50% between 1950 and 1960, and by another 50% between 1960 and 1970. By 1960, more than three-quarters of American families owned at least one car, and 15% owned two.

A wealthy Tennessee homebuilder named Kemmons Wilson took his family on a road trip to Washington in 1951, a trip that journalist David Halberstam later dubbed "the vacation that changed the face of the American road." Wilson was irritated at the lousy and uneven quality of roadside motels. He was outraged that he had to pay extra for each of his children and had to drive away from the motel to find a restaurant to feed them. Assuming that other dads were similarly annoyed, Wilson opened his first Holiday Inn in 1952. Four years later, Congress approved President Dwight D. Eisenhower's ambitious interstate highway construction program that eventually would pave an area equal in size to the state of West Virginia, and would route cars away from downtown hotels to locations like those that Wilson favored. By 1964, there were 500 Holiday Inns.

"Life in America, it appeared, was in all ways going to get better," Halberstam wrote in his book, *The Fifties.* "A new car could replace an old one, and a larger, more modern refrigerator would take the place of one bought three years earlier. . . . Thus, the great fear of manufacturers, as they watched their markets reach saturation points, was that their sales would decline; this proved to be false. . . . The market was saturated, but people kept on buying—newer, improved products that were easier to handle, that produced cleaner laundry, washed more dishes and glasses and housed more frozen steaks."

Optimism and abundance fueled an unprecedented and unexpected baby boom. Returning GIs and their wives made up for lost time: 20% more babies were born in 1946 than the year before, and the fecundity lasted until 1964. More babies were born in the United States in 1957—4.3 million—than in any year before or since.

In *The Affluent Society,* which gave a label to the times, economist John Kenneth Galbraith pondered something that economists never before had had the luxury to contemplate: a system that was producing enough food, clothing, and shelter for the bulk of its population. Galbraith observed disapprovingly, in the 1958 book, that contemporary economists and businesses had managed to transfer the sense of urgency once felt for producing food and shelter "to a world where increased output satisfies the craving for more elegant automobiles, more exotic food, more erotic clothing, more elaborate entertainment—indeed for the entire modern range of sensuous, edifying, and lethal desires."

Advertisements sometimes have a way of distilling the mood of a nation; no one has more of a vested interest in plumbing the middle-class psyche than the ad agencies that serve America's corporate giants. A 1958 Chevrolet television commercial opened with a young man, who resembled teen-idol Tab Hunter, rushing out of his house in a white dinner jacket, obviously on his way to a high school prom. His dad, mom, and younger sister watch at the doorway. The boy heads toward his jalopy, but suddenly notices a brand-new convertible parked in front of the house. For the first time, the announcer speaks: "If it's happened once, it's happened a thousand times." The boy looks at the convertible, then at his family in the doorway. Dad smiles and reaches into his pocket for the keys. The boy drives off to pick up his date, played by then-unknown actress Shirley Knight, who won an Oscar two years later for her performance in the film *Elmer Gantry*. The announcer speaks again: "What a gal. What a night. What a car. The new Chevrolet." This was a commercial made for an age of economic optimism and ever-greater affluence, even if it exaggerated.

Contrast that message to the advertisements that Cigna Corporation, an insurance company, ran in the mid-1990s to peddle life insurance and retirement plans in the Age of Anxiety. A magazine ad, printed in sepia tones like an old-fashioned photo, shows an adult baby-boomer couple sitting on their front porch with two doe-eyed girls, one perhaps five years old, the other seven. "Help," reads the headline. Then in smaller type: "How did your parents ever do it? Pay for the dentist, school, even manage to put a little something aside for the future? Maybe life was once about getting ahead. Today it's more about keeping up." Then the pitch for the product, followed by the spirit-lifting laugh line: "So maybe you can do something really extravagant tonight. Like taking in a movie. That is, if you can find a sitter."

As enviable as the economic performance of the Eisenhower years looks today, after twenty-five years of slow growth, it didn't impress John F. Kennedy's activist economists in 1961. Even though living standards were improving as the economy rode the ups and downs of the business cycle, Eisenhower had presided over three recessions in eight years. With unemployment at 5.5%—roughly, what passes for "full employment" today—New Frontier economists declared it to be unacceptably high and persuaded President Kennedy to propose a tax cut. Congress adopted it after Kennedy's assassination, and the pace of economic growth quickened, just as Keynesian textbooks had predicted. The results enhanced the confidence of economists—and of a public still scarred by the Great Depression—that experts understood how the economy worked and that a wise government could rev it up. Economists of the era genuinely believed that the post-World War II pace of economic growth could be sustained indefinitely, provided the government was prepared to step in periodically.

At about the same time, the benefits of advances in technology—in air travel, for instance—spread to the middle class. In 1955, only a quarter of all Americans had ever flown on a commercial flight. By 1973, more than half of them had. In 1950, fewer than 700,000 American civilians traveled overseas; in 1973, nearly 7 million did.

The jet age arrived at the end of the 1950s, inaugurating quieter, more comfortable, and more efficient airplanes. On August 26, 1959, President Eisenhower traveled on a jet—the first Air Force One—for the first time in his life. He found it an "exhilarating experience," according to biographer Stephen Ambrose. "As the big jet went into its 'silent, effortless acceleration and its rapid rate of climb,' whatever doubts Ike had about the wisdom of spending most of the remainder of this term on world travels vanished. He was hooked." Millions of Americans had similar experiences in the 1960s as the airlines deployed jets first on transatlantic and then on shorter, domestic flights. Pan Am wooed the middle class with the first "Fly Now, Pay Later" marketing campaign. Charter airlines offered low fares to popular middle-class destinations such as Las Vegas. And Southwest Airlines, in a tantalizing hint of the fare wars that would come later, offered $10 fares on late-night flights between Dallas and Houston. Frank Borman, the astronaut who became president of Eastern Airlines, declared in the 1970s: "We have become mass transit."

For most Americans, the economy worked well in the quarter century after World War II. Their wages rose faster than inflation did. Their jobs increasingly came with health insurance and pensions. They bought houses at reasonable prices and low interest rates—and watched their wealth swell as the value of their houses increased. They looked forward to retiring on Social Security benefits. "This was an era during which the American dream was fulfilled for most families," wrote economists Peter Gottschalk and Sheldon Danziger.

At times, there was an uneasiness about the price of prosperity. Sloan Wilson's 1950s best-selling novel, *The Man in the Gray Flannel Suit,* captured the discomfort of rigid conformity and the gnawing lack of fulfillment even among those who were materially comfortable. "I don't know what's the matter with us," Betsy Rath says one night to her husband, Tom, a public relations man for a big New York City company. "Your job is plenty good enough. We've got three nice kids, and lots of people would be glad to have a house like this. We shouldn't be so *discontented* all the time."

The 1950s and 1960s were not a golden age for many American women, despite widespread improvement in their material well-being. For those who had paying jobs, opportunities were limited and their wages were considerably below those of men. Women made little progress in closing the wage gap, even when they worked at jobs similar to those that men held. Legal barriers to hiring married women vanished almost entirely in the 1950s, but most married women—70% in 1960—didn't have paying jobs. Women's magazines described the married woman as "gaily content in a world of bedroom and kitchen, sex, babies, and home," Betty Friedan reported in *The Feminine Mystique*. But many women didn't see life from the magazines' perspective.

Friedan called it "the problem that has no name" in her 1963 book, which shattered the mirage that American stay-at-home moms were happy, fulfilled, and content. "The problem lay buried, unspoken, for many years in the minds of American women," wrote Friedan, who had become a suburban housewife after the left-wing labor newspaper for which she wrote fired her when she got pregnant. "It was a strange stirring, a sense of dissatisfaction, a yearning that women suffered in the middle of the twentieth century in the United States. Each suburban wife struggled with it alone. As she made the beds, shopped for groceries, matched slipcover material, ate peanut butter sandwiches with her children, chauffeured Cub Scouts and Brownies, lay beside her husband at night—she was afraid to ask even of herself the silent question—'Is this all?'"

As the baby boomers reached adolescence in the 1960s, discontent spread to the college campuses. Whatever fueled the youthful campus rebellion and unrest of the decade, it wasn't deprivation. The "Port Huron Statement," issued by the Students for a Democratic Society in 1962, began: "We are people of this generation, *bred in at least modest comfort,* housed now in universities, looking uncomfortably at the world we inherit" (emphasis added).

Still, others lacked that "modest comfort." Blacks were often excluded from the American dream. Dennis Kerley remembers that blacks were admitted to one Chattanooga amusement park, but were banned from its swimming pool. Another park filled its swimming pool with concrete rather than allow blacks to swim in it. Only one in three black households in the surrounding county owned its own home in 1970, roughly half the proportion of white households. The typical black man with a full-time, year-round job in 1973 earned two-thirds of the amount the typical white man earned.

In the 1950s and early 1960s, poverty was hidden and ignored to a degree that is hard to imagine today when welfare, homelessness, and the brutality of urban life are staples of the nightly television news. In

1962, Michael Harrington's book, *The Other America,* made poverty visible. In the opening paragraphs of the book, Harrington held up a mirror to the middle class: "There is a familiar America. It is celebrated in speeches and advertised on television and in the magazines. It has the highest mass standards of living the world has ever known." Even its anxieties, he wrote, were "products of abundance."

"While this discussion was carried on," Harrington added, "there existed another America. In it dwelt somewhere between 40,000,000 and 50,000,000 citizens of this land. They were poor. They still are."

The reaction to Harrington was extraordinary, especially given today's cynicism about the ability of government to fight poverty. There was an almost unbounded optimism about the nation's capacity to cure poverty and all other economic ills. With the middle class taken care of, the only remaining economic challenge was to eradicate "pockets of poverty," as they were called, and that was seen as a manageable task. "The United States," President Lyndon Johnson's Council of Economic Advisers declared in the heady days of the War on Poverty, "is the first large nation in the history of the world wealthy enough to end poverty within its borders." James Tobin, a Kennedy economic adviser who would later win the Nobel Prize (though not for his forecasting ability), put a date on it. His article in the *New Republic,* in 1967, carried the headline: "It Can be Done! Conquering Poverty in the US by 1976." He was counting on sound macroeconomic policies and a "negative income tax" to help the poor; the government delivered neither. "The promised land receded," Tobin wrote years later. "We'll be lucky to reach it by 2026."

It wasn't just poverty that would be licked. Recessions would be abolished, too. Believing that the cycle of recession–recovery–recession was over, the government renamed its monthly "Business Cycle Digest," dubbing it "Business *Conditions* Digest." *TIME* gushed in 1969: "The amazing U.S. economy may defy even the law of physics: what goes up need not necessarily come down." *Fortune* ebulliently predicted in 1967 that wages would increase by 150% over the next twenty-five years. (*Fortune* was off by a factor of six. Including fringe benefits, total compensation for all workers in the United States actually rose by only 25% between 1967 and 1992, and wages for the typical worker rose much less.)

In what would later prove to be the closing scenes of the Golden Age, Paul Wilkes, a *New Yorker* writer, spent most of 1972 with a family he chose because it was as close to a real-life embodiment of the Census Bureau's average as he could find. The Neumeyers, as he called them in the book he wrote, *Trying Out the Dream,* lived in suburban Long Island and were modestly fulfilling the American dream. Art was foreman at a small, family-owned manufacturing company. Betty didn't work, though she talked frequently about getting a job. Her husband discouraged her: "He said she didn't have to and that she should enjoy herself at home, that she has earned it," Wilkes wrote.

Like many of her suburban counterparts, Betty Neumeyer was restless, and periodically depressed for reasons she didn't understand. Only one of her three children was still at home; she wondered what she would do with the rest of her life. Like many women of her generation, she didn't even know how to drive.

The older two of the three Neumeyer children were rebelling, rejecting their parents' suburban lifestyle. "It has become more and more apparent to Martha and Richard [20 and 18 years old, respectively] that their parents' lives are not the kinds of lives they want to have," Wilkes observed. "Martha does not aspire to be a mother and a homemaker; Richard does not want his life revolving around something as ephemeral as a job, steeped with responsibility, cemented in sureness."

One recurring scene in Wilkes's chronicle of his year with the Neumeyers was Betty's guilt about her malaise. After all, her family had so much more than she had ever dreamed: a three-bedroom home, the first backyard pool in the neighborhood, a week's vacation at the shore or in the mountains each year, and eight cameras, including one for shooting family movies.

Whatever its frustrations, the American economy had paid off for the Neumeyer family. Betty hadn't any doubt about that. Reflecting on how much her circumstances had changed over 22 years of marriage, Betty found her own way to sum up the Golden Age of the middle class: "I love the affluence of being able to rip off a big sheet of aluminum foil and not have to worry about washing it and using it again."

6

The Age of Anxiety

A disappointing quarter-century for the middle class,
1973–1996.

As the Golden Age closed in 1973, Dennis and Ann Kerley looked back at their parents' lives and at their own childhood and saw that they were better off—much better off. When Jim and Ann Marie Blentlinger, a Chattanooga couple a generation younger than the Kerleys, take a similar look back today, they wonder if the middle class has made any progress at all.

Can it really be true that couples living at the middle of the middle class today are worse off than couples in the same stage of life twenty years earlier?

The gloomy portrait of the American middle class painted in the press and in political debates often suggests the material standard of living for the middle class actually deteriorated between the 1970s and the mid-1990s, and only recently has begun to improve. An alternative portrait, popular among some economists, is that middle-class life has improved enormously, but that flawed official statistics hide the progress. A third view, best presented in books by *Newsweek* columnist Robert Samuelson and British-born journalist Michael Elliott, is that Americans complain too much and don't realize how good they have it now.

None of those views is right; all those explanations are far too simple. The experience of the American middle class over the past twenty-five

How life has changed since the early 1970s...

PEOPLE	1973	1996
% of women 15-19 years old who've ever had intercourse	29%	50%
% of births to unmarried mothers	10.7%	32.4%
legal abortions	616,000	1,267,000
% of mothers who breast feed	30.1%	58.1%
% of high school seniors who say they've used any illicit drug (other than marijuana) in past 30 days	15.4%	9.5%
% of high school seniors who say they've smoked cigarettes in past 30 days	36.7%	34.0%
% of income going to top 5% of households	15.5%	21.4%
% of income going to bottom 20% of households	5.5%	3.7%
households with incomes over $100,000 (1995 dollars)	2.9 million (4.2%)	8.3 million (8.2%)
black households with incomes over $100,000	63,400 (0.9%)	327,000 (2.7%)
children 18 and under living in poverty	9.6 million (14.4%)	14.5 million (20.5%)
persons over 65 living in poverty	3.4 million (16.3%)	3.4 million (10.8%)
% men between 25 and 34 living with parents	9%	15%
% of children under 18 living with two parents	82.1%	68.7%

CONSUMERS		
number of items in the average supermarket	9,000	30,000
U.S. residents who traveled overseas	6,933,000	19,767,000
foreigners who visited U.S.	3,554,000	22,454,000
pounds of red meat consumed per person	131.8 lbs	111.9 lbs
pounds of poultry consumed per person	33.7 lbs	64.3 lbs

HEALTH		
cases of measles	26,690	508
new cases of AIDS	0	52,200
% of population overweight	24.9%	33.0%
% of population with high cholesterol	27.2%	19.5%
death in first year of life (per 1,000 live births)	20.0	7.2
maternal death in childbirth (per 1,000 live births)	21.5	6.3
deaths from motor vehicle injuries (per 100,000 people)	26.9	16.5
deaths from suicide among 15-24 year olds (per 100,000)	8.8	13.3
life expectancy at birth	71.4	76.1

ENVIRONMENT		
% of aluminum cans recycled	15.2%	63.5%
tons of carbon monoxide emissions (million short tons)	144.8	92.1

WORKPLACE		
strikes involving 1,000 workers or more	317 strikes	37 strikes
workplace fatalities	14,200	6,112

EDUCATION		
high-school graduates in college the following fall	46.6%	61.9%
maximum federal "Pell Grant" to college students	$3,089	$2,308

How many hours of work does it take to buy a...

	1973	1996
First class stamp (1 oz letter)	$.08 — **1 min.**	$.32 — **1.1 min.**
Gallon of unleaded gasoline	$.39 — **4.9 min.**	$1.23 — **4.3 min.**
5-minute call from Dallas to Seattle	$2.19 — **27.9 min.**	$1.60 — **5.7 min.**
1 lb of chicken breast	$1.02 — **13 min.**	$2.02 — **7.1 min.**
McDonald's Big Mac and large fries	$1.05 — **13.4 min.**	$3.17 — **11.2 min.**
Movie ticket	$1.89— **24.1 min.**	$4.35 — **15.4 min.**
Monopoly board game	$3.97 — **50.6 min.**	$10.99 — **38.8 min.**
Men's dress shirt from Sears	$4.99 — **1.1 hrs.**	$23— **1.4 hrs.**
Best-selling novel	$7.95 — **1.7 hrs.**	$26.95 — **1.6 hrs.**
Amtrak one-way ticket from Boston to NYC	$9.90 — **2.1 hrs.**	$43 — **2.5 hrs.**
H&R Block tax preparation fee	$13.33 — **2.8 hrs.**	$66.23 — **3.9 hrs.**
Zenith 19-inch color TV	$439 — **12.6 days**	$239 — **2.5 days**
San Francisco 49ers season tickets	$85 — **2.4 days**	$450 — **3.9 days**
American Airlines round-trip ticket, NY to LA	$336 — **9.6 days**	$450 — **3.9 days**
Obstetrician's childbirth fee	$300 — **8.6 days**	$1,742 — **15 days**
One year's tuition at Brown University	$3,250 — **4.3 mo.**	$21,592 — **8.5 mo.**
Average cost of a car, including financing	$4,687 — **6.2 mo.**	$23,991 — **9.5 mo.**
Median price of house in Des Moines, Iowa	$21,000 — **2.3 yrs.**	$96,000 — **3.2 yrs.**

Based on average hourly wage of $4.71 in 1973 and $16.98 in 1996 years can't be summarized with a simple arrow pointing up or pointing down. A comparison of the lives of the Kerleys and the Blentlingers shows the true story is more nuanced. During the past twenty-five years, economic progress has been disappointingly slow, especially in comparison to the preceding decades. That isn't whining; it's reality— and it's why middle-class families are so disheartened. The past two decades of middle-class life have been gloomier than young couples like the Blentlingers had reason to expect. Although middle-class families today have more and better cars, more sophisticated appliances, and grander vacations, and are better off materially in many other ways, these gains have come at great cost and have been accompanied by relentless uncertainty and insecurity. These pressures won't disappear, but they will ease in the next twenty years.

For typical married couples, incomes did rise between 1973 and 1996. But the Blentlingers arrived at the middle of the middle class only because both Jim and Ann Marie work. This isn't simply one more fact; it is central to what happened to the American standard of living. Although many wives worked in the 1970s, most couples got by on a single paycheck. Today, the typical couple has two paychecks—but isn't living twice as well. Neither Jim nor Ann Marie Blentlinger earns as much as Dennis Kerley earned at DuPont in the mid-1970s, after adjustment for inflation. It's only because of the second paycheck that the Blentlingers are living better than the Kerleys did twenty years earlier.

The Blentlingers also rely on easy credit far more than the Kerleys did in the early 1970s. Credit cards and home-equity lines make it easier to buy the trappings of a middle-class life, and simpler to cope with financial emergencies, but easy credit also tempts families to borrow more than they can pay back. Despite a reasonably strong economy and the lowest unemployment in decades, 1.1 million people filed for personal bankruptcy in 1996, breaking the previous record of 900,000, set in 1992.

A close look at these two middle-class Chattanooga families— similar in many ways, but separated by twenty years—shows both the economic disappointments and the accomplishments of the Age of Anxiety. The comparison shows why—despite the wonders of cheap electronics, modern medicine, and a cleaner environment—so many middle-class families feel shortchanged. During the Golden Age, families lifted their incomes by getting paid more per hour, not by working more hours. In the Age of Anxiety, families got ahead primarily by work-ing more hours; hourly wages rose only slightly—or, for some, actually fell. The next twenty years will be better. Living standards won't improve as rapidly as they did in the Golden Age. But in the coming Age of Broadly Shared Prosperity there won't be any debate about whether life is getting better for most Americans; it will be obvious that it is.

In the 1990s, Jim and Ann Marie Blentlinger and their sons, Matthew and Luke, are living roughly at the median income for married couples, which the Census Bureau says was $49,700 in 1996. In some years, they make a little more than the median; in other years, a little less. In many respects, the Blentlingers *have* more and *want* more than the Ker-leys did back in the 1970s—but they pay a price for this ambition. With both parents working, tensions over housework and childcare, the chores that stay-at-home moms handle routinely, are inevitable. The credit cards that allow middle-class families to live beyond their means cause an uneasy sense of running to stay in place. And with 50-plus channels of cable television come an ever greater awareness of what others have, and a hard-to-fulfill longing to see more, do more, and have more.

Jim Blentlinger graduated from high school in 1983, and then worked, among other jobs, as a counselor in a Christian youth organi-zation and as a mental health aide. He moved to Chattanooga in 1990 to marry Ann Marie, then a student at the University of Tennessee at Knoxville. He was 25; she was 22. While working as the caretaker for a local church camp, Jim went to Chattanooga's community college and, in 1994, earned a degree in computer-aided design. Even before gradu-ation, he got a job designing, on a computer, restaurant layouts for a restaurant-supply business. The job at the small firm was more satisfy-ing and more flexible than Dennis Kerley's factory job ever was, and Blentlinger even got an occasional commission. There was a time clock on the wall, but no one ever punched it. If he arrived a few minutes late, no one noticed. Some of Blentlinger's classmates went to work for big companies, but he chose the small firm deliberately. "Guys at DuPont get laid off all the time. Their chances of not having a job next week are a lot bigger than mine," he explained early in 1995.

But just before Christmas of that year, the restaurant-supply firm closed. And unlike Dennis Kerley, who expected to be recalled by DuPont when he was laid off, Blentlinger knew his job was gone for good. He could have drawn unemployment benefits while he hunted for another job that used his computer skills, but he didn't. "I pretty much decided a long time ago there was no chance of my going on unemployment," he said. "I'd work at a McDonald's before that."

He took a $6-an-hour stock clerk's job at an office-supply firm owned by a member of his church, and a few months later began selling office supplies to small businesses on the outskirts of Chattanooga. For several months, Blentlinger, who never met anybody he didn't want to talk to, drove his '88 Jeep Cherokee, which had already traveled 103,250 miles, from one small office to another, peddling office adding-machine tape, manila folders, and used chairs. One hot, sunny Southern day, he chatted with 20 or so receptionists and secretaries in northern Georgia, but didn't close a single sale. Most of them politely told him they didn't need anything. When folks at a Georgia Farm Bureau office asked about buying a "customer parking only" sign, Blentlinger suggested where they could have one made. Afterward, he wondered aloud if he should have bought the sign himself and sold it at a markup. "Maybe I'm too idealistic to be a successful salesman," he said.

For whatever reason, the job was a bust; it lasted only about nine months. He quit when the placement office at Chattanooga State Technical Community College called with a tip that an air-conditioning manufacturer was looking for someone to do computer-aided design. Despite the 45-minute commute—and the cost of fueling his thirsty Jeep—Jim leaped at the $25,000-a-year job. But he stayed less than ten months, leaving with mixed feelings when Chattanooga State passed along word of a position with a consulting engineering firm located much closer to his home. The pay was better, too. This job pays $29,000 a year, more than Jim has ever made, but not as much, adjusted for inflation, as Dennis Kerley earned in the early 1970s.

Now in his early 30s, Jim Blentlinger is fighting an on-again, off-again battle to trim a bulging waistline, which reminds him he is no longer a kid. But he maintains a refreshing, youthful confidence that everything will work out. "Most people would like to make lots of money. We just like to do all right and do what we want to do. I'd rather work at one place for 20 years. But," he adds quickly, "Ann Marie tells me: 'If you make a little bit more, I won't have to work.'"

Working mothers with young children—women like Ann Marie—aren't exceptional today; they were during the Golden Age.

In Chattanooga, the 1970 census found that only 33% of women with children under six years of age were working. By 1990, in Chattanooga and elsewhere, the rate was up to 60%. Ann Marie Blentlinger, 2½ years younger than her husband, is a fair-skinned woman with a round face and an inviting smile. She followed her mother and grandmother into public-school teaching, and gives her three-syllable last name as an extra-credit spelling word on tests.

The Blentlingers had hoped to time their first pregnancy so the baby would come at the end of the school year, allowing Ann Marie to spend the summer caring for him, but Matthew arrived in February 1992. Ann Marie worked until the day before she delivered, then took four weeks of paid sick leave and two weeks of unpaid leave before returning to the classroom. She would have liked more time, but the couple needed her income.

In contrast, Ann Marie's mother stayed home until her only child was a sophomore in high school. Ann Marie likes teaching most of the time, but is ambivalent about working. "I wouldn't feel productive if I didn't work," she says, "but I figure I only have one chance at raising Matthew." The Blentlingers timed the arrival of their second child better. Luke was born at the end of May 1997, allowing Ann Marie to take some of her forty-eight days of sick leave at the end of one school year and to spend the summer with her two children. But there isn't any more talk about quitting work altogether.

Ever since he was six weeks old, Matthew has been in day care or in school all day. As an infant, he went to a day care center at Chattanooga State where his grandfather, Ann Marie's father, is a dean and math teacher. Some of Jim's jobs allowed him to drop Matthew at the day care center on his way to work. But when he had to leave home before 6:00 A.M. to put in a few hours unpacking boxes at the office-supply company to supplement his salesman's pay, Ann Marie had to drive across town to leave Matthew with her father at 7:15—because the day care center didn't open until 7:30—and then drive back across town to be at her school by 7:35.

Ann Marie fantasizes about starting her own in-home business because that would allow her to stay with Matthew and Luke—and save the $300 a month they spend on day care. She talks about selling invitations and stationery printed on her personal computer, and the couple spent their $1,000 tax refund in 1996 on paper and other supplies.

But they both know that Ann Marie isn't likely to make anywhere near the $29,000 she is now earning as a seventh-grade reading teacher. "She has to teach until the van is paid off," Jim used to say, laughing but not joking. The van is now paid off, and Ann Marie is still teaching.

Twenty years earlier, in the early 1970s, Dennis Kerley was a burly, blond dad. Ann was a slim, serious, stay-at-home wife. Their first two boys were born close together, in 1968 and 1969; the third boy arrived in 1974. It wasn't easy for the Kerleys to make ends meet, but they thought the boys would benefit if Ann stayed home. Besides, Dennis didn't want his churchgoing wife to deal with the foul language and "vulgarity" of a factory job. "I liked her being at home," he says today. "Having dinner ready for him at 4:30," she interrupts.

In the early 1970s, DuPont automatically disqualified women from factory work requiring manual labor. Application forms for these jobs were marked with an asterisk and the words, "Male only." Twenty years later, Dennis Kerley's workplace partner is a young woman who hoists a heavy electric wrench to change machine parts that weigh as much as forty pounds apiece. Dennis and his partner carry the same workload and pull down the same paycheck.

Ann Kerley didn't even drive until she convinced her husband to teach her when she was 27, and giving her even this smidgen of freedom frightened him. "It was a control thing. I didn't want her independent," he says candidly. Ann was hardly unusual. In 1970, one in four women—but only one in ten men—didn't drive. She now buys herself a new car every few years. With her children grown, Ann Kerley works full-time at $9 an hour in a carpet mill in nearby Dalton, Georgia, and enjoys the independence and extra money. By bringing home an additional paycheck, she says, "You can have a little more, and you don't have to worry so much."

The Kerleys' life was marked by a disciplined, self-sacrificing frugality. They still have neat bundles of twenty-year-old checks that document how carefully they spent. Dennis earned $9,740 at DuPont in 1973. Thanks to overtime and a couple of substantial raises, his earnings jumped to $12,332 in 1974—roughly what the typical married man earned that first year of the Age of Anxiety. Dennis had been haunted his whole life by his father's debts and reluctance to share information about family finances with his wife. Dennis was determined to be different. So Dennis and Ann took out a ruler every month and drew a grid on a steno pad. On the left, they noted all the bills they had to pay and the date each payment was due. Each week, they would make a budget. The Kerleys may have been extreme, but their determination to live within their means was more typical of the Golden Age than of more recent times.

Judging strictly by possessions and conveniences, the Kerleys certainly had far less in 1973 than the Blentlingers have today. They spent more of their family budget on food, ate out less often than the Blentlingers do, settled for a car and appliances that are primitive by today's standards, had many fewer options for how to spend their free time, and had neither the means nor the inclination to travel.

Look inside the two-bedroom yellow bungalow that the Kerleys rented in a Chattanooga suburb in the early 1970s: The fifty-year-old house had a washer, a double-door refrigerator, a 21-inch color TV, and a window air-conditioner, but no vacuum cleaner and no dryer. "I hung clothes out on the line," Ann recalls. "In the winter I'd go to the Washeteria to dry them."

The Blentlingers' house in the 1990s has all that the Kerleys' had and then some: a washer plus a dryer, a dishwasher, even a bread-baking machine. Fruits of the electronics revolution are everywhere; everything electronic is far cheaper and far better than anything the Kerleys had. They have a 21-inch TV in the living room and a 13-inch set in the kitchen, both with cable television. Ann Marie Blentlinger does things Ann Kerley couldn't imagine in the early 1970s: She tapes "As the World Turns" on a VCR for later viewing, and turns out custom birthday cards on her color printer. In the kitchen, the Blentlingers have a cordless telephone and a microwave oven. They listen to singer Amy Grant on a compact-disk player, which offers crisper sound than the cabinet-size record and tape player on which the Kerleys listened to the Oak Ridge Boys. Adjusted for inflation, the $169 CD player cost 40% of what the Kerleys' stereo did twenty years before.

To feed the family, the Blentlingers spend less of their paychecks on food than couples like the Kerleys did twenty years earlier—even including the cost of eating out. The Kerleys figure they spent $35—roughly, one day's pay—each week on groceries in the early 1970s, when they had two young boys. "Most nights we'd have meat," Ann recalls. "He thinks he's starving if he doesn't have meat." Only rarely did they treat the family to dinner at a hamburger joint or take the kids for soft ice cream at Dairy Gold.

The Blentlingers spend just two-thirds what the Kerleys spent on groceries, adjusted for inflation. One reason, of course, is that one of the younger couple's children is still an infant. The typical middle-class family today has fewer members, so the same income, adjusted for higher prices, goes a little further. But having one, or even two, fewer children doesn't compensate for the excruciatingly slow growth of income. After adjusting family income figures to reflect shrinking family size, economists Sheldon Danziger and Peter Gottschalk concluded that median income per family member still was only 8% greater in 1993 than it was twenty years before.

Eating out more often is a distinguishing feature of today's middle-class lifestyle, one of those improvements in American living standards that often escapes public discussion. Perhaps twice a month, the Blentlingers dine at a family restaurant such as Bennigan's, a national chain with several Chattanooga outlets, which charges $5.59 for a hamburger and fries. Once a luxury for the middle class, eating out is now so common that the number of restaurants in the Chattanooga area grew by more than 40% between 1972 and 1992.

Measured against family incomes, however, some important emblems of middle-class life, such as houses and cars, have grown more expensive over the past twenty years. In 1976, after years of putting every raise Dennis got into a savings account, the Kerleys managed to accumulate $1,500 in the credit union. With that, and another $1,000 borrowed from the same credit union, they made a down payment on a $26,000, three-bedroom, split-level house a few miles north of Chattanooga. The Kerleys avoided the city itself because they wanted no part of the court-ordered school busing aimed at integrating Chattanooga's public schools. The house cost roughly twice Dennis's annual earnings at the time, but he thought it was worth it. The one-year-old home had a roomy backyard, central air-conditioning, wall-to-wall carpeting, a big basement, and the first dishwasher the Kerleys ever owned. "It was nicer than anything my parents ever had," Dennis says.

For a young family at the middle of the middle class, it was easier to buy a house in the early 1970s than in the early 1990s. In 1973, the median house in the United States sold for about 2.2 times the income of the typical married couple—again, most families earned only one paycheck. Twenty years later, the typical house cost close to 2.5 times the median married couple's income, even though the modern couple was more likely to have two paychecks. Largely because of that, home ownership among families headed by people in their 30s and early 40s has fallen.

The Blentlingers have achieved the embodiment of the American dream—home ownership; many of their peers haven't been so fortunate. After living rent-free when Jim worked as caretaker for a church camp, and then renting for about a year, they bought a house, in June 1995, on a quiet, shady block in the blue-collar suburb called Red Bank. They paid $70,455—less than twice their combined annual income. Like an increasing number of young couples, the Blentlingers couldn't have afforded the house without help from Ann Marie's parents, who gave them $4,000 toward the down payment. Data compiled by the Chicago Title & Trust Company show that such gifts account for a growing fraction of the down payments of first-time home buyers. In the late 1970s, 8.5% of the average down payment was a gift, usually from a relative; in the early 1990s, it was 13.1%.

The Blentlingers' split-level house has three bedrooms and a dark-paneled family room off the kitchen. It's roughly equivalent to the house in which Ann Marie Blentlinger grew up, the house in which her parents still live—one of the reasons that the Blentlingers suspect the middle class isn't improving its lot as rapidly as earlier generations did. The house, however, came with central air-conditioning and an alarm system, a feature that didn't even make the Kerleys' wish list in the 1970s. And, at last, the Blentlingers have a two-car garage, something they've wanted ever since they were married.

Cars cut more deeply into middle-class budgets today than they did during the Golden Age. In late 1973, as gasoline prices shot up, Dennis Kerley traded his roomy Ford Galaxie for a 1973 Datsun station wagon barely big enough for the family of five. It cost $3,195—three months' pay—and was the family's only car. They paid it off in just three years. But car owners today get more for their money; the cars are safer and more comfortable, and they perform better. The Blentlingers have two cars: the used Jeep that Jim bought from his fastidious boss at the restaurant-supply house, and a 1993 Dodge Caravan they bought new.

The minivan boasts a tape player, an airbag on the driver's side, and electric locks, features that didn't exist or were only for the wealthy twenty years earlier. But Jim and Ann Marie paid for the extras: The minivan cost $18,000, or four-and-a-half months of the Blentlingers' combined income. Because it cost so much, they paid it off over five years.

Higher car prices are one reason that middle-class families today rely so much more on credit than did families several decades ago—to better and worse effect. Easy credit is a key both to middle-class life and to middle-class anxiety. For big purchases in the 1970s, the Kerleys kept an account at a local store, and paid off each new appliance before buying another. They used credit cards only for children's clothes, and then only when Ann Kerley didn't sew them herself on a sewing machine her mother-in-law had given her. Their canceled checks show only a handful of MasterCharge payments, and those were only about $40 each.

For many, that kind of frugality started to crumble in September 1958. Bank of America mailed 60,000 unsolicited cards to the citizens of Fresno, California, a watershed in American economic life. The cards took years to catch on, but when they did, they became indispensable to middle-class families. In 1970, only 15% of American families carried general-purpose credit cards—Visa, MasterCard, or other cards that could be used almost anywhere. By 1986, more than 55% of families did. And by 1992, 63% did. "Consumers seem to have taken the television commercial to heart: Very few ever leave home without one," says Lewis Mandell, historian of the credit card. Credit card solicitations now arrive in the mail—or in dinnertime phone calls—with the regularity of sunset. "We get a credit card application every day, or at least once or twice a week," Jim Blentlinger says.

The Blentlingers, although not overburdened with debt, ran up a $2,000 Visa tab over a three-year period before they swore off plastic. It had become too easy to live beyond their means. Ann Marie arranged for the teachers' credit union to automatically deduct from her salary: $80 each month to pay off Visa, $70 for a loan they took to buy a personal computer, and another $367 for the van.

Couples like the Blentlingers do shoulder a heavier tax burden than similar couples in the 1970s did, but the difference isn't nearly as great as is popularly believed. The problem for the middle class is not that taxes are increasing, but that *income before taxes* is increasing very slowly. In 1973, according to U.S. Treasury Department estimates, the typical family of four had income of $13,710 and paid about $1,300 in federal income taxes and $630 in Social Security and Medicare payroll taxes. These federal taxes ate up 14.2% of their income. As payroll taxes rose to finance an increasingly expensive Medicare health-insurance program for the elderly and to bolster Social Security, the federal tax bite for these families climbed to 18.4% in 1981. Then things began to improve. Tax reform in the mid-1980s cut income tax rates for the middle class. By 1995, the typical family of four paid 16.8% of its $47,700 income in taxes—about $4,375 in income taxes and $3,650 in payroll taxes.

A more comprehensive Congressional Budget Office analysis covered federal taxes on liquor, cigarettes, gasoline, and airline tickets, as well as taxes paid by businesses, income taxes, and payroll taxes. It found that the overall tax bite on families in the middle of the middle class didn't budge between 1977 and 1994. Federal taxes claimed 19.5% of their incomes in 1977 and 19.4% in 1994. For middle-class families with children, the 1997 tax cuts shaved their tax bills a bit from those levels.

Middle-class satisfaction reflects not only what people have, but what they want. The Blentlingers of the 1990s have a lot in common with the Kerleys of the 1970s: a hardworking seriousness, a strong desire to see their children succeed, and a deep commitment to their church. Recreation for the Kerleys in the 1970s was mostly free: softball games at Dennis's parents' house, and church gatherings where the men would grill hot dogs and the women would bring covered dishes of food. The Kerleys rarely went out without their children. But neither do the Blentlingers. With both of them working and dividing the household chores, it isn't only the money; it's the energy. They rent videos from time to time, but Ann Marie confesses that she usually falls asleep before they're over.

But the Blentlingers have more choices now and want more in the future: travel; private school for their sons. They have a more expansive sense of the world and a clearer sense of what they would do with more money. They are less satisfied with what they have—and that, together with the stress of two jobs, nagging worries about debt, and the disparities between ordinary Americans and the very wealthy, adds to the discontent of today's middle class.

The yen to travel illustrates rising middle-class expectations. The Kerleys loved to camp in the 1970s, but rarely strayed far from home. "We've never been farther north than North Carolina. Never been out West," Dennis Kerley says without regret. Although they made two pilgrimages to Walt Disney World in Florida, a typical 1970s vacation was four nights of camping about twenty miles away on the shores of Chickamauga Lake, within sight of the cooling towers of a nuclear power plant. Dennis's parents would go along, and after the kids were put to bed, the adults would build a fire and toss out fishing lines. (One unpleasant feature of the times: The river was so polluted that they could see the debris float by.) In the winter, Dennis would work a couple of days of readily available overtime, then drive the family to Daytona, Florida, for a long weekend at the cheapest beach-front motel they could find.

The Blentlingers, by contrast, have been as far away as a remote corner of British Columbia, where they met at a Christian youth camp. Vacations in the 1990s mean flying to Texas or Illinois to visit Jim's family, or long weekends in North Carolina or South Carolina with Ann Marie's parents—but they long for more. They describe their one long weekend in New York City as if doing a tourism promotion ad ("I thought riding the subway was great," Jim says). In 1994, Ann Marie's parents paid her way to Paris, where her mother and grandmother were chaperoning a group of Chattanooga high school students. "This trip opened my eyes," she says.

Gauging standards of living means more than taking an inventory of a family's possessions and comparing vacations. Broadly defined, living standards go beyond vacuum cleaners and television sets to the quality of the air that people breathe, the health of their children, their safety, and their sense that they are doing as well as their neighbors are. By such measures, the story of the middle class over the past twenty-five years is mixed.

The shuttering of a big ammunition factory, production cuts at other plants, and an aggressive local anti-air-pollution campaign brought a welcome change to Chattanooga's air, deemed the nation's dirtiest by the federal government in 1969. "You'd go across Missionary Ridge and, on a typical day, there'd just be a cloud and it was bad. We were a very industrialized city," says Ann Marie Blentlinger's father, Herb Hooper, who grew up not far from Chattanooga and has lived in the city since the early 1960s. "It looked like pictures of the L.A. smog that you used to see," adds his wife, Brenda. Today, the air is clean and the city, which operates one of the nation's largest fleets of electrically powered buses, is trying to promote itself as a center for environmental research and technology. One of the city's grungiest factories, U.S. Pipe & Foundry, is even growing pine trees around its perimeter to present a greener face to motorists passing by on the interstate.

But in cleaner, healthier Chattanooga, crime is a far greater worry to the Blentlingers than it was to the Kerleys twenty years before. In 1992, Ann Marie's father was shot as he ran fleeing from a mentally disturbed college student who suddenly pulled a gun from her purse. He wasn't seriously hurt, but the incident has made him far more cautious than he had been before. More recently, Jim and Ann Marie Blentlinger were shaken—and still are—by an incident they witnessed in the church parking lot downtown, in the summer of 1994. A car drove up, a young man got out, asked a group of teenagers for a cigarette, and then punched one of them in the jaw without any apparent provocation.

And it isn't just crime that makes the Blentlingers uneasy. They correctly sense a disturbingly large gap between themselves and the best-off Chattanoogans, the ones living in the posh new houses that have been built in the mountains overlooking the city. They wonder how some of the other young families in their Baptist church can afford so much more than they can. "If I could afford it, I'd like to be on Signal Mountain. There are so many good neighborhoods, and it's a good area as far as schools go," Ann Marie says. Signal Mountain, where the median household makes twice as much as the median household in the Blentlingers' Red Bank neighborhood, is favored by Chattanooga's new money, by DuPont managers, and by up-and-coming lawyers.

In the 1970s, few hourly workers even thought about living near the boss, so such disparities weren't much of an issue. "It was almost like a caste system," says Ray Childers, the former DuPont supervisor. But if some social and psychological distance between workers and managers has narrowed over twenty years, the economic distance has widened. In 1973, DuPont's chief executive earned 29 times the median earnings of male American workers. Twenty years later, the CEO earned 41 times as much. According to the 1990 census, 3,500 Chattanooga families had incomes more than triple the local median family income—that is, over $100,000. By this rough definition, the number of affluent families increased by 60% over twenty years, a period in which the overall number of families grew by only 16%.

Middle-class resentment shows itself differently in Chattanooga today than it did during the early 1970s, when the city's restive blue-collar workforce was ready to walk off the job during fights with management. It now focuses on institutions identified with the expanding affluent class—in particular, a $45-million aquarium. The privately financed aquarium is the focal point for the city's ambitious downtown rejuvenation, but many longtime residents see it as a plaything for the suburban elites. "I like to go to aquariums, but I never go to Chattanooga's," says Ray Catlett, a middle-aged machinist who has lived in the area his whole life. He calls the aquarium "the bull's eye" for populist resentment.

Some of the inequality of the past twenty-five years reflects unusual economic forces that probably will prove unique to the Age of Anxiety. The decline of labor unions removed one of the floors that kept wages from falling. Twenty years ago, close to 25% of all public and private employees were union members; today, less than 15% are. A wave of immigration—the greatest in 70 years, adjusted for the size of the U.S. population—widened the gap between the well-paid and poorly paid by vastly increasing the pool of unskilled workers, even as it enriched Americans in other ways. The demographics also were unusual: The baby boom entered the workforce, and so did millions of working moms. Nearly two-thirds of all mothers of children under six years old are in the workforce, twice the proportion twenty years ago. None of these forces will persist with such strength for another twenty years: unions can't get much weaker. Americans won't permit as much immigration. And, whatever the economic consequences of the baby boom and the rise of the working mom, both have been absorbed by the economy already.

Today, Chattanooga's economy—like much of America's—is on the rebound. But the uneasiness has yet to dissipate, despite the euphoric reports about the economy in the press, and President Clinton's boastful speeches.

DuPont is investing in its Chattanooga nylon plant again: modernizing machinery, adding product lines, and even hiring new workers, though largely to replace retiring older ones. But the memory of the hard times of the 1980s hasn't faded for Kerley and his colleagues.

Ominously, in their view, the company is relying on outside labor contractors to do a growing portion of what it calls "peripheral" work—tasks like shipping and receiving. The company insists these cheaper workers will be laid off first if business turns sour; Kerley and his coworkers worry that DuPont won't keep its word.

Still, Dennis now has substantial seniority and is finally getting the opportunity to become an electrician, the highest paying blue-collar job at DuPont. He is taking college courses at the plant, and the company pays for the training. But, to save money, the company isn't paying wages for the hours Kerley logs in the classroom, as it did for earlier groups of workers. Most weeks, he is expected to put in 40 hours at DuPont plus 16 unpaid hours in the classroom. Given the choice of training to be an electrician or a maintenance technician, both of which pay the same, Dennis chose electrician because he figures that's a more marketable skill, should he ever have to leave DuPont.

Jim Blentlinger still maintains his unshakable optimism, even though he has been forced to change jobs so often. He lifts his wife's spirits when they sag. But when her father, Herb Hooper, reflects on his daughter's and son-in-law's prospects, he frowns. "They'll have to work as hard as Brenda and I have worked," Hooper muses, "but they won't have the income to show for it. I think they'll continue to live with more uncertainty—just because of the times."

7

The Computer Paradox

Why computers haven't paid off—yet.

The central economic mystery of our time is why an economy that delivered so much for its middle-class majority through 1973 took such a disappointing turn. Why did productivity gains peter out? Why didn't a hard-working couple like Jim and Ann Marie Blentlinger make bigger strides, measured against the previous generation?

The mystery deepens because it coincides with an extraordinary burst of technological creativity. Since the 1970s, microprocessors, personal computers, biotechnology, global communication networks, and a host of other seminal inventions have begun to transform homes and industries. Economists and nearly everyone else figured that computers, especially, would power the economy. Since the invention of the microprocessor in 1970, U.S. businesses have spent $2 trillion on information technology, much of it for personal computers, software, and communications equipment. If computers had come close to living up to the promises made in the glossy, glowing ads in news magazines and business publications, the United States would be enjoying a productivity boom. It's not. Productivity has been increasing at a pitifully slow pace of 1% a year, on average, since 1973.

Productivity experts find it easier to exonerate suspects than to convict them for causing the slowdown. At first, economists blamed the oil shock. But oil prices came down, and productivity failed to rebound. Then they accused the flood of inexperienced workers, both baby boomers and women returning to the workforce. But the youngest baby boomers are now past 30, and most women in the workforce have been working for a while; yet productivity still lags. Next, they blamed the torrid inflation of the 1970s and early 1980s. But productivity didn't turn up even after inflation was licked in the 1980s.

Then, some economists turned back to the time-worn complaint about the fading American work ethic. But that isn't any more compelling now than it was in the past. After productivity scholar Edward Denison, of the Brookings Institution, admitted in a published interview that he didn't know the reason for the decline in productivity, he got lots of phone calls from people who were sure they knew. American workers "don't want to work any more," the callers told him. Denison was unpersuaded. "My skepticism," he wrote in 1979, "is largely attributable to having heard similar generalizations all my life and having read them in the works of observers who wrote long before my birth."

In some parts of the economy, especially in manufacturing, productivity has begun to turn around. But why do the companies that employ the 100 million Americans who work outside of manufacturing, including the Blentlingers, have so little to show for the enormous investments they have made in computer technology? Why is productivity stalled in America's vast service sector, the 80% of the economy that includes everything from hardwood-floor professional suites to linoleum-tile bodegas?

Fortune technology columnist Stewart Alsop pondered this productivity paradox, as economists have labeled it, and blamed computer technology. "The trouble with software is . . . it sucks," he concluded. A flip answer, to be sure, but one that reflects the hard-learned wisdom that computers have been failures, so far, in bucking up productivity. Like a frustrated detective searching for clues, Nobel Prize-winning economist Robert Solow remarked: "You can see the computer age everywhere but in the productivity statistics."

It's hard to think straight about computers, with all the hype and hope surrounding them. Microprocessors, the chameleon-like computer chips that can be programmed for different tasks—writing reports, calculating finances, changing streetlights from red to green—ushered in the microcomputing era in 1970. Packaged with memory

The elusive payoff of computers

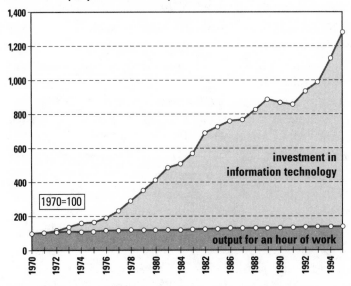

"You can see the computer age everywhere but in the productivity statistics," says Nobel laureate Robert Solow. Since 1970, investment in computers and other information technology has soared, but growth in output for each hour of work has not. Source: *Economic Report of the President 1997.*

chips and other equipment, microprocessors became the brains of personal computers, compact disk players, computer games, robots, and machine tools. Computers have accomplished great things over the past few decades, especially when lashed together as networks. Automated teller machines make cash available around the clock; bar-code scanners let supermarkets track and sell thousands more items than they used to carry; airline reservation systems handle millions of calls efficiently and reduce the cost of airline tickets; electronic-mail systems link correspondents around the globe, obliterating notions of time and space; computer networks let kids tap libraries of information once reserved for scientists.

But those accomplishments don't justify the awe that computers inspire. Many people venerate personal computers. When they sit in front of the screens, they feel plugged into the future. Others are intimidated. They demand that their schools buy more PCs so that their children won't be left behind, even though schools are frequently baffled about how to merge computers into their curricula. The media reinforce the fear and adoration. *TIME* named the personal computer the "Machine of the Year" in 1982, even though computers of that time were too primitive to make a big difference in society. (*TIME* should have realized it was ahead of reality when the article's author chose to bat out his computer paean on a typewriter.) More recently, to launch its Windows 95 software, Microsoft mounted a television-ad campaign that would have made P. T. Barnum proud. Backed by pulsing Rolling Stones music, the campaign had teenagers talking, in the reverential tones once reserved for hot rods, about a software program that did little more than arrange other software programs. The effect of all the hype is twofold: People believe that computers are some kind of pass to the future, and when computers don't deliver much, they blame themselves, not the machines.

It's not surprising, then, that many people believe computers have made their working lives more productive. Far from it. Microcomputers have been a bust so far, in lifting productivity throughout the economy. To be sure, there have been some successes. Manufacturing productivity has recovered from the slump of the late 1970s and early 1980s, and is now growing at better than 3.5% annually, in part because factories have figured out how to unleash the potential of computers. But productivity growth in the vast sectors of the economy outside of manufacturing has averaged a paltry 0.6% per year since 1973, according to government statistics.

Productivity scholars rightly point out that those statistics probably misstate recent productivity improvements. There are straightforward ways to gauge manufacturing gains—the number of tires produced during an hour of work—and the government probably overcounts efficiency gains here. But because it's harder to estimate gains in the service sector, the government often undercounts them. Is a doctor more productive if he sees more patients in an hour, or if he sees fewer patients but cures more of them? Is a law firm more productive if it revises a legal brief eight times in the length of time it used to take to revise the document twice?

Nevertheless, the chasm over the past twenty-five years between the technological advances of the microcomputer era and the broad productivity disappointments isn't simply a reflection of poor measurement. Even if the measurements were perfect, the mystery would remain: Why hasn't the computer revolution done more to raise the living standards of the American people during the past twenty-five years? In good measure, it's because computer systems are so complex, and computer and software designers are so out of touch with computer users that the systems are bound to fail.

Computers drive people crazy, even smart people. They're hard to use and they're poorly designed. "Not a day goes by that I don't want to throw my computer out the window," Mitch Kapor used to say when he was running Lotus Development Corporation, then a giant in the software field. Humorist Dave Barry captured the frustration: "In 1578, Da Vinci sketched the following diagram, which, although simple, contains all the fundamental elements that we find in modern computers," he wrote. Underneath was a sketch of a computer screen displaying the message: "ERROR, ERROR." Computer-industry doyens like to think of themselves as the sprinters of the economy, bursting past the laggards on their way to prosperity and productivity. In reality, the computer-driven economy moves more like a fox-trot: two steps forward, one step sideways.

Think about icons, the tiny computer-screen sketches that substitute for typed commands. Using a mouse to click on an icon of a trash can saves a computer user from having to type "delete active document," or something even more obscure. When Apple's Macintosh computers pioneered icons, they freed users from memorizing opaque commands. But now computers are so chockablock with icons that it's impossible to remember what they all mean. Rather than boost efficiency, they stymie it. Clifford Stoll, a best-selling computer critic, complained that his engineering-design software has 50 different icons and five different palettes of color. "I'm literally navigating through a maze of twisty passages, all different, without signposts or maps," he writes. Some programs try to fix that problem by labeling icons with text-filled balloons, thus scrapping the original idea that icons could be wordless guides to computing. Call it the Frankenstein factor: Computer designers try to help improve society, but manage to screw things up in the same way that Dr. Frankenstein tried to create life through technology but produced a monster instead.

Reliance Insurance Company has had a long struggle with the Frankenstein factor. Entranced by the ability of personal computers to write and send paperwork electronically, Reliance declared in 1979 that it would be "Paper Free by 1983." The Philadelphia insurer spent millions on new computers and an electronic mail system. To rev up employees, it printed the paper-free slogan on wall posters, coffee cups, stationery, and lapel buttons. At the appointed time, though, Reliance was buried in computer printouts. Like most companies, it was using *more* paper because employees printed out draft after draft of reports. These days, Reliance no longer talks about being paper-free; it merely hopes to save money on printing costs by posting manuals on its computer network. Gloats a spokesman for Xerox, which profits from paper-clogged offices: "There will be a paperless office when there is a paperless bathroom."

Bank managers are aware of Frankenstein's monster. Automated teller machines (ATMs) seemed to be a clear productivity winner, but they have had ghoulish consequences for banks. At first, banks were pleased: automated deposits and withdrawals cost about one-fifth as much as teller-processed ones, and the public loved the convenience. What could be better? But banks didn't realize that ATMs would radically change the way customers use banks. Instead of waiting in a teller's line once a week to withdraw $150, customers now pop over to the ATM several times a week to withdraw $30 at a time. Scowling tellers, it turns out, kept bank expenses down.

Now the banks are stuck. They can't pull out ATMs or customers will desert them. But if they expand ATM services, customers won't have any reason at all to go into bank branches and chat. As banks discovered too late, customers who mill about the lobby are often the ones who decide to take out home-equity loans, buy stocks, or use other services that banks make money on. Searching for a way out of the bind, branch employees at First Union Corporation in Durham, North Carolina, are cold-calling bank customers to sell them car loans and retirement plans, hoping that phone calls will substitute for the personal encounters lost with ATMs.

Repeated over and over again, the Frankenstein factor and other problems cancel out many of the productivity gains promised for the economy. Many times, the solutions are achingly obvious: Software designers should talk to software users before they design new programs. But the obvious is overlooked, something we've seen firsthand in the Washington bureau of *The Wall Street Journal,* where we work. The *Journal* is a technologically savvy company that pioneered the use of satellites to produce a national newspaper. But it stumbled badly when it upgraded the software in Washington in 1995 without conferring with the bureau's news staff beforehand.

The new software allowed reporters and editors to do some things they had never done before, such as send e-mail. But when it came to the most basic task of a newspaper bureau—moving a story from a reporter's desk to an editor's—the new software was awful. Reporters couldn't tell whether editors had received their stories. Editors couldn't easily tell what the story was about, who had sent it, or whether it had been previously edited—all things the old software used to tell them. After some fast consultations with apologetic technicians sent from New York to train the Washington staff, some fixes were made. But the system still is slower and more cumbersome than the one it replaced.

Ron Shafer, a bearded, 35-year veteran of the newspaper, stares at a computerized index of stories filed to him. "Here's 'Ratart.doc,' whatever that means," he sighs, nodding at the screen. He calls up the story, which turns out to be the chart material, or "art," illustrating a story about the balanced budget amendment. "Rat" was short for "ratify." Neither the old nor the new system could handle a more obvious name—"Ratify-art," let's say—because file names can't be longer than seven letters. But the old indexing system listed the first line of an article, so the editors could see what the story was about. Next, Shafer turns to another, even more inscrutable file: "MS2354." For reasons he can't figure out, stories sent from the *Journal's* New York headquarters are named like that. MS2354 turns out to be a headline, but the bewildered Shafer says of the new software system: "It's all one incomprehensible mess."

The *Journal's* computer team waited months—until after the software was installed—to dispatch fifteen technicians to interview Shafer and other senior editors about how they did their jobs. They clustered around the editors like students in the Greek agora surrounding Socrates. "What is it that you do?" Shafer says they asked him. "They had no idea how the Washington bureau operated."

The problems continued. To guard against a crash in the computer network that linked the several dozen reporters and editors covering the 1996 presidential conventions, the newspaper assigned a half-dozen technicians to the convention sites in San Diego and Chicago. No matter; the system sometimes crashed on deadline anyway. Meanwhile, convention reporters communicated with Washington mainly by using the old, supposedly obsolete computer network that the new system was supposed to supplant. "Organizing *The Wall Street Journal's* coverage of this year's national political conventions wasn't quite as complicated as the planning of the liberation of Kuwait, but considering the number of people deployed, and the number of different departments and companies involved, it came close on a per-capita basis," one of the senior computer managers wrote in the company's newsletter, without a note of irony.

Walter S. Mossberg, the *Journal's* computer columnist, sent scathing reviews of the new system to higher-ups in New York. The problem, he says, is that the computer designers and technicians didn't understand how reporters and editors work, and didn't take the time to find out. "It's been a techie-driven process," he says.

John Coston, a veteran New York editor, was put in charge of the six engineers and four journalists who oversee the *Journal's* project to upgrade software throughout the company. He says the new software is "unacceptable" and has made him a "pariah" in the news department. But he asks for understanding: The new software was meant to work only as an interim measure while the *Journal* developed still newer software to tie together the company's far-flung operations. Having learned its lessons, the software group is interviewing editors like Shafer before the latest version is installed. "The system that's coming will allow reporters to do their job better," he promises. About two years after the software package was first installed, for instance, the *Journal* added a program for reporters to browse the Internet.

Across town, at Georgetown University Hospital, a center for high-tech medicine, a similar communications problem sandbagged new hospital software. At the very least, the designers didn't understand what the newborn nursery needed. When nurses entered the weight of a newborn, the system would convert kilograms into pounds and round off to the nearest whole number. The problem: The computer would list the weight of a three-pound baby as equal to the weight of a stronger newborn who weighed 3 pounds, 7 ounces. In the neonatal ward, where every ounce makes a difference, that was a crucial flaw, so the program was scrapped within a month. A replacement version had problems too, especially for patients with unusual diets. "You can't be a diabetic and a vegetarian with this computer," says a frustrated Georgetown nurse. "It only gives you one choice—vegetarian or diabetic. You can't mix." By mid-1997, the computer system for ordering medicines was also scrapped, and nurses had to use old-fashioned paper forms to place orders.

As odd as it may seem, software writers who design projects for companies rarely talk to the people who will use the software they're creating. That's part of software's loner ethos, where programmers imagine themselves as the cowboys of the information age, riding the high plains of cyberspace with a Gary Cooper-like aversion to chit-chat. Programming attracts twice the proportion of introverts and three times the number of intuitive thinkers as are in the general public, according to one study. They rely on their own thoughts and imaginations to solve problems; that's an admirable personal quality, but a potentially disastrous one in designing useful products. "Imagine choosing a career in which you become so involved in solving logic problems that you would fail to engage in RL [real life] for months and even years," Stewart Alsop, the *Fortune* columnist, wrote about programmers.

Software managers reinforce the keep-your-distance attitude. Thomas Landauer, a computer expert at the University of Colorado, says a software firm insisted on one stipulation when it wanted to hire him to help write a complex information-retrieval program: No testing the software on anyone who might actually use it later. That would only slow down the work, the company figured. As for the customer: Caveat emptor. There's a financial interest involved too: So long as software is complicated, those who write and oversee it can command higher salaries. "People left things purposefully difficult, so they could be paid more to master it," says Peter Kelly, a computer manager at First Union, the banking company. "It was an elitist thing."

It's not only the programmers' fault, of course. Sometimes, companies have outlandish expectations. U.S. manufacturers thought they could computerize and automate their way out of trouble in the 1970s and 1980s when they were being battered by competition from Japan and Germany. Buyers throughout the country were concluding that foreign-made meant better-made in the auto, steel, semiconductor, and machine-tool industries. "America does indeed have a serious productivity problem," a widely publicized report on U.S. manufacturing, called *Made in America,* warned in 1989. "Left unattended it will impoverish America relative to other nations that have adapted more quickly and effectively to pervasive changes in technology and markets."

The problem, U.S. manufacturers argued, was overpaid U.S. production workers. The solution was robots and other computerized machines that would work without sick days or union hassles. Manufacturers and their consultants pursued "lights-out manufacturing." Factories could be so automated, manufacturers believed, that the lights could be turned off, and perfectly made goods would roll off the conveyor belt. In *Comeback: The Fall and Rise of the American Automobile Industry,* two *Wall Street Journal* reporters described the attitude of General Motors executives toward GM workers, an attitude reflected in many other U.S. companies. GM would "automate away from those assholes," the carmaker's executives boasted.

GM Chairman Roger Smith was the truest believer. A technology buff who toyed with a home computer well before other executives did, Smith spent tens of billions of dollars on new robots and other technology. The results were disastrous: Money was wasted; productivity declined. In one new factory, called "Buick City," GM preached its new "sociotechnical systems approach" of marrying people and robots—at the same time that the heavy-handed robots were smashing the windshields they were supposed to install. *Comeback* describes GM's vision for its plant in Hamtramck, Michigan, a community nicknamed Poletown because of its large Polish-American population. "Poletown was Roger Smith's thundering reply to the negativists wringing their hands over the decline of American industry . . . [Cars] would be assembled using state-of-the-art technology in a superefficient, sparkling clean factory. Parts would arrive 'just in time' and be toted by robot-guided carriers known as AGV's [automated guide vehicles] to the right spot on the line. Engines would be ferried to the car bodies by AGV's too. Robot arms would do all the painting, and apply all the caulk and sealer to the bodies so they would be perfect every time. Massive welding machines called robo-gates would stitch together car bodies in seconds."

But Poletown's performance never matched the technodream. As GM sped up the line during the mid-1980s, the robot-guided carriers strayed off course. In a Charlie Chaplin-like series of mishaps, spray-painting robots began spraying each other, rather than the cars. Panicked GM managers trucked the cars to a 57-year-old Cadillac plant for repainting. One of Smith's top lieutenants sent him a blistering letter before resigning, complaining that GM had tossed technology at its problems when what it should have done was try to reform itself. "We have relied almost exclusively on 'clean slate' strategies that ignore the internal obstacles and end up trying to circumvent rather than transform GM's organization and culture," wrote the executive, Elmer Johnson.

Reached at his Florida retirement home, Roger Smith says he has been misunderstood. He says he deliberately introduced too much automation in some factories, so GM could test how far it could go in replacing workers. When GM found the limit, it would scale back, as it eventually did throughout its manufacturing empire. "When the pioneers went out west, a lot of them died," says Smith. "Does that mean they were wrong and should have stayed in New York City and waited until 1999 to go to the other side of the Hudson? Does that mean no one should ever try?"

Other automation "pioneers" were killed too. In the Carolinas, textile manufacturers installed robots even though the aisles and ceilings of their antiquated mills were too cramped for the machines. By the mid-1980s, chastened executives there dismissed the machines as "functional idiots" because they didn't have visual or tactile sensitivity to inspect fabric. General Electric automated its light bulb factories and found that production was awesome when the robots were working well—but they rarely were. One GE motor factory in Linton, Indiana, installed a robot in the early 1980s to handle oven-hot steel parts, and discovered to its horror that the robot would sometimes fling hot, laminated steel at the terrified workers, says a former GE manager. The solution: GE put the robot in a cage.

As manufacturers discovered, software is devilishly difficult to design and update. Computers are run by layers and layers of software, which must somehow work with each other. Some software tells each piece of hardware how to behave; other software translates the programmers' instructions into the ones and zeros that computers can understand; another program routes the computer users' keystrokes to the correct devices; still another manages all the other software. To work right, software requires the coordination of a ballet corps. Inevitably, though, someone trips up and the dance isn't nearly as smooth as choreographed.

Many software designers don't even bother to write down the steps. Consider the problem of fixing mainframe computers so they can recognize the year 2000 without going bonkers. One reason that this seemingly small change will cost companies billions of dollars is that the people who created the old programs rarely wrote down explanations of what they did. Now, a new generation of programmers-turned-sleuths must analyze each line of code—some mainframe programs have tens of millions of lines—to see whether it is linked to a date. If it is, the programmers must rewrite the code so the computer realizes that "00" means the year 2000, not 1900. (If a computer assumed it was 1900, it would file current information as if it occurred a century ago, and forever mess up its ability to make sense of data.) Allstate Corporation, which has assigned 100 programmers to handle the year 2000 problem, discovered that former programmers had named parts of their mainframe code after rock lyrics, girlfriends, and members of the Beatles, making analysis a funky nightmare.

Overall, U.S. companies canceled about 40% of large software projects, according to a survey of 360 firms in 1996 by Standish Group International Inc., a software consultant in Dennis, Massachusetts. Another one-third of the projects were completed at great angst: They were late, cost about twice as much as budgeted, and had about half as many features as promised. Only 27% of the projects were rated as successful—and that's an improvement over 1994, when only 16% were completed on time and on budget. Standish's chairman, Jim Johnson, complains that companies are trying to cram too many features into new software, which makes them unmanageably complex.

Productivity also suffers because lots of people use the machines at work to goof off. Take a look around the office. How many people are playing computerized Solitaire? How many are dashing off e-mails to kids in college? How many are toying with new software? There isn't a precise estimate, but a San Francisco-area software firm surveyed customers and found that office workers spent 5.1 hours a week "futzing" with their computers. The time was split pretty evenly among waiting for the computer to run programs, checking or formatting printed pages, helping co-workers with their computer problems, organizing old files, and playing computer games. Nielsen Media Research Inc. found that employees at IBM, Apple, and AT&T together logged onto *Penthouse's* site on the World Wide Web 12,823 times during one month in 1996. At an average visit of 13 minutes each, that equaled 347 eight-hour days in lost work.

Even when the software is designed well, productivity gains often prove elusive. After the Internal Revenue Service bought laptops to help agents with field tests in 1988, the number of cases each agent handled weekly actually declined. The agents spent extra time noodling with spreadsheets and revising reports. (Agents' "prestige, credibility, and self-image" rose, however, according to a review of the project.) Similarly, when twenty-six business school students were split into two teams and asked to create an efficient factory production schedule, the team that used a computerized spreadsheet was far more confident about its results than the team that wasn't allowed to use computers. Trouble was, the spreadsheet team's schedule turned out to be more costly; relying on the software made the computer jockeys too cocky. Using a spreadsheet program creates the illusion of control, wrote the three researchers conducting the experiment.

Even word processing hasn't yielded the productivity boon it is commonly believed to have. Thomas Landauer, the software expert, reports on two studies of word processing in his book, *The Trouble with Computers.* In 1981, an IBM researcher asked ten IBM managers to write four letters the old-fashioned way—penning an original, and handing it to a secretary to type—and then had the managers use a word processor to write four letters themselves. Letters produced by computer were revised 41 times; handwritten ones only eight, canceling out most of the expected efficiency gains. Overall, the computer-produced letters were completed about six minutes faster than typewritten ones. But they weren't noticeably better written, and they cost slightly *more* to produce because managers spent more of their time composing the computer-written letters than the typewriter-written ones.

A Xerox researcher who couldn't believe those results repeated the experiment three years later, using a better word-processing program. The results were pretty much the same, but the computer-produced letter turned out to cost one-fourth *less* than the typed one. That's progress, but a puny return for an office technology as fundamental as word processing.

Americans have settled for far less from computers than they should have. "When people tell me something [in software] is wonderful, they usually mean it's up and running," says Landauer. "People don't tell me they're getting anything useful out of it."

FUTURE

8

Forward to the Future

Why computers finally will power faster economic growth.

The future has had a lot of false starts. "Computers are no strangers in business today—but the new industrial revolution they herald has hardly begun," a *Business Week* special report declared in 1958, just four years after the first computer designed exclusively for business was installed. But the magazine warned that the computer age wouldn't really lift the economy until "today's old-timers [are] gone and today's computer kids sit in their place."

Those "computer kids" that *Business Week* touted are probably retiring from their jobs—if they haven't been downsized out of work already—but the productivity payoff from computers is still elusive. No matter; many computer magazines predict that *today's* computer kids—the Nintendo-playing, Netscape-browsing crowd—finally will realize the computer's promise. Ever hopeful, *Business Week* forecast at the end of 1996 that today's video-game wizards will boost tomorrow's economy because "in 10 or 15 years, they will bring their attitudes and skills into a workplace filled with fast-changing technology."

There are some lessons here for future-gazing—other than the lesson that journalists sometimes make lousy predictions. Despite technology's reputation for speed, technological change ripples slowly through the economy. Progress doesn't depend solely on a new generation of tinkerers growing up and replacing their fuddy-duddy elders. Rather, society must learn how best to use the new technology of the time.

As the history of electricity and other technologies demonstrates, developing the best use often takes decades. In the early part of the century, Maytag foremen complained about new motor-driven machine tools. Only later did they realize that these tools would revolutionize factory production. Around the same time, telephone customers regularly cursed their phones because the lines went dead and conversations were garbled. Within a few decades, telephone service had greatly increased office efficiency and had become synonymous with reliability. For technologies as fundamental as electricity, telephones, and microcomputing, there's a tortuous process of hype, disappointment, and, finally, progress. Computers are starting to pay off now; over the next few decades, the gains will be dramatic and impressive.

In this section of the book, we look toward the future, identifying the nascent trends that will mature during the coming years and will produce a better life for the American middle class. This chapter, and the two chapters that follow, describe how the early stages of the productivity surge will create wealth at a faster clip over the next twenty years than has been realized over the past twenty years. This chapter tells how technology, particularly computer-network technology, is raising productivity in factories and is beginning to do so in the service-sector companies that employ the vast majority of American workers. Chapter 9 shows how pioneering companies are realizing remarkable gains in productivity by reorganizing the workplace and giving frontline workers more say in what they do. Chapter 10 exposes as a fallacy the commonly held view that the Federal Reserve will stand in the way of faster economic growth. Fed Chairman Alan Greenspan has resisted pressure to raise interest rates, in part because he expects information technology to pay a significant productivity dividend.

The growth of computer networks, which store millions of pages of information and can speed them around the globe, holds particular promise for enhancing productivity. Workers now share information once hoarded by senior managers and locked in glass-encased computer rooms. The broad dispersement of the information places on managers and employees the extra burden of figuring out ways to use this deluge of data efficiently. Their predicament is similar to the trial-and-error process that bedeviled factory owners early in the twentieth century, when they began to tear down belt-and-shaft factory systems. Some companies already have made the transition. Factory computer networks manage production with greater precision than before; trucking networks direct fleets across the country as if the vehicles were images in a computer game; global office networks knit together coworkers who don't know each other and coordinate their work on common projects. The systems change the ways people work and share ideas. The productivity potential is immense.

No single example is conclusive, but both academic and anecdotal evidence suggests that American managers and workers finally are figuring out how to unleash the productivity-enhancing potential of computers and software. But the $7 trillion U.S. economy is so vast that the changes will need time to spread before they can lift productivity nationwide.

The computer-driven upsurge is underway. Studies by MIT economists Erik Brynjolfsson and Lorin Hitt, who analyzed the information technology spending of 367 large firms from 1987 through 1991, have convinced skeptical economists that computers finally are delivering long-predicted productivity gains. By 1991, the researchers calculated, the payoff from a dollar invested in computers was substantially greater than the payoff from other types of investment—evidence that computers were increasing productivity throughout private industry. Columbia University economists Frank R. Lichtenberg and William Lehr studied federal government spending and found a similar, hopeful pattern. Agencies with the fastest rate of productivity growth between 1987 and 1992 were those that were computerizing most rapidly.

Brynjolfsson forecasts additional growth of 0.5% a year, which, as we've already seen, can greatly improve living standards when compounded annually over a decade or two. Stanford University economist Paul Romer, one of the nation's leading theorists of economic growth, thinks the gains from computers may be far greater than Brynjolfsson imagines. In the long run, Romer says, productivity and growth feed off innovation. Computers help thinkers think; they organize vast libraries of data, simulate new processes and inventions, and run different kinds of scenarios. Those capabilities may permanently lift the rate of innovation and economic growth in the twenty-first century, he believes. "Computers raise the productivity of the knowledge-generating sector," he says. "They let us discover new things faster. Instead of creating a one-time burst [of productivity] . . . the underlying rate of growth could be speeding up in the next century."

In manufacturing, the productivity surge has arrived. After a decade of stagnation that ended in the mid-1980s, manufacturing productivity is now rebounding at a clip of more than 3.5% annually. Even if the federal government's statistics overstate the gain somewhat, that's still a smart turnaround. As the economy's far more numerous service companies create a similar surge, robust economic growth will be ensured. To engineer a turnaround, factory managers first had to learn a painful lesson that service companies must now take to heart: Technology alone won't solve all their problems.

There's evidence that service companies are starting to catch on. During the twelve-month period that ended in the fall of 1997, service sector productivity rose briskly, by 2%. That's three times as fast as the average annual gain in service productivity since 1973.

Manufacturers discovered that their problems went far beyond those caused by lazy workers and wacky robots. The mass production model pioneered by Henry Ford—stamp out carbon copies of the same product twenty-four hours a day—had become outmoded. Manufacturing operations had to meet the new demands of efficiently making a variety of different products, in smaller production runs. Companies that successfully transformed their factories could catch mistakes early during assembly, speed products to market, and reduce burdensome inventory costs. The results were higher productivity, and lower costs for consumers. Computer-controlled technology aided immensely in the transition, as did worker training. Manufacturers had to invest substantial amounts of time and money in teaching workers how to run advanced machinery and how to take responsibility for the factories' operations.

"It isn't enough to throw technology at the existing production system," says Richard K. Lester, one of the coauthors of the best-selling *Made in America* study, which warned of a productivity slowdown in the late 1980s. "Everything about the production system has to change."

The Allen-Bradley Company, in Milwaukee, is emblematic of the transformation of U.S. manufacturers. The company sits at the epicenter of U.S. manufacturing: It makes the innards of the industrial world. Allen-Bradley computer modules, sensors, switches, and controllers track engine parts in factories, sort packages in mail rooms, regulate conveyor belts' speeds, and even measure the amount of cheese sprinkled on frozen pizzas. Allen-Bradley has never made anything as sexy as a robot. But Allen-Bradley devices are assembled into the computerized control systems that oversee production in auto factories, chemical plants, and dozens of other industries.

The question for Allen-Bradley became: How does the automation expert automate itself?

For years, the answer was: It doesn't. Founded in 1903, Allen-Bradley grew rich producing handmade, solidly built products that lasted for decades. The company's management was stolid and paternal. Harry Bradley, the chairman, lived in an apartment atop the factory until the early 1960s. Along with a formal dining room and a hardwood-paneled library, the suite included an octagonal room with a small patch of grass for Bradley's poodle, Monsieur Dufy. An insomniac, Bradley would prowl the factory at all hours, Monsieur Dufy at his side, and chat with assembly workers. Inside the factory, he built a hospital and a marble-tiled cafeteria for the workers; outside, he topped the eight-story building with a nine-story clock tower. The huge, four-sided clock face is larger than London's Big Ben and could be seen all over the south-side neighborhood where many Allen-Bradley employees lived; it was promptly nicknamed "the Polish moon."

But Allen-Bradley changed in the 1980s. After a struggle among Bradley's heirs and longtime managers, the company was sold to Rockwell International Corporation in 1985, ending its run as a coddled, privately owned firm. Allen-Bradley also faced mounting competition. It was late introducing electronic versions of its mainstay products. Customers were fleeing big clunky Allen-Bradley motor controllers and buying sleeker German-made ones that didn't last as long but cost one-fourth the price. Even more frightening, some large clients were starting to build their own automation systems, cutting out the supposed automation expert.

Allen-Bradley had to rethink its manufacturing strategy, especially how it intended to compete in electronics. At the heart of all electronic products are green plastic boards honeycombed with microprocessors and soldered circuits, which function as the brains and central nervous system. Allen-Bradley needed a ready supply of printed circuit boards for products ranging from bar-code readers to computerized motor starters. In 1988, Allen-Bradley was making small volumes of circuit boards in its customary way—largely by hand. But a company study forecast that, to meet projected demand, the firm would have to ramp up production twentyfold by 1992. The company later realized that demand would quintuple again by 1996.

To make the process even more daunting, Allen-Bradley would have to manufacture these boards in lots ranging from a few dozen to a few thousand each, which was a break from convention. Many large circuit board manufacturers run millions of copies of the same design, in an electronic version of an automobile assembly line. But Allen-Bradley's catalog listed hundreds of thousands of different industrial gadgets. To be of any value, the company's new automated manufacturing would have to emphasize flexibility.

Allen-Bradley has shown how combining smart work organization and modern technology increases productivity, boosts profit, and enhances wages. Allen-Bradley's electronic circuit board center in Milwaukee, called the Electronics Manufacturing Strategy (EMS), now cranks out annually about $15 million worth of circuit boards, which are assembled into hundreds of different Allen-Bradley products. Productivity has soared. EMS can turn out prototypes for a new product in a week, rather than the four months it used to take. Between 1995 and 1996, EMS placed one-third more components per hour on circuit boards, and the cost of each placement dropped by about one-third. Cheered by the results, Allen-Bradley has opened five other EMS sites around the country.

The computerized products have yielded big gains in output for customers. With Allen-Bradley's electronic motor controllers, Appleton Papers Inc., a large paper mill in Appleton, Wisconsin, can run its new paper-coating machines at twelve times the speed of older models. The Allen-Bradley system uses computers to coordinate the movement of forty-six different motors, and makes sure the enormous press doesn't rip the paper or spray chemicals helter-skelter—"painting the machine," Appleton calls it.

Allen-Bradley's workers benefit, too. EMS operators in Milwaukee make $17.52 an hour and can earn another 50 cents an hour if they complete six college engineering courses. That's 20% more than the plant's average pay. With overtime, EMS operator salaries top $50,000 a year. The EMS philosophy of continuing education is spreading. Allen-Bradley and its union have opened what they call a learning center—factory classrooms crammed with computers—to help bring workers up to high school standards and pass exams to get EMS jobs.

To achieve those gains, the company attacked with two weapons: technology and organization. Allen-Bradley manufacturing experts toured circuit board facilities at computer and auto-parts companies in the United States and Japan, to learn about the latest technology. And Allen-Bradley learned what *not* to do from one of its longtime customers, General Motors.

Randall Freeman, an Allen-Bradley marketing vice president, had worked, early in his career, with GM's highly automated van factory in Baltimore. The plant's assembly line was geared to produce about sixty-five vans an hour, he says, but its fancy new computer system was so overlogged with data that it could process only seven vans. The vehicles would sit idly for minutes at each manufacturing station, waiting for computerized instructions. Freeman was part of a team that, in 1981, had to disconnect the computers to increase production. GM chairman Roger Smith "was both our hero and our villain," says Freeman. "He spent billions on factory automation, but he gave automation a bad name" because it delivered so little for GM.

Allen-Bradley made its share of mistakes too, including plunking down $5 million to buy a robotic cart to deliver parts, and then realizing that the factory stocked so many parts that the cart got confused. The company eventually tore out the system and turned the work back to forklift operators.

More importantly, Allen-Bradley was forced to rethink how it organizes work. For many Allen-Bradley workers outside of EMS, work today consists of screwing components into assemblies, one after the other, until they reach their quota. Then comes a cat-and-mouse game with foremen. Workers slow down, hide in the bathrooms, or chat with friends. Working harder is taboo because that only prompts management to increase daily workloads. Employees also are rigorously segregated by function. If an assembler notices that a wire is bent the wrong way in a component he is attaching, the assembler is instructed to call the foreman, who notifies a wire specialist to fix the problem. The system reinforces the power of factory foremen, who divvy up assignments, and of the union, which insists on strict job classifications.

But old-style work habits would be disastrous for the new circuit board line. Workers there have to think for themselves in order to keep the expensive machinery running smoothly. Changing habits is daunting, especially for workers at old-line factories where routines stretch back decades and are preserved by union work rules. A study

of thirty-one circuit board factories came to the mind-bending conclusion that the factories that spent the most money on new, flexible machinery had the worst record on flexible manufacturing. The new
machinery made it easier for workers to keep doing what they were
used to doing: cranking out high volumes of the same old product.
"When flexible technology meets an inflexible workforce it is often the
machines, not the people, that are forced to adapt," wrote Erik Brynjolfsson, the MIT economist.

Sometimes, extraordinary measures are necessary to get workers and
managers to use new technology productively. Brynjolfsson and his colleagues studied a New Jersey medical-goods manufacturer they called
by the pseudonym MacroMed, which makes sterile adhesives. Desperate to reduce the time it took the factory to change from producing one
kind of adhesive to producing another, MacroMed cooked up an elaborate plan. To create a stir at the plant, MacroMed built walls around the
new, flexible-production equipment it was installing. A hand-picked
SWAT team of workers and managers labored behind the walls to
debug the machinery and get used to the new style of production. They
fanned out and trained others at the plant. MacroMed then tore down
the walls surrounding the new machinery, symbolically demolishing
the division between the old and the new. The forethought and training
helped MacroMed slash the time required to prepare production machinery for a new run by 67%, and reduced waste by 65%. MacroMed
was so convinced that the new machinery gave it a competitive edge
that it painted the windows black so competitors couldn't see what it
was up to.

At Allen-Bradley, most of the factory looks little changed from the
1940s. Walls are grimy; ancient steel shelving is stuffed with cartons of
parts; workers hunch over their workbenches, tightening bolts with
pneumatic screwdrivers. On hot days, the place is sweltering; overhead
fans provide the only relief.

The circuit board manufacturing center, opened in 1989 within
the same plant, is different. EMS is brightly lit, air-conditioned, and
humidity-controlled. The clean, blue-paneled machinery is laid out in
a backward "S" configuration in a space about as big as a basketball
court. Because the boards manufactured there are only 9.4 inches wide,
everything is a miniature size. One slim conveyor belt carrying the thin
green panels runs about waist-high; another belt runs overhead so circuit

boards can be routed past operations that aren't required. At different spots, automated machines grab tiny electronic components—some as small as peppercorns—and glue or staple them into place. For a factory, the place is quiet; the rapid-fire rat-tat rat-tat of the stapling machine can be heard in the background. Techniques pioneered here—how to protect against static electricity, how to redesign workbenches—were later applied to the older part of the factory.

A computer network oversees the operations. Circuit board designs created four floors below are routed electronically into EMS computers, which track 800 different orders over 90 days. The computers produce instructions that tell the assembly machines where to place components on each board. Bar-code readers track the boards' passage through the system. At two assembly stations, operators looking through a thick lens or a microscope check that parts are aligned, and then type their findings into a computer database. When one of the main assembly machines crashed for a week, EMS technicians were able to load the assembly instructions onto a computer disk, walk to another circuit board manufacturing center within the factory, and begin stamping out the boards there.

The EMS computer system is linked to others that track inventory at Allen-Bradley, so the company can forecast upcoming purchases. Suppliers are updated every Saturday, by computer. Meanwhile, the company publishes on the Internet its plans to use new technology, to give designers and suppliers advance notice. All this has helped Allen-Bradley reduce its inventory of supplies, and the costs of stocking and financing the inventory. Lead time is now two and one-half weeks; it was ten weeks before EMS was built.

The system wouldn't work smoothly if Allen-Bradley hadn't emphasized worker training. Employees who want to work on the EMS line must pass tests in math, logic, and mechanical skills. Nancy Bores, a longtime Allen-Bradley hand, was an early recruit. She had been laid off twice from Allen-Bradley in the 1980s. Once, when her husband was laid off too, they were forced to sell their boat and car, as well as the possessions of her husband's late mother. Getting a job that required more training, she figured, would reduce the odds she would be laid off again.

Allen-Bradley pays the tuition for EMS workers who take electronics courses on their own time at a local engineering school. Few of them have ever taken college courses; most have been out of high school for years. Completing the courses helps them understand the rudiments of electronic theory, and gives them the confidence to work without close supervision. Prior to taking college computing courses, says Bores, "I had no way to communicate without being afraid of asking questions and appearing stupid."

EMS is designed to handle 250 different kinds of circuit boards, so the sixty-one operators are trained with flexibility in mind. Teams of five workers are assigned to oversee different assembly operations. They print out the upcoming schedule and arrange the components, which come on long reels of tape, so the machines can move smoothly from one order to the next. At the end of the line, one team hand-assembles the few odd-shaped parts that the machines can't handle. Another team uses a microscope and electronic test equipment to search for defects and then replaces faulty components.

Change still comes hard, though. Allen-Bradley's difficulty in convincing even motivated workers to change their work routines mirrors problems faced by firms across the economy and explains why the payoff from technology has been delayed for so long. For several years, EMS operators were trained to inspect each board after a machine laid components on one side. Frequently, they would nudge a component or two with tweezers. When Allen-Bradley replaced the machine with a more precise one that also worked 20% faster, operators were told they didn't have to tweak the components so often. After a four-week trial run, the managers and technicians were sure the machine worked properly. But the workers weren't, and they continued the time-consuming inspections and tweezer-nudging, even though they weren't necessary.

EMS's young, sprightly manager, Alicia Fernandez-Campfield, figured the operators were balking because they feared the faster machine would eliminate some jobs. She assured them it wouldn't. But they kept to their old routines anyway, even when she ordered them to stop. Ellie Turman, a thirty-year veteran at the plant, says the workers were simply trying to make sure quality remained top-notch. It took two months before the operators became convinced that the machine worked as advertised. When they did, productivity jumped at that manufacturing station.

Giving operators more responsibility is worth the effort because they learn more about the manufacturing system and about working in teams. After surveying 584 factories, Carnegie Mellon University manufacturing expert Maryellen R. Kelley concluded that the most productive factories are those that rely on operators, rather than managers or engineers, to work out the kinks with automated machinery.

Allen-Bradley's experiences are becoming more and more typical in manufacturing as plant managers experiment with ways to reduce inventory, increase production, and cut turnaround time—and pressure their suppliers to do the same. In Milwaukee, a lunchpail town that has one of the nation's thickest concentrations of factories, supervisors swap stories about new manufacturing techniques at Chamber of Commerce meetings. A local coalition of companies and unions, called the Wisconsin Regional Training Partnership, prods firms to train operators to use new technologies. Harley-Davidson Inc., the motorcycle maker and one of Milwaukee's largest companies, even hosted $300-a-day seminars to teach other companies what it had learned about factory technology and organization.

A few companies also are experimenting with a more radical kind of flexible manufacturing: custom-tailoring goods at mass-production prices. The Primus subsidiary of the McGraw-Hill Companies assembles individualized textbooks for idiosyncratic college professors, allowing them to select from the hundreds of different articles in its computerized database. Levi Strauss & Co. has a "Personal Pair" line of jeans. Customers at its company-owned stores are measured for their waist, hip, crotch, and inseam and fitted with a sample pair of jeans. A Levi plant in Tennessee receives the measurements by computer and sews a pair of jeans to fit. At $65, the jeans are pricey. But Levi is betting that customers will appreciate the better fit.

Erik Brynjolfsson, the MIT economist, points to the Levi system as a precursor of productivity improvements to come. Computer technology "allows you to keep track of customers and respond to customers in better ways," he says. "You're playing from strength." But one new buyer of Levi's custom-fit jeans in Washington, D.C., isn't enamored with the change. She used to buy her jeans snug, to tuck in her stomach. Now, she says, the new jeans fit so well that what's there shows.

Many service companies face more daunting challenges than Allen-Bradley did when it revamped its factories. Manufacturers have been forced to change; with competition from abroad, factories had to innovate or die. Service companies may face tough competition at home, but they are largely insulated from overseas foes. No chain of Tokyo department stores threatens Sears; no group of British pubs challenges T.G.I. Friday's. Without an invasion by technologically advanced competitors from abroad, service companies took a more leisurely attitude toward productivity. Now they have to catch up.

Offices are harder to automate than factories. For decades, manufacturers have been clocking assembly workers in hopes of shaving a few minutes off one process or another. Computers are the latest innovation, but they are part of a long tradition. Not so in many offices and service companies. Alan Monahan, a Xerox manufacturing vice president who has studied with Japanese productivity masters, says he could easily boost the productivity of the white-collar workers who assemble quarterly financial reports, but Xerox never asked him to. The payoff was paltry compared to the potential returns from factory automation. But just as manufacturers finally mastered computer technology to chalk up impressive productivity gains, so have some service companies, and many more will follow.

In some service industries, deregulation provided a life-threatening impetus, just as foreign competition had prodded manufacturers. The once-coddled telecommunications and trucking industries, which were riven by savage domestic competition in the 1980s after government controls were lifted, have seen some of the largest productivity gains since then. No manufacturer has outperformed Wal-Mart Inc. in using computerized inventory control and satellite technology. Wal-Mart was pushed to automate because its Bentonville, Arkansas, headquarters, and its rural store locations, put it at a geographic disadvantage when competing with city-based retailers such as Detroit's Kmart. Wal-Mart used information technology to even the score; the retailer now transmits data from checkout scanners to headquarters and suppliers by satellite, so they all know promptly what's hot and what's not.

Target discount stores tell trainees that the cash register is a terminal, and that "the most important thing the terminal does is help your store reorder merchandise." During the 1996 Christmas rush, the Dayton Hudson Corporation subsidiary tripled its order for "Olympic Barbie" after analyzing computerized cash-register data and discovering that the dolls' sales exceeded projections.

In Green Bay, Wisconsin, Schneider National Inc., one of the nation's largest truckers, is using computers to work out complex logistical problems that would be impossible to solve by hand. The system makes the nation's transportation system run more smoothly, which saves fuel, speeds deliveries, and ultimately reduces prices—the rewards of greater productivity. Factories and stores can keep inventories at a minimum because of Schneider's computerized on-time delivery; consumers can count on quicker turnaround when they order goods.

Schneider turned to satellite communication in the late 1980s, when it was reeling from the effects of deregulation. Before, communication with truckers was hit-and-miss. Truckers were supposed to check in every few hours by phone. Sounds easy, but they had to pull their rigs off the highway, make the call, and usually wait on hold while a dispatcher juggled a half-dozen other callers. With the satellite system, drivers get messages beamed to the trucks' keyboards; they can respond with a few taps of the keys. Dispatchers in Schneider's octagonal control room—it looks like NASA's Mission Control Center, only larger—can route drivers from one pickup to the next, eliminating lengthy delays.

Schneider trucks turn up regularly at a Chrysler factory that assembles Dodge trucks. "As soon as the supplies are unloaded, they go into production," says the company's president, Don Schneider. "There's no back-up warehouse; you have to assure them you will be on time."

At first, some drivers were suspicious. Computer tracking meant that headquarters would know where they were at any moment. If they were driving when regulations said they should be sleeping, corporate Big Brother would find out. To escape detection, some drivers ripped out the satellite antenna's wiring, covered the antenna with galvanized metal buckets to block transmissions, or installed burned-out fuses. But the rebellion was short-lived as drivers saw the benefits of staying in touch. During the 1994 Los Angeles earthquake, one of Schneider's drivers, James Crim, was scheduled to make a delivery in Simi Valley, the epicenter of the quake. Frantic, his wife called Schneider, which quickly reported that Crim had already left L.A. and was rolling past the Arizona border. Another driver, Kimberly Trent, tells about the time her tires caught fire on Interstate 40 in North Carolina. The blaze was too large for the on-board fire extinguisher. She grabbed her keyboard, typed "63," the signal for an emergency, and a repair van pulled up promptly.

Taking its service a step further, Schneider is now contracting with customers to take over their entire logistics operations, whether shipments go by truck, rail, or overnight delivery. Schneider applies sophisticated computer analysis to pickups and deliveries—parts of the manufacturing chain that often are overlooked. Thousands of potential carriers charge different rates, based on different measurements. Some charge by the mile, others by zip code; all give discounts for favored routes. Schneider had to develop logistics software that could handle the variation and make the best choice. The resulting software is based on concepts used to develop complex airline reservation systems and, before that, U.S. air-defense systems in the 1950s.

Daniel Ross, a former Schneider manager, estimates that a product may be handled as many as twenty times during shipment and warehousing. Each handling adds to the cost. "The vision of the future is a more seamless and fluid pipeline," says Ross, now a transportation consultant at Mercer Management Consulting in Boston. "A product is manufactured; it goes right on a truck, right onto a shelf, and right into a buyer's hand."

General Motors, the company that gave automation a bad name, has contracted with Schneider to handle $300 million worth of spare-parts shipments annually. It's an enormous task involving 3,300 different GM suppliers, 385,000 parts in inventory, 16 giant warehouses, and 9,300 dealers and wholesalers. For all that, says Schneider, GM knew precious little about where products were going and when. "People at GM weren't working with computers and computer models," says Larry Sur, president of Schneider's logistics business. They couldn't track shipments instantaneously. "Two months after the fact, they could tell you what they had done."

Schneider was able to collect information quickly with its enormous computer network; it then used its logistics software to pick the most cost-effective carrier. Within a year, Schneider says, it had shaved 10% off GM's shipping costs, a savings of $30 million. (GM agrees that costs have declined, but not as much as Schneider claims.) Although outsourcing generally has a reputation as a job killer, Schneider replaced GM's forty-five-person shipping department with sixty Schneider logisticians, including many who were more highly paid than GM employees had been. "Our focus is on the heart of the problem," says Sur, looking out at the control center from a glass-walled conference center. "We're cutting out unnecessary movements and making our savings. I have [computer] systems people who can get on a computer and make it sing."

Promising as all this sounds, the greatest productivity benefits from computing are still to come. Most of the gains so far have involved automating muscle—Allen-Bradley's circuit board machines work faster than hand assemblers; Schneider's truck drivers make more deliveries when talking to headquarters by satellite. The greatest potential, however, lies in leveraging intellect—using computers to revamp the way in which people work together. That's a task for which computer networks are uniquely suited. A few companies are exploiting the technology already; many more will follow over the next few decades.

To leverage intellect, companies have to rethink their operations. How should a company best be organized to take advantage of computerized technology? Who should be responsible for decisions? What's the job of managers if computer networks make available to underlings the information once reserved for managers? For decades, information was centralized in big computers housed in headquarters buildings. Until recently, blue-suited managers at the Armonk headquarters of International Business Machines Corporation, for instance, could be assured that the information stored on the company's mainframe computers was reserved primarily for their use. With their unrivaled overview of the firm, they exercised tight control over major decisions. But the development of networks of personal computers heralded a historic shift. Now, information is available globally, forcing companies to tear down old hierarchies.

Johnson & Higgins, a big New York insurance broker, has made such changes and is reaping the rewards. J&H uses a worldwide network to link 300 brokerage offices, which employ 15,000 people. Over the past few years, J&H has scored solid gains in one of the conventional measures of productivity: revenues and profits per employee. But it's the unconventional gains that are more telling.

The network technology let J&H smash its century-old structure, where all information was stored and hoarded in New York. The network gives distant brokers in South Korea and Atlanta as much information to negotiate and close deals as the most plugged-in broker in New York, demolishing some of the disadvantages of working at a distant location. The technology also blurs the distinction between client and customer; both are connected by the same network, call up the same information, and make changes. This ability to change work habits and organization holds the most potential for productivity gains.

In 1990, when Johnson & Higgins dispatched David Kim to open a branch in his native Seoul, South Korea, the Columbia Business School graduate was cut off from the company's New York headquarters by thousands of miles and a fourteen-hour time difference. To get information for the big Korean companies and U.S. subsidiaries that he was courting, Kim did what other distant J&H brokers are supposed to do. He contacted headquarters in New York or J&H's big London office. Then he waited for a response while his message was passed around those offices. But secretaries sometimes misplaced the messages, and responses were haphazard. There wasn't any systematic way to pick the brains of J&H's far-flung organization.

Then Kim had an inspiration. Trying to figure out how to insure a Korean chemical maker against product recalls in June 1995, he posted a message on J&H's international network, asking for help. He got answers from around the world—from brokers he didn't know, and from offices he wouldn't have thought to contact. A broker in Richmond, Virginia, suggested contacting a subsidiary of insurance powerhouse American International Group Inc., which insured food processors; a broker in Charlotte, North Carolina, proposed an insurer in Switzerland with whom he had worked before; a broker in London told him to contact J&H's Singapore office; and the broker in Singapore tipped him off to another AIG subsidiary, thus creating the possibility that Johnson & Higgins could get two subsidiaries of the same company to bid against each other. Kim says he used all that advice to win the Korean company's business.

"We harnessed the latent potential of the worldwide network and brought it to life," he says. Without the network, "how would I have known that any of these people had experience in this area? I would have had to send 100 faxes; I wouldn't have done it. I would have sent a fax to NY and [missed] the untapped experience and knowledge."

Kim's ability to contact so many sources was possible because of a program called Notes, which organizes communications globally. Developed by Lotus Development Corporation, now an IBM subsidiary, Notes creates a global repository of information that is continuously updated, easy to search, and permanently archived. The system posts messages worldwide, collects responses, and displays them. On the computer screen, the dialogues look like a series of e-mail messages that are stored according to subject matter and can be searched by key words.

The dialogues become a permanent record that can be searched with the click of a computer mouse. Brokers can research insurance questions according to industry, region, or type of insurance, and see how others have handled problems. The company's most valuable resource—information about customers and their insurance problems—is mined, not lost.

The Johnson & Higgins system shows in small scale the power of global networks to store and display massive amounts of material. In *Computer: A History of the Information Machine,* Martin Campbell-Kelly and William Aspray traced the lineage of computer networks to the French philosopher Denis Diderot's creation of the first encyclopedia in the eighteenth century. "The idea of making the world's store of knowledge available to the ordinary person is a very old dream," the authors wrote. In the 1930s, science-fiction writer H. G. Wells urged the creation of a "World Brain"—a repository of enlightened thinking, captured on microfilm, that people could consult to refute claims made by fascists. After World War II, Franklin Roosevelt's science adviser, Vannevar Bush, sketched a plan to use microfilm readers to scan libraries of information. But that technology proved to be too expensive and inadequate for the task.

Now, a half-century later, computer networks are the most recent embodiment of the Enlightenment idea. For $9.95 a month, anyone can tap into the Internet, with its uncountable collection of facts stored in computers around the world. J&H's efforts are an offshoot of the World Brain idea, except that the information stored on J&H's network is specialized and reserved for employees, clients, and others connected to the firm.

Johnson & Higgins is an unlikely pathfinder. Founded in 1845, the broker last pioneered technology in the 1880s, when it signed up as an early customer for Thomas Edison's first generating plant. Even when Wall Street had a reputation for rectitude, J&H was considered stodgy. During the Civil War, company regulations forbade "loud talking, laughing or gossiping"; during the 1980s, J&H urged employees not to imbibe at lunch. J&H, with $1.1 billion in annual revenue, is the insurance broker to the Fortune 500; it brokered coverage for the ocean liner *Titanic,* Andrew Mellon, the racehorse Secretariat, and each generation of Boeing jetliners. When the director of the film *Carlito's Way* wanted to film an office suite that symbolized wealth and power, he chose the mahogany boardroom at J&H. During the spring of 1997, J&H ended its long history as a privately owned company when it was purchased by Marsh & McClennan Companies, an even larger, publicly traded insurance broker. A J&H executive has been put in charge of merging and updating the technology used by the two companies.

For years, Johnson & Higgins was dismissive of personal computers. PCs were considered machines for secretaries and other low-paid help. Asked whether he wanted a PC, one of J&H's most senior executives curtly declined. "I'm not a chauffeur; I ride in the back," he said. But by the late 1980s, J&H realized it had to change. Its competitors were expanding globally, and J&H lagged behind. William Wilson, a young, red-haired broker with a flair for technology, was transferred from J&H's Cincinnati office to New York and put in charge of updating the firm's technology. He discovered Notes at a computer trade show, and oversaw the creation of the network in 1991 and its expansion since then. While many in the company were seduced by the jazzy new technology early on—the Smithsonian Institution picked J&H for its first round of technology awards in 1993—it wasn't until 1995 that the network impressed bottom-line types.

Then, a broker in Stamford, Connecticut, was trying to help a non-profit organization, Save the Children, insure workers it hired to dig up land mines in Angola. Most workers' compensation policies exempt "bodily injury" due to war; digging out land mines seemed to fall under the exclusion. Having no idea where to turn, the broker sent a message on J&H's computer network. A London broker, nicknamed "Daz" and experienced in handling war-related policies, responded the same day. Within six months, J&H had sold Save the Children two new policies to cover its workers. "At last, tangible success," Daz wrote to Wilson—and the New York technology guru made sure others in the company learned of the results. "This is like chaos theory," says Wilson, who does most of his work out of a Manhattan apartment outfitted with two high-speed telephone lines. "There's no way to predict how this will work out."

Now the network is abuzz with conversations. Some are exotic. A London broker wants to insure a Russian shipper against "mysterious disappearances" of cargo during transport from St. Petersburg. Several respondents suggest London insurers, but a Washington, D.C., broker includes a tip about a company that insures Russian shipments of enriched uranium to U.S. factories that turn it into power-plant fuel; those shipments must be protected from foes who want to steal enriched uranium to make nuclear weapons.

Some dialogues are bizarre. A Philadelphia broker frets that her client, a software company, wants thrills and chills at its company picnic. She says she succeeded in talking the client out of renting jet skis to ride the waves, but, to her horror, the company decided on trampolines instead. "Of course, my reaction to this was less positive than the wave runners, but I wasn't able to convince them not to do it," she says, pleading for advice. A Richmond, Virginia, colleague responds: "Between trampolines and the wave runners—I'd go with the wave runners." As for trampolines, the Virginian advises a "no somersault" rule. After receiving formal warning from Johnson & Higgins, the software company eventually canceled the trampolines. "Whatever happened to volleyball?" asks the J&H broker, Linda Helman.

As information spreads globally, the brokerage system becomes more efficient. Power shifts to distant brokers, who no longer rely as much on information and guidance from headquarters. Atlanta broker Mark Swank turned to the network to dig out information about insuring a cigarette company that wanted to sponsor an Indy-style racecar. Looking under the listings "sponsorship" and "advertising" in a Notes database, he found a J&H broker in Houston who had handled a similar request, and put together a deal within a week.

But getting good results requires information sharing, and that's harder to encourage than it seems. Wanda J. Orlikowski, an information technology professor at MIT, profiled a company she identified as Alpha Corporation, but is actually the accounting firm of Price Waterhouse. Consultants there said they had no intention of sharing information—by computer or any other way. Their value and their pay were linked to their unique knowledge, they believed. Why in the world would they give that away?

"I'm trying to develop an area of expertise that makes me stand out," said one. "If I share that with you, you'd get the credit, not me." Added another consultant: "Power in this firm is your client base and technology. . . . Now, if you put all this information in a Notes database, you lose power." But Sheldon Laube, Price Waterhouse's chief information officer at the time, says Orlikowski exaggerated the discontent. Eventually, Price Waterhouse consultants realized that if they contributed to the network, they would bolster their standing in the company and get promoted. "Where there's new technology, there's uncertainty," he says.

J&H has overcome these obstacles partly through its tradition of sharing resources. For years, the company wouldn't charge, say, the Atlanta office for the time brokers in New York and Pittsburgh spent on an Atlanta account. Sharing by computer network fit smoothly with that structure. To make sure it did, the company's vice chairman, Richard A. Nielsen, says he participated in the early computer dialogues to let everyone know that top management was watching. (Nielsen became so entranced by the technology that he later created his own Internet site dealing with tarpon fishing.) For younger brokers, who make about $40,000 a year, answering network queries became a way to build reputations.

Not that J&H hasn't had problems. Some managers fiddle with the network so often that they neglect the rest of their business. Others are still frightened by the technology, especially when they are forced to communicate with clients. One broker kept two sets of books: one for his internal use, and another, prettied-up, for the network, negating any productivity gains.

Then there's the cost. Like many other companies, Johnson & Higgins underestimated computer networking costs. Lotus annually charged about $100 a person for Notes and other software. J&H also had to buy a new personal computer for each broker, and hundreds of more powerful computers called servers, to store and route information along the network. Still other computers, including microcomputers and mainframes, serve as host computers, the main repositories for information.

Computer network vendors once promised they could slash costs by replacing $1 million mainframe computers with hordes of $5,000 microcomputers. But networks haven't yet produced big savings because they're still fragile and need a lot of maintenance, driving up overall costs to mainframe levels. Companies spend $8,170 a year to manage each PC in their network, estimates Forrester Research Inc., in Cambridge, Massachusetts. Of that, only $2,000 is the cost of the machine; software and training add another $2,340. The rest of the cost—nearly half the total—goes to administration, computer downtime, work lost when coworkers are asked to solve computer problems, and time taken to prevent computer disasters and to recover from them when they happen anyway.

J&H calculated that it cost $30,000 to set up one of its clients with a small network using Notes software, obviously reducing the number of clients willing to link up. The Internet made J&H's network plans practical, a lesson many other companies are learning. Since J&H has redesigned its network to make it compatible with the Internet, customers can call up J&H's website, enter a password, and connect to the J&H database that contains their files. Nearly every company has some computers devoted to Internet access, greatly expanding the reach of the J&H network. The Internet connection lets J&H share information more widely, pulling customers into the teams that it creates to solve problems.

How big a productivity gain can Johnson & Higgins expect? It's hard to say. Unlike Allen-Bradley, which precisely measures its circuit board output, J&H hasn't developed a reliable way to gauge the impact of technology. There are micro measurements. It used to take J&H 200 minutes to send faxes to twenty people; now it takes ten minutes, or one-twentieth the time. And there are macro measurements. J&H looks at how much revenue it collects for each dollar of employee-related costs it expends servicing its midsize clients. (Those clients are assumed to benefit most from the computer network.) By that measurement, productivity has increased about 9% a year since 1992, the year J&H started to expand its network—a substantial gain by the standards of service companies.

But no numbers are needed to prove that J&H is improving productivity, as are many other service companies that are exploiting computer networks. Wowed by the network technology, J&H's customers are setting up similar systems, accelerating the spread of the technology throughout the economy. "Within 30 days we saw the value of it," says David Strode, assistant treasurer of Northrop Grumman Corporation. Now, Northrop's insurance department has its own network linked to brokers outside of J&H. Multiplied thousands of times, those kinds of technology purchases will yield productivity breakthroughs and lift the rate of growth throughout the economy.

Recall the path electricity took. It was decades before electricity transformed the economy—far longer than optimists had predicted. But when the payoff came, it was profound—far greater than skeptics believed possible. The same is true with computing. The change has begun.

9

The Secret: No Bosses

How reorganizing the workplace will boost productivity.

It's midnight at Miller beer's Trenton, Ohio, brewery, which rises from the cornfields between Dayton and Cincinnati. The quiet of the night is shattered by eerie, amplified recordings of screeching birds, a way to discourage real birds from nesting in the grain-laden silos. Inside, amid a beer-scented maze of conveyer belts and the rattle of thousands of bottles of beer, workers tend machines that brew, pump, and package Miller Lite and Red Dog.

One thing is missing: bosses.

There are no managers here at midnight. They're home in bed, confident that a union crew will work diligently through the night and handle any problems that crop up. With substantially the same equipment as Miller's five other breweries, Trenton makes 50% more beer per worker than Miller's next-most-productive brewery.

The secret hasn't anything to do with technology; computers aren't the only reason to be optimistic about productivity. The secret is this: Miller trains workers to do the job and then lets them do it. The traditional foreman has been banished; an overseer is as unnecessary as someone who shovels coal. The technicians, as they're called, work in teams and handle chores that once were the foreman's exclusive domain. Because workers are trained to maintain their own machines, the plant operates with a lean thirteen-member maintenance team; not so long ago, Miller breweries needed maintenance crews numbering 150 or more.

Smarter deployment and better training of workers are boosting productivity in scores of American firms. Sometimes this new style of management combines with computer technology, as at Allen-Bradley. (See Chapter 8.) Sometimes it produces remarkable results without new technology, as it does at Miller's Trenton brewery. In a totally different arena, Xerox Corporation technicians who fix copiers in offices in Columbus, Ohio, showed similar results in a reorganized workplace. Xerox has done away with the supervisors who used to deploy, monitor, and nitpick the repair personnel. Work groups who manage themselves have turned out to be substantially better and more productive at their jobs than they were when managers were constantly looking over their shoulders. As more employers and employees catch on to this approach, productivity will increase more rapidly—and wages will rise accordingly. Miller and Xerox, the focus of this chapter, aren't isolated examples; they are harbingers of a new, more productive way of work.

In an earlier era, business executives, influenced by Frederick Winslow Taylor and his *Principles of Scientific Management,* sought to improve productivity by treating workers as mindless components in efficiently designed machine systems. In the late nineteenth and early twentieth centuries, Taylor used a stopwatch to time the most efficient workers and, based on their routines, established complex sequences for other workers to follow. Time-and-motion studies were used to set piecework pay rates in factories around the nation. The precisely defined jobs gave workers little flexibility and little reason to show enterprise, beyond trying to beat the system. "In our scheme," Taylor said in a 1906 lecture, "we do not ask for the initiative of our men. We do not want any initiative. All we want of them is to obey the orders we give them, do what we say, and do it quick." Taylorism fit neatly with Henry Ford's vision of the factory as a giant machine, and with the military-style hierarchies that dominated American corporations for most of the twentieth century.

Henry Ford and Frederick Taylor turned workers into cogs in vast assembly lines, managed by better-paid bosses. Today, Miller asks the cogs to manage the machines—and each other. Practices once popular only with socialist academics and Scandinavian manufacturers are now moving into the mainstream of American management, particularly in the manufacturing sector. About half of all manufacturing companies surveyed by the U.S. government in 1995 were experimenting with self-directed work teams. "Almost every major company has some plants managed by 'empowered workers' with no foremen. This is a big deal," says Harvard Business School professor Quinn Mills. What once was radical is now conventional. In a book published in 1995, the president of the National Association of Manufacturers offered factory owners ten steps to success. The very first step was to give workers more responsibility and authority.

It's easy to deride all this as a fad—the latest product of buzzword junkies and management consultants. But something significant and enduring is happening inside the most successful companies. First, there is a permanent sense of urgency in companies once distinguished by their complacency—Xerox, for example. "For the first time," suggests Edward F. Lawler III, a professor at the University of California Graduate School of Business, "we are in a change-or-die environment." Second, there is an accompanying realization that reorganizing the workplace isn't a quick fix, the hallmark of a fad. Instead, reorganization takes years to pay off—yet companies are committing themselves nonetheless. "The changes today are not just micro fine-tuning of traditional systems; they represent a new paradigm for management thinking that is bringing an end to the command-and-control, old-logic approach that has dominated organizations since large bureaucracies first emerged," Lawler writes.

Those who master the changes post impressive results. Examining a 1994 Census Bureau survey of 3,000 employers, economists Lisa Lynch and Sandra Black found that the factories with the largest measurable gains in productivity give employees more say in what they do. They also "benchmark," or set targets based on other plants' performance. Three other academic researchers compared forty-five steel-finishing production lines scattered from New York to California, in an effort to figure out why some were so much more productive. The half-dozen that resembled Miller's Ohio brewery—where teams of workers had flexible, broadly defined duties, job security, and extensive training—were substantially more productive and made higher-quality steel. Steel plants that went part of the way (the bulk of the plants) were only modestly more productive than the half-dozen old-fashioned plants with rigid hierarchies.

Successes like those at Miller and Xerox offer a tantalizing preview of the changes that will work their way through the U.S. economy in the next decade or two. Change comes slowly. But as these practices pay off for the companies that try them, other companies are bound to copy. Susan Morman, a colleague of Lawler at the Center for the Study of Effective Organizations, in Los Angeles, says the changes at companies like Miller and Xerox will soon be irreversible. Rebuilding the hierarchies of foremen—and foremen's foremen—is too expensive to contemplate; it would be akin to abandoning voice mail and rehiring squads of telephone operators.

Miller's experiment demonstrates just how large the payoff can be. The Trenton brewery was built in 1983, but its opening was delayed until 1991 because beer sales were lower than anticipated. Dennis Puffer, a veteran Miller manager who had been experimenting with newfangled ways to organize work at a Miller brewery in Irwindale, California, was put in charge. A slight man with white hair and fair skin, Puffer has the demeanor of a bookkeeper. By Miller standards, he is an industrial radical. (It doesn't take much to be a radical at Miller. Puffer was able to shock his peers by coming to work without a coat and tie.) The first time he explained his plans for the Trenton brewery to other plant managers, they laughed so hard, he says, that "it was hard to keep them from falling off their chairs."

The other plant managers aren't laughing anymore, and they're not wearing ties either. When Miller beer sales dropped, in the fall of 1996, production at other Miller breweries was cut back to four days a week. Trenton worked overtime because it produces beer at lower cost.

Compared to the traditional breweries, the Trenton brewery's productivity record reflects two fundamental differences. First, it has substantially fewer nonproduction workers—fewer maintenance electricians sipping coffee and waiting to be beeped; fewer front-office paper shufflers; fewer upper-level supervisors managing other supervisors who manage the people who make beer. Because it has fewer idle workers, Trenton produces 15,500 barrels of beer per employee annually; other Miller breweries produce fewer than 10,000 barrels.

Second, Trenton's machines break less frequently and are repaired more rapidly when they do break, primarily because the brewery workers are responsible for them. A worker at a traditional brewery is like someone who is driving a rental car, hears a knock in the engine, and ignores it. A Trenton worker who hears an engine knock gets it fixed. Because the machines are down less often and are operated more hours a week, each of Trenton's nine production lines pumps out 160 barrels of beer an hour, on average, compared with 140 or so at the best of the other breweries.

On a sunny fall afternoon in Trenton, the fourteen members of the second-shift team that runs the returnable-bottle production line trickle into a cluttered conference room just off the factory floor. Messages from the first shift are scrawled on a white board in one corner. All the brewery's production crews work nine hours a day and get paid time-and-a-half for the first hour, which is devoted to a team meeting. "If they're going to make decisions, they have to have time to make them," Puffer says.

Monica Venney, the technician assigned by her peers to coordinate the discussion, calls the meeting to order at 2:30 P.M., methodically following an agenda on a laminated card that is taped to the table. The session begins with some snarling about a team member who has called to say she won't be in—again. Each team is responsible for making its own attendance rules. Some permit a worker to call at the last minute to take a vacation day; others require that vacations be scheduled in advance. All must make sure that the production line is adequately staffed to do the work, and must decide how to allocate sometimes-unpopular weekend overtime. A lean workforce means fewer people to share weekend overtime duty. That pumps up paychecks—production workers earn $20.80 an hour straight time—but exhausts workers.

Besides their duties on the production line, each worker is assigned to be a "star point"—that is, to assume what used to be a management responsibility, such as personnel or maintenance. Miller wants workers to do more maintenance themselves, so that productivity will continually improve. Team managers must step carefully; if the managers assume too much responsibility, the workers won't take any. This remains a work in progress, and progress is sometimes frustratingly slow.

At the meeting, one worker asks about a stubborn gauge that has been causing problems at the point on the production line where beer is poured into bottles. Another man, a Miller lifer who transferred from another Miller brewery, says he has made a temporary fix. But he wants

Rocky, one of the plant's small team of maintenance experts, to tap into the computer that controls the gauge, and fix the problem permanently.

Charlie Korth, a manager who oversees the forty-three workers who run the returnable-bottle line during three shifts, pipes up: Maybe the team should do the job itself. Adjusting a gauge with the computer isn't any more difficult than adjusting an old-fashioned gauge with a screwdriver, he says. The workers bristle. "When you adjust one thing [on the computer], you adjust something else. Don't give me that screwdriver mentality," Venney snaps. The other workers hoot at her sharp-tongued putdown.

Korth backs off. "I was trying to get them to go ahead and give it a whirl," he explains later with a shrug. "They didn't have the confidence to do so."

But then a peacemaker suggests that someone should watch Rocky so he doesn't have to be called the next time the gauge needs adjusting—precisely the sort of practical step that's required to keep productivity improving. It's one of the small victories that build over time and eventually change the way entire companies operate.

Peer pressure keeps the plant functioning. "At my old plant, the supervisor was the only person I had to please," says Cheryl McCormick, whose team runs a beer-canning line. "Here, I feel like I have eight bosses I have to please. If you walk in late, you've got eight people who want to know where you were." Which system does she prefer? "It's easier to please one person, but all in all, I have to say I like this better." Other workers echo her sentiment.

Over coffee and cigarettes in the lunchroom, one notorious malcontent complains about the fatigue that comes from working rotating shifts, the pressures of weekend overtime, and his frustration that management won't add workers in the bustling warehouse. But after reciting that litany, he reaches a surprising conclusion: "If this country doesn't go to some form of this concept, we're all going to be sitting here twiddling our thumbs, and we won't be able to buy shit." Despite his bellyaching, somehow he has figured out that these pressures are the price of protecting and lifting the American standard of living.

Although the Trenton plant's stated goal is to give each worker eighty hours of training a year, monitoring is haphazard. A good deal of learning at Miller occurs informally, on the job. The plant manager, Dennis Puffer, seems to write off as "learning experiences" what other plant managers would consider expensive mistakes. When a 33,000-gallon hot-water tank collapsed because a worker made a mistake, the brewery was shut down for a day and a half. No one was disciplined or fired. No one even shouted, according to Pat McGowan, a utility-house worker. "They said, 'Can we do anything to help you?'" he recalls, still incredulous.

Another time, production workers, reluctant to call for help in the middle of the night, pored over blueprints seeking a failed electrical relay—unaware that the plant engineer had a more up-to-date blueprint. The engineer had the machine fixed five minutes after he arrived in the morning. The price of the workers' pride: four hours of lost production. "Sometimes they'll go down with the ship before they'll ask for help," Puffer says. "I told them: 'It's OK to ask for help.' In the old days, you'd go rant and rave. You felt good, but you still lost the production time."

The Trenton experiment isn't painless. Although teams do their own hiring, plant management is pressuring them to be racially diverse, causing friction with one team that is entirely white and another that's mostly black. Workers on those teams accuse management of tolerating only those workers' decisions with which it agrees.

Trenton workers benefit from their plant's productivity. Overtime pay boosts their average annual earnings to around $58,000, but even more important, their jobs are more secure. They aren't threatened with four-day weeks. And because the work involves the challenges of management, not just the monotony of running a machine, workers find their jobs more interesting. But the Trenton workers want more: a higher hourly wage than workers at less productive breweries. The United Auto Workers, which represents all the brewery's workers, had negotiated a promise that Trenton workers would be paid extra for learning new skills. But after two years spent struggling to find a workable formula, union and management gave up and are looking for another way to reward Trenton workers for their productivity.

Managers of Miller's other breweries slowly are copying Trenton's techniques—even though they're hobbled by more restrictive union contracts than Trenton's and by older workers who are set in their ways. Already, top Miller management has peeled away layers of salaried management at the breweries, a step that doesn't require union approval. Three of the other five breweries have adopted something close to Trenton's "star point" system of pushing onto production workers what were formerly management duties. The other two breweries soon will do the same. Quality checks are routinely done by frontline technicians instead of by a separate squad of quality checkers. This labor-saving step also prods technicians to avoid mistakes in the first place.

Eighty-five miles away from Trenton, in an office building next to the interstate that rings Ohio's capital city of Columbus, Xerox repair personnel are proving that well-trained frontline workers can boost productivity in a very different setting.

Not so long ago, Xerox, a pioneer in the copying business, was floundering. Customers were defecting, unhappy with the company's products and service. Japanese competitors were cutting into its market share. Shortly after he became chief executive in 1982, David Kearns worried that he might preside over the extinction of one of America's postwar corporate legends. "I didn't know whether Xerox would be able to survive the '80s," he wrote a decade later. "I frankly thought Xerox was on its way out of business." Kearns launched an expensive and ultimately successful campaign to improve product and service quality.

Xerox went through an extraordinary period of introspection. The company assigned Alan Monahan, now a manufacturing vice president, to learn from two eminent Japanese productivity experts who were advisers to Honda and Toyota. During the $30,000-a-day sessions, the plain-spoken Monahan came to appreciate how much waste there was in Xerox's manufacturing system—and how much of it was the fault of poor management.

The Japanese experts criticized Xerox's managers, not its workers, says Monahan, who still keeps his mentors' photos by his desk. During one session, to which Monahan had invited Xerox's chief executive, Honda's coach, Noriaki Kano, tore Monahan apart. "A lot of people thought I would lose my job," he says. But Xerox, mindful of how much it needed to improve, later promoted him instead.

Like many other big U.S. companies, Xerox had experimented with teams, but the serious push in the Xerox service organization began in 1986, led by Chuck Ray, a service technician who had moved into management. "Ray realized that technicians could improve their productivity greatly if responsibility for decision making moved closer to the point of customer contact," according to a brief history written by the American Society for Training and Development.

"The challenge was to meet customer demands without driving costs so high that we couldn't afford it," says Michael Tutko, who took over Xerox's troubled southern Ohio region in 1982 and enlisted in Chuck Ray's crusade in 1986. Improving service without increasing costs is a working manager's definition of improving productivity. The solution: Create teams of technicians responsible for a roster of machines, and tell them to dispatch each other, monitor their own performance, and consult management only when necessary. Now, although the ranks of Xerox service technicians are growing, the ranks of middle managers aren't.

Tutko oversees four offices, each of which used to have its own boss. In the Columbus office, a team of five "field managers" is responsible for 127 technicians; a decade ago, it would have taken ten supervisors to manage that number. Xerox simply stopped paying supervisors to handle mundane decisions about who should respond to a service call, or to referee disputes over vacation time.

Getting rid of the supervisors is just part of the formula. Service technicians say they do their daily jobs better and more efficiently in teams, despite having to endure the occasional interminable meeting at which the workers do what the managers once did.

Old-timers draw a sharp contrast between the way management treats them today and the way it used to treat them, and they're quick to enumerate the advantages of today's workplace. Supervisors used to tail repairmen and wait in the parking lot to see how long they spent on a job. "I was fond of telling the supervisor: 'I know my job better than you, so let me do it,'" recalls Tim Billips. "Then Jaime [Simpson, the group's current supervisor] comes along and says, 'You know your job better than I do. Do it.'" Billips was stunned.

Jaime Simpson is a former technician who now supervises twenty-one technicians organized into three work groups; he is part of a management-level team responsible for the Columbus territory. Simpson measures the success of the reorganized workplace by simple indicators. "My phone rings less. My customers are happier. And this translates into more machine sales," he says.

On Tuesday, at 8 A.M., the eight Xerox Corporation service technicians of Work Group Six sit in a conference room so colorless it could be a rent-an-office suite. The men look like middle managers; each has a neatly knotted tie and a small leather-bound organizer. They talk for three hours, dickering over how to decide on a vacation schedule, whom to send to company-sponsored training, and how best to evaluate each other's performance. It's hard to believe that this is actually a way to *increase* productivity, but it is.

For the first half hour or so, the meeting is a corporate dream come true. Without a boss looking over their shoulders, technicians who earn a base salary of up to $46,500 manage the day-to-day business and strive to improve their performance. One member distributes photocopied printouts—this is Xerox, after all—detailing the number of parts the team used in October (above budget), and out-of-pocket expenses (below budget). At great length, Brian Guerra explains how he avoided replacing an $8,000 component in a high-volume copier at a local copy shop simply by turning an alignment screw. A third technician alerts the team that technicians last month took two and a half hours to arrive at 5.5% of their customers' calls. No customer is supposed to wait that long.

Then the meeting bogs down. Only one of the eight work-group members is trained to repair the sophisticated Xerox copiers that are hooked into the latest office computer networks. Someone else needs to be trained at the Xerox training school in Leesburg, Virginia, but who?

"What are the selection criteria?" asks Don Rogers, the 23-year Xerox veteran who has been designated by his peers to run the weekly meetings. The candidate must be someone who is computer-literate and has completed the required computer courses, the group agrees after some back-and-forth discussion. After several moments of uncomfortable silence, it becomes clear that three of the eight want to go. Don Rogers suggests reserving one seat in the eleven-day course, and deferring the choice. No one agrees. Then talkative Brian Guerra suggests that the team train *two* members and schedule the training as early in the year as possible, to avoid conflicts with summer vacations. That proves popular. A couple of dates are selected. The group agrees that Guerra will attend the course and defers choosing the other candidate. "That was fairly painful," Rogers says with a grimace. He then turns the meeting to what will prove to be yet another time-consuming matter: how to decide who takes vacation when.

In all, the training discussion consumes about twenty minutes of eight workers' time, or nearly three work-hours that otherwise could have been spent repairing machines. An old-fashioned supervisor could have made the decision, albeit arbitrarily, in one minute. But Tutko, the work-group champion who oversees Xerox customer service in southern Ohio and West Virginia, is neither surprised nor concerned when the session is described to him. "As they work through making those tough decisions," he says, "the next time, the time it takes is cut in half."

His optimism is well-founded. In Tutko's territory, inflation-adjusted service revenue per employee climbed 37.7% between 1993 and 1996, a rate of productivity increase that has made Tutko something of a hero inside Xerox. "We have made a clear connection statistically that people who feel empowered have better [personal] satisfaction, customer satisfaction, and business results," says Tony Manasseri, who helps Xerox units improve their performance. Xerox customer satisfaction in southern Ohio, where the teamwork concept is most mature, is higher than almost anywhere else in the country. Xerox estimates from its surveys that by the ultimate test—the reliability of copying machines—the most empowered workers are about 8.5% more productive than those who are the most alienated.

Technology plays a limited role. The biggest innovation, hardly high-tech, was initiated by a work group that bought itself CB radios to stay in touch, rather than relying on a central switchboard to relay messages. Now, all the technicians carry radios to communicate with each other, beepers to alert them when a customer reports a problem, and cellular phones to call customers.

Although Xerox copiers are studded with computer components, and Xerox technicians are now beginning to carry laptops, Xerox's productivity gains have often come in spite of computers, not because of them. For now, technicians use the laptops mostly for record keeping. As Don Rogers waits at a Kinko copy shop for his laptop to boot up and display a section of a repair manual, he complains that he probably could save time by getting the paper manual from his car. When Rogers finishes fixing the Kinko copier, he dutifully types the information into the laptop and sends it over the phone line to a central database where any other laptop-carrying technician can retrieve it. But he also records the same information in a logbook that is kept at the Kinko store, as well as in a notebook he carries with him. "We're so enamored with the technology that we always make a paper backup," he jokes.

Working in teams didn't come naturally to the Xerox veterans. For years, Xerox technicians were responsible for repairing machines in their own defined geographic territory. They were reluctant to help another technician for fear that they would be busy when a customer on their home turf called. Complaints from customers—and there were many—went to the supervisor. So did every technician's problems.

To make the transition, Xerox had to train the loners to work together. In one early exercise aimed at building a group approach, Work Group Eight picked the ten worst machines on its list. "We asked, 'What do we need to do to make these home runs? What do we need to do to make these customers happier?'" recalls team member Roger Tedrow. Each team member was given a half-day a week to concentrate on one of the team's worst-performing copiers. "One account was constantly calling the sales manager," Tedrow says. The team explained the new approach, telling the customer that the team would make the machine run 10% better. "Now we get hugs," Tedrow says—and dinner at the customer's expense at Christmastime.

The members of Work Group Eight agree, without hesitation, that the hardest thing they've done so far was confront a peer who wasn't doing his job, a task that once was the exclusive province of management. Maintenance of various components of a copier is supposed to be done every so-many copies, much as oil is supposed to be changed in a car every 5,000 miles. Each technician has a roster of machines to tend routinely. If another technician is called to fix a machine, he expects to find all the routine maintenance chores completed.

One Group Eight technician, a veteran repairmen, was consistently negligent. After several private conversations between individual team members and the offender failed to produce results, the other members of the work group drew up a list of offenses. Each signed the list. They consulted their supervisor, but didn't involve him. Finally, they confronted their peer. "We were all scared to death," says Lee Bugbee, a 31-year Xerox veteran with more than a passing resemblance to Santa Claus. "You don't know how a person is going to react when you do that."

The malingerer read the list, took his glasses off, and, to the relief of his peers, said: "It looks like I've got some work to do." Later, in an unrelated reshuffling of work groups, the offender moved to another group where he is performing well. Although the target of the criticism remembers some of the specifics differently, he expresses surprisingly little hostility toward his former teammates. He doesn't think vacuuming the innards of a Xerox machine on every service call is necessary; to him, once every 250,000 copies is sufficient. But the team felt differently, and he had agreed to go along with the team decisions.

"If you buy into the group, you just do it," he says, though he acknowledges that he "blew off steam" for three or four days after the team confronted him. Is it better hearing such criticism from peers than from a boss? Maybe not, but it's much more effective, he says. "If a manager tells you to do something, you go back and complain to everyone else."

In the old days, each technician had a performance review, and raises were awarded to the best performer. The switch to work groups required a substantial rethinking. Today, technicians are measured exclusively on how their groups perform. Groups that do well on a common set of measures—machine reliability, customer satisfaction, parts usage, response time—get raises as much as 50% higher than the average group. Groups that do poorly get raises as much as 50% lower than the average amount. And any group that achieves preset goals, known as "work group excellence," on the various measures gets a bonus of $1,000 per technician. Mike Tutko says that about 50% of the groups in his territory qualified for bonuses in 1997. "It's an aggressive target," he insists, "not something you'll make by simply coming to work every day." Counting bonuses and larger raises, members of the best performing work groups can make as much as 10% or 12% extra.

But, surprisingly perhaps, technicians say that pride and control are motivators as much as money. "You don't want to be the lowest group on the totem pole," says Lee Bugbee. "I like having a say in my destiny," he adds. One of the most telling changes in the past several years has been a marked decline in absenteeism. Mike Tutko estimates that half the technicians in his territory never miss a day of work. Responsible not to a boss but to each other, the technicians are much more reluctant to miss work.

10

Alan Greenspan, Optimist at the Top

Why the Fed won't be an obstacle to faster growth.

Political cartoonists invariably draw Alan Greenspan, the chairman of the Federal Reserve Board, as a small, owlish man with over-sized black-rimmed glasses, thinning hair, and a dour demeanor. On an otherwise sunny beach, Greenspan is drawn standing under a storm cloud. On an empty highway, Greenspan is a flagman holding a sign that says: "Slow." He is standing beside another sign that warns: "Caution: Inflation Ahead . . . Somewhere"—even though the road stretches to the horizon without obstruction.

The cartoons reflect the popular wisdom: Even if the U.S. economy does prove capable of faster growth, as we expect, Greenspan and his fellow inflation-phobes at the Fed will interfere, raise interest rates, and prevent the middle class from enjoying the benefits.

The popular wisdom is wrong. The Fed won't stand in the way of a productivity-produced economic boom. Alan Greenspan cannot boost productivity himself, but he has the clout to prevent Americans from enjoying the benefits. He won't use it.

His public image notwithstanding, Greenspan is an economic optimist. In the face of skepticism from a substantial cadre of prominent economists who study such things, Greenspan concludes that the official productivity numbers clearly understate reality, and, more important, he expects the pace of productivity to quicken in the years ahead as American companies and workers figure out how to get more out of their computers. He says "an undetected delayed bonus" from the "massive advances" in computer and telecommunications technology is showing up already and should be nurtured, not squelched. Greenspan's surprisingly upbeat view of the economy's potential already has kept interest rates from rising faster, and likely will continue to do so even after he is gone.

Greenspan is notoriously cagey when he talks in public about interest rates. "I spend a substantial amount of my time endeavoring to fend off questions, and worry terribly that I might end up being too clear," he once told a black-tie crowd. They laughed, but he wasn't joking. Presidential candidates prize sound-bites that are so pithy that they are guaranteed to make the 7 o'clock news. Greenspan envelops himself in sentences so long and intricate that even *The Wall Street Journal* can't quote them in their entirety.

But Greenspan is explicit when he talks about the next decade or two. He has done more than anyone to popularize the views of Paul David, the Stanford economic historian who draws the analogy between electricity and computers and argues that technology soon will open a new era in economic growth. In 1996, when Greenspan was resisting pressure from inside the Fed to raise interest rates, he talked frequently in public and with his colleagues about the promising prospects for the American economy. "The rapid acceleration of computer and telecommunication technologies can reasonably be expected to appreciably raise our productivity and standards of living in the twenty-first century, and quite possibly in some of the remaining years of this century." Are these the sentiments of a congenital pessimist?

Coming from anyone else, the statement would be interesting chatter. Coming from the chairman of the Federal Reserve, it has enormous significance. The United States concentrates more economic power in the Federal Reserve system than in any other institution. By raising interest rates or otherwise contracting the supply of credit in the economy, the Fed discourages or prevents businesses and families from borrowing. The less Americans borrow, the less they spend. And the less they spend, the fewer jobs there are in the economy.

No mighty commercial bank, no industrial giant, no software powerhouse comes close to having so much power. Except for the Supreme

Court, no other arm of the government is so independent. The President can launch nuclear missiles on his own, but he is almost powerless to steer the economy without the consent of Congress and the cooperation of the Fed. The Supreme Court overturned parts of Franklin Roosevelt's New Deal that had been approved by Congress, but it has never moved to restrict the Fed's freedom to raise interest rates. Congress and the President have the constitutional clout to force the Fed's hand by passing a law, but they never have.

The prevailing theory of political economy holds that a democracy is prone to inflation. To fight that tendency, Congress has delegated its constitutional right to print money and set interest rates to the Fed, which is deemed wiser and less influenced by public opinion. Despite its enormous influence, the Federal Reserve is one of the least understood institutions of government, and it likes it that way. The Fed, as one historian put it, is "an intentional mystery." Because few people understand what the Fed does and how it functions, it has far more flexibility to do whatever it wants.

One thing is abundantly clear: What matters more than anything else at the Fed is what the chairman thinks, even though other top Fed officials legally could outvote him. Greenspan, an intellectual, inquisitive business economist who served as President Ford's top economic adviser, was picked to succeed Paul Volcker as chairman of the Fed in 1987. Ronald Reagan's economic advisers thought Volcker was focused too much on fighting inflation and too little on fostering economic growth. At the time, William Greider, a journalist who chronicled the Volcker years, wrote that Greenspan "didn't have the personal stature of Paul Volcker, either in Washington or Wall Street." Reflecting the conventional wisdom of the time, he predicted Greenspan "would be unable to dominate the Federal Reserve Board the way Volcker had . . . [and] less able to intimidate the politicians."

A decade later, Greenspan's stature in Washington is unrivaled. Unlike the 6-foot-7-inch Volcker, the slight, balding Greenspan isn't physically imposing. He sets the economic agenda in Washington through a shrewd sense of how politics in the capital is played. Authority over interest rates comes with the job. Greenspan also freelances as a Washington wise man, a conservative counselor to presidents and legislators of both parties. He has pushed reluctant politicians to overcome their natural inclination to spend more money, and has convinced them to reduce the federal deficit instead. He has persuaded many members of Congress that the government is overcompensating Social Security beneficiaries for inflation. And he has steered them away from investing Social Security funds in the stock market.

Greenspan, although a Republican, is a bipartisan pro. "Greenspan has about as good a 'bedside manner' with people in power as anybody I've ever seen—one of the reasons being, he's very smart," says William Seidman, who was President Ford's economic policy coordinator. "But he also speaks in ways that sound profound even if you don't understand what the hell he's talking about." Greenspan celebrates his birthday each year with an unlikely threesome who share the same March 6 birthdate: former Democratic Speaker of the House Thomas Foley, Republican Senator Kit Bond of Missouri, and former FBI Director William Webster. He skillfully cultivates the press, and in 1997 married a television news reporter, Andrea Mitchell of NBC.

In person, Greenspan is unassuming, soft-spoken, and gentle. When a Steinway piano, a wedding gift from Andrea Mitchell's parents, was delivered, she was on the other side of the world, covering the travels of the Secretary of State. He telephoned her, placed the receiver near the piano, and played a tune so she could hear it. He disarms critics with flattery and an appearance of being keenly interested in their thoughts. When Greenspan begins his response to a particularly stupid question from a member of Congress by saying, "That's an extraordinarily interesting question, Congressman," he never sounds condescending.

Former Labor Secretary Robert Reich, in his memoir of four years in Washington, describes his first encounter with Greenspan: "One look, one phrase, and I know where he grew up, how he grew up, where he got his drive and his sense of humor. He is New York. He is Jewish. He looks like my uncle Louis, his voice is my uncle Sam. I feel we've been together at countless weddings, bar mitzvahs, and funerals. . . . How did my Jewish uncle get to be the most powerful man in the world?"

"I actually like the guy," Reich writes, sounding surprised.

The conference room where Alan Greenspan presides looks like a place where momentous decisions are made. Greenspan sits at the head of a massive, oval mahogany table under a giant Seal of the United States. Once every six weeks, Greenspan and the six other members of the Board of Governors of the Federal Reserve join the presidents of the twelve regional Fed banks, created by Congress in 1913, to talk about the economy and decide what to do about interest rates.

There isn't any knob marked "Interest Rates" that the Fed twists to make rates go up or down. Decisions made around that table are conveyed to the Federal Reserve Bank of New York, a fortresslike building in lower Manhattan with a basement vault full of neatly stacked gold bars that foreign nations give to the Fed for safekeeping. Upstairs, traders linked by telephones and computer screens to dealers in government securities manipulate the "federal-funds interest rate"—the rate banks charge each other for overnight loans. When the federal-funds interest rate moves, other short-term interest rates move along with it.

When the Fed wants to push interest rates down, Fed traders buy U.S. Treasury bills and pay for them by putting money into checking accounts of securities dealers, literally creating money by tapping a few computer keys. When you write a check, the money moves from your account to someone else's; when the Fed writes a check, the money comes out of thin air. When the Fed wants to push interest rates up, Fed traders sell U.S. Treasury bills from the Fed's hoard, taking money out of the economy. This is known as *monetary policy,* to distinguish it from tax and spending decisions that are known as *fiscal policy.* It's said that President John F. Kennedy remembered which was which by associating the "m" in monetary policy with William McChesney Martin, the Fed chairman at the time.

The Fed is guided by a simple and longstanding bit of economic logic: Over the long run, the economy can grow as fast as the growth of the labor force, plus the rate of productivity improvement. Fed staff economists regularly chart these trends for their bosses. The labor force has been growing around 1% a year, and, productivity, as officially measured, has been increasing at around 1% a year. So Fed staff economists lately have argued that the economy can safely grow, without accelerating inflation, at only around 2.0%, on average—perhaps 2.25% at best. The economy, however, has stunned Fed experts. In the first three quarters of 1997, it grew at a 3.8% annual rate with barely a hint of inflation.

Greenspan insists that he doesn't set an inflexible speed limit for the economy. But he concedes that having a sense of how fast the economy can safely grow over the long run is helpful. The economy, of course, can grow very rapidly when it is coming out of a recession and lots of workers are unemployed. But, in 1997, with unemployment at a twenty-four-year low, that wasn't the case. Greenspan addressed the point in an interview: "If there is evidence that the economy is growing at a rate that you believe to be faster than the long-run sustainable

growth rate, you will be far more sensitive to looking for signs of inflation." A Fed chairman, like Greenspan, who believes that the pace of
productivity—and, thus, "the long-run sustainable growth rate"—is
likely to improve is far more likely to tolerate faster growth than a productivity pessimist.

The toughest task for the Fed is to decide whether a quickening of
economic growth is based on a sound foundation or on an unsustainable gush of excess credit. Telling the difference is what monetary policy is all about; that's where Greenspan has an edge, and where his
worldview matters most. In public statements, in newly released transcripts of Fed deliberations, and in accounts of present and former Fed
insiders, Greenspan's words suggest his secret for divining the economy's direction lies in understanding the thousands and thousands of
numbers that describe its complex workings.

Greenspan reads numbers-laden Fed-staff reports in the bathtub
before going to work, a habit acquired twenty-five years ago when a
doctor prescribed long, hot soaks for an aching back. He once told a
U.S. Senator that the best thing about being the nation's most powerful economic policy maker is that it gives him access to "the data." He
complained to the Big Three auto makers in 1994 that their decision
to stop reporting auto sales every ten days "significantly diminished
our ability to monitor business activity." Although any of the Fed's 232
economists would respond instantly to a Greenspan query, he nevertheless keeps two computer terminals on his desk—one to monitor financial markets and the other to tap the Fed's huge database. The Fed's
domestic economic-research unit tracks 18,500 data series, 3½ times
as many as before he arrived.

But despite what he says, scrutinizing numbers isn't the true key to
Greenspan's success. Rather, he relies on a sophisticated seat-of-the-
pants approach, informed by nearly fifty years of pondering the way the
economy works. That approach, hard even for Fed insiders to understand, has led Greenspan to the conclusion that productivity is growing
more rapidly than official measures suggest.

This was apparent when Fed officials gathered around their oval
table in the summer of 1996. Several were deeply worried that the
United States was on the verge of economic growth so strong that inflation was about to accelerate—the very thing that they were hired to
fight. The unemployment rate had fallen to 5.4%, and the economy

had expanded at a 4.2% annual rate in the spring quarter. At those levels, history suggested, employers faced labor shortages and would be forced to increase wages faster than the underlying pace of productivity. Behind closed doors, the presidents of several of the regional Fed banks argued that inflation was inevitable. Indeed, by mid-September, eight of the twelve regional Fed banks were petitioning for higher interest rates, a gesture that conveyed the urgency of their concern. But, month after month, Greenspan refused to raise interest rates. It was a gutsy call, but proved to be the right one.

Edward Boehne, a thoughtful economist who joined the staff of the Federal Reserve Bank of Philadelphia thirty years ago and has been its president since 1981, sided with Greenspan. "We have really taken some risks on the growth side," he said in late 1996. "The first rule is: Do no harm. If the economy can grow faster, if the unemployment rate can go lower and we're not seeing inflation, so be it."

What gave Greenspan the confidence to take risks on the growth side? The Fed chairman gave many reasons. The economy was about to slow on its own. Workers were so insecure about their jobs that they weren't pressing for wage increases. Firms were unable to raise prices because of intense competition. All these factors undoubtedly contributed to his decision.

But so, too, did his hunch that productivity was likely to turn up, and that the economy could safely grow faster than the conventional wisdom at the Fed suggested. Gary Stern, president of the Federal Reserve Bank of Minneapolis, and an inflation foe who has spent 23 of his 53 years at the Fed, said Greenspan was wrong—and voted to raise interest rates. In an explanation written for the Fed's records, he challenged Greenspan's argument head-on, saying he didn't believe there was "a substantial and sustained improvement in productivity."

But Greenspan reasoned that no matter what the detailed government data on productivity showed, production was up, profit margins were widening, labor costs were steady, and prices were stable. Productivity had to be improving. Verbatim transcripts of Fed deliberations are kept secret for five years, but the published summary of a September 9, 1996, meeting records that Greenspan observed that the "previous relationships" between prices and the level of economic activity were "undergoing changes that required careful study." That's Greenspan-speak for: The old rules don't apply. Throughout 1997, the same arguments surfaced when the unemployment rate fell to levels not seen since Richard Nixon was in the White House. Some Fed veterans grew anxious about the risks of inflationary wage increases. Again, Greenspan held his colleagues back. A summary of their May 20, 1997, deliberations records that they "focused on the possible role of faster-than-reported increases in productivity as a key explanation for the benign behavior of inflation in current circumstances."

Over and over again, Greenspan lays out the optimistic case for productivity. Businesses are spending heavily on computers and telecommunications gear, and on software, he notes, but the productivity payoff is elusive. "Either we are spinning our wheels for a lot of this frenetic activity and going nowhere," he told Congress in July 1996, "or—and this is what I expect is really the case—the productivity acceleration is being delayed in a manner not dissimilar to the way the productivity gains from the development of the electric motor were delayed at the early part of the twentieth century." Once businesses and workers figure out how to harness the computer's potential, he predicted, productivity would accelerate. "We are living through one of those rare, perhaps once-in-a-century events," he proclaimed. "The advent of the transistor and the integrated circuit and, as a consequence, the emergence of modern computer, telecommunication and satellite technologies have fundamentally changed the structure of the American economy."

By early 1997, Greenspan was growing more confident, talking as if the gains in productivity that he had predicted were at hand. Productivity growth usually slows after the economy has been expanding for a few years, he said. With a shrinking pool of unemployed workers to draw from, employers are forced to hire less desirable workers, who usually aren't as productive as those already on the job. But in the seventh year of the Greenspan expansion, productivity growth wasn't slowing. "This pattern is contrary to our experience," he said. What it suggested, he said, is that the underlying, long-run pace of productivity might be improving. The U.S. economy need not settle for the meager growth of the past two decades, and the Greenspan Fed won't force it to do so.

Greenspan's views on productivity aren't universally accepted at the Fed, or on Wall Street, or in academia. The more conventional economists who populate the Fed remain skeptical, and quietly fear

Greenspan's vision may be a mirage. Former Fed Vice Chairman Alan Blinder, who distinguished himself from hard-line Fed inflation foes by emphasizing the Fed's legal charge to maximize employment as well as keep prices stable, derides Greenspan's arguments as a "Brave New World" thesis—that is, as futuristic fiction. After Blinder left the Fed, he wrote a paper titled, "Waiting for Godot: Information Technology and the Productivity Miracle?" Even if Greenspan is right, in the long run, about the potential for computer technology to boost productivity, Blinder argued, "we may be condemned to an extended period of transition in which the growing pains change in nature, but don't go away."

The Fed at times has been an obstacle to rising living standards, a fact that Fed officials don't often acknowledge. When the Fed is preoccupied with resisting or reducing inflation, it can deliberately cause a recession that undoes years of economic progress. Paul Volcker did just that in the early 1980s, when inflation approached double-digit levels. In a single-minded campaign to force down the inflation rate, he triggered the worst recession since the Great Depression. But the Fed won't have to fight that war again anytime soon. With inflation at historically low levels, the Fed lately has shown little interest in reducing it further. By official measures, consumer prices are climbing about 3% a year; by Greenspan's estimates, the measures are so flawed that the actual inflation rate is below 2% a year, close to the nirvana of "price stability" about which the Fed so often talks. The Fed's current strategy is to keep the inflation rate from rising in good times, and to take advantage of the inevitable recessions to get inflation down a bit more.

But that raises a question: If Greenspan is so optimistic about the economy's potential, why did he raise interest rates in March 1997? Greenspan still believes there is some point at which the demand for goods and services in the economy exceeds the capacity of the economy to produce them. At that point lies inflation, and that's still the enemy. Businesses would be unable to increase production fast enough to meet demand and would start raising prices instead. Workers might get higher wages, but their fatter paychecks wouldn't buy any more if prices went up, too.

Thomas Melzer, president of the Federal Reserve Bank of St. Louis, makes the point with this example: "Suppose a retailer suddenly experiences more traffic in her store—more customers are buying whatever she has to sell. The retailer may call her supplier and request an increased shipment of goods. If the supplier has been operating at substantially less than capacity, he may be glad for the extra business and willingly supply the additional goods at the usual price.

"If, on the other hand, he is already operating close to capacity, the supplier may demand a higher price from the retailer, or he may simply refuse to ship any more goods. The retailer, in turn, may determine that her best course . . . is to raise her own prices, and expect to sell about the same quantity as before," Melzer says. The same is true for the overall economy. "Because monetary policy has the potential to boost output in the short run, some may be tempted to push for faster and faster growth by stepping on the monetary accelerator. Output may indeed go up for a time, but eventually inflation will be the only outcome."

In the spring of 1997, Greenspan decided that the risks of inflation had risen to the point where he couldn't ignore them. The growth of the economy had reduced the unemployment rate. Overtime hours were rising. There was little spare capacity in factories. Greenspan raised interest rates by ¼ percentage point. Although offering no guarantees, he said that he wouldn't choke off economic growth over the longer run— and surprised many of those who make a living predicting Fed moves. He held interest rates steady for the rest of the year.

At today's levels of inflation, the Fed won't *intentionally* hold the economy to 2.2% annual growth, provided it is convinced that productivity is improving rapidly enough for the economy to grow faster. Not even Gary Stern, the Minneapolis Fed president who argued forcefully for higher interest rates in 1996, wants that. "Were productivity improvement to accelerate, so that the economy could grow at, say, a 4% rate over the long run, monetary policy would certainly welcome it," he has said.

But workers are hurt if the Fed's inflation phobia leads it to *unintentionally* prevent the economy from realizing its potential. Indeed, American workers have more to fear from Fed clumsiness than Fed cruelty. Economic data are always confusing. Greenspan inevitably describes the current state of the economy, no matter what the circumstances, as "extraordinarily uncertain." Measured productivity, unlike some other important indicators of economic vigor, jumps around from one quarter to the next. And the Fed makes its share of mistakes. In retrospect, the Greenspan Fed contributed to the 1990–1991 recession by moving too cautiously to lower interest rates. And it prolonged the peculiarly sluggish nature of the recovery that followed by being slow to cut interest rates still further.

How will the Fed distinguish productivity-driven economic growth from unsustainable, inflation-threatening economic growth? As Greenspan put it, in a May 1997 speech: "How can we be confident we at the Federal Reserve are not inhibiting the nation reaching its full growth potential?"

The usual Fed answer, articulated by Greenspan and by Fed bank presidents Stern, Boehne, and others, is that if the Fed were restraining the economy too much, the Fed soon would see a declining inflation rate or a rising unemployment rate. But at any particular moment, these measures can send contradictory signals.

Ultimately, the Fed's ability to avoid mistakes depends on the judgment and instincts of its chairman. A doom-and-gloom chairman—one who believes the United States must settle for the disappointing economic growth rates of the past two decades—will have little problem realizing that outcome. But Greenspan believes that technology will yield a productivity dividend, and he will embrace it when it arrives.

Greenspan turns 72 in March 1998, and his term as chairman expires in June 2000. Before President Clinton leaves office, he'll either reappoint Greenspan for a fourth four-year term or replace him. What happens if Clinton replaces him? All the evidence suggests that the Greenspan legacy will continue.

Paul Volcker cast a shadow over the Fed for years after he left. He had instilled in veteran Fed staff and policy makers a determination to avoid the mistakes of the late 1970s, which produced the double-digit inflation of the 1980s. Future Fed officials will be much less likely to let inflation creep up to 8% or 9%. They know how much pain Volcker inflicted on America to reduce inflation.

Greenspan's legacy will be far different. He forced skeptical colleagues at the Fed to take seriously the possibility that the economy was poised for "a once-or-twice-in-a-century phenomenon that will carry productivity trends nationally and globally to a new higher track." He ran a bold experiment when he allowed the economy to grow more, and unemployment to fall lower, than other inflation-fearing Fed officials and economists thought prudent. The economy grew more, employers hired more, workers enjoyed more—and inflation remained surprisingly benign. Greenspan was correct, and that record will have a lasting effect on his successors. "Everyone of us listens to the chairman," says one Fed veteran. "It helps when his views are backed up by what's happening to the economy."

Because of Greenspan's incessant preaching about the prospects for greater productivity and the inadequacies of official productivity measures, the post-Greenspan Fed will be much more likely to spot and nurture a pickup in productivity. At his urging, Fed economists have dissected the official—and discouraging—productivity measures to show that they can't possibly be accurate. Greenspan has enormous credibility inside the Fed, in financial markets, and among world leaders. His endorsement of an argument that might otherwise be dismissed as naïve optimism forces others to take it seriously—and that will continue even after he leaves.

More than other big institutions, the Federal Reserve is notoriously resistant to change; the institutional inertia is strong. It took a decade of internal discussion before the Fed hesitantly decided to publicly announce changes in interest rates, instead of signaling financial markets by the manner it bought or sold Treasury bills. But ultimately, *results* matter at the Fed. Good results—and Greenspan's results certainly qualify as good—gradually change the way Fed officials and influential staff economists view the economy. They already have forced veterans of past inflation wars to recognize that the economy is changing, and that the pace of productivity improvement may be quickening.

"The current adult generations are having difficulty adjusting to the acceleration of the uncertainties of today's silicon-driven environment," Alan Greenspan says. "Fortunately, our children appear to thrive on it. The future accordingly looks bright." He has made optimism respectable—even at the Fed.

11

Dream Catchers

How community colleges will foster prosperity and equality.

Since the mid 1970s, the dividends of prosperity have been paid disproportionately to those who already have wealth and education. This trend, particularly the widening of the wage gap in favor of people with college educations, is one big reason the American middle class hasn't done better over the past twenty years. The next twenty years will witness greater economic equality. The prosperity we foresee will be broadly shared.

The previous three chapters explained why the economy will grow faster. This chapter and the next tell why the forces of supply and demand will divide the spoils more equitably. Here, we tell the encouraging story of how the 1,100 community colleges across the country are creating a growing pool of workers who have precisely the skills that command good wages in today's economy. In Chapter 12, we tell how computer technology will be simplified so that it increases employers' appetite for less skilled workers, making it possible for them to get good-paying jobs that have been out of their reach until now.

What goes on at a school like Cuyahoga Community College, in Cleveland, Ohio, and similar institutions across the country, is more important to the American middle class than what happens at Harvard. In the early twentieth century, the expansion of high schools improved living standards and narrowed the gap between well paid and poorly paid workers. Community colleges are beginning to do the same today, and their economic influence will expand in the future. In an avalanche of bad news about schools, community colleges are the exception. Although celebrated by employers nationwide and championed by President Clinton, community colleges remain underappreciated by the public and, often, by the state legislatures that fund them.

But workers like Ken Bohla understand their importance. In the early 1980s, Bohla immigrated to the United States from Guyana at age 17, with his mother and nine siblings. He worked in a succession of $9-an-hour factory jobs through the 1980s and early 1990s. Around 1989, he vowed to enroll as a full-time student at "Tri-C," as Cuyahoga Community College is known locally. But, because he couldn't afford to stop working, he could squeeze in only a course or two at a time. In 1993, he discovered a Tri-C model factory that pays students while they learn to operate computer-controlled machine tools. Now 31 years old, his apprenticeship complete, Bohla is making $17.78 an hour—$35,000 a year before overtime—operating a computer-controlled machine tool on the third shift at a Lucas Aerospace Inc. plant in Aurora, Ohio. Although he still is taking courses toward an associate degree in mechanical engineering, he already is cashing in on his Tri-C investment.

To Bohla, a community college degree is a more likely guarantee of economic security than a job at a big company. "A job, especially the way business is run today, in my view, is not there forever, whether it's Ford, GM, or AT&T. So long as you have them, they're good. But you don't depend on them," says Bohla. "This degree, this document, will help me to do better in the future."

That simple but irrefutable logic, echoed by 5.5 million community college students across the country, is cause for optimism about the prospects for middle class workers. People respond rationally when wages for educated workers rise far above those of workers without education: *People go to school.* The trend is clear; as recently as 1982, only half of all high school graduates went to college full-time or part-time the following fall. Today, about 62% go.

Nearly half those freshmen enroll in community colleges, the institutions that bridge the gap between high school and the job market, between $9-an-hour and $17-an-hour jobs. "Workers aren't going to get by with a high school education and a good attitude," says Frank

Doyle, who retired in 1995 as General Electric Company's top personnel executive. "The graduates of name colleges, they're going to make it anyway. Community colleges are going to help with education that makes a difference."

Community colleges are doing what other educational institutions in America *aren't* doing: preparing people, often those with mediocre basic schooling, to get well-paying, middle-class jobs. The proof is in the paycheck. In 1996, the typical man who had a community college degree and was working full-time earned $35,201—nearly 20% more than a worker who didn't go beyond high school. For women, the payoff was even greater. Those with community college degrees earned an average of $27,311—33% more than high school graduates.

In many ways, the market for workers resembles the market for anything else. In the past twenty years, the supply of educated workers hasn't kept up with surging employer demand. Because of that shortage, employers have been forced to pay a higher premium to hire these choice workers. In 1980, the typical man with a four-year college degree earned 26% more than a man with just a high school diploma; in 1997, a college graduate earned 52% more. The story for women is similar. Historical comparisons for community college graduates aren't available, but the trend is undoubtedly similar.

The lure of higher pay is encouraging more people to get educated. That trend has important consequences for the wages of all workers, with or without a college education. As the pool of educated workers continues to grow, the pool of less educated workers shrinks. College-educated workers will continue to earn more than their less educated counterparts, but the gap between their wage levels will diminish.

Why? With a growing supply of college-educated workers, employers won't have to pay quite so much of a premium for college diplomas as they pay today. Meanwhile, the glut of less educated workers will diminish. All workers will enjoy rising wages; improving productivity will see to that. But those who have been battered during the past twenty years—workers without college education—will see their wages move closer to those of their better educated and better paid peers. Prosperity will be widely shared.

Recall the image, in Chapter 1, of the two teams of mountain climbers. The college-educated trekkers have reached a height on the side of the mountain; the high-school-educated climbers remain stuck at the base.

In the coming era of broadly shared prosperity, high-school-educated climbers will ascend at a faster pace, closing the distance between themselves and the college-educated climbers as both groups make their way toward the peak.

This isn't wishful thinking. It is already beginning to happen. The gap between high-school-educated and college-educated workers has stopped widening. This important change shows up more clearly among younger workers because the surge in college enrollment has been greatest among those just out of high school. Looking at government data on wages of workers who have been on the job between one and five years, Kevin Murphy, a University of Chicago labor economist, says the size of the wage bonus for college graduates rose from about 40% in the late 1970s to nearly 80% around 1990, and has begun to head downward since then. He credits the expanding ranks of college-educated young people. "Based on my reading of the evidence, it would

The wage bonus for going to college
For workers with one to five years work experience

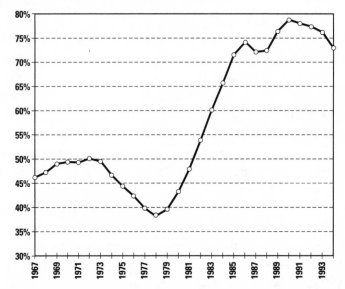

The amount of extra wages employers paid college graduates, compared to what they paid high school graduates, soared in the 1980s as employers' demand for educated workers outstripped the supply. Because of increases in the pool of college graduates, the bonus they earn has begun to shrink recently. Source: Kevin Murphy, University of Chicago.

seem that growth in the wage gap has probably run its course," says Murphy, who, with Harvard colleague Lawrence Katz, did definitive work on how changes in the supply of and demand for educated workers explain the increased wage inequality of the 1980s.

The notion that more widespread college education will foster greater wage equality is confirmed in Canada, where the economy is close to a mirror image of the U.S. economy. The same forces of technology that increase U.S. employers' appetite for educated workers have been at work there. But the wage gap attributable to education level didn't widen in Canada during the 1980s, largely because the pool of educated workers has expanded rapidly. This development has been reinforced by stronger unions and a higher minimum wage, but, most significantly, compared to the United States, a greater percentage of young Canadians enrolled in community colleges and other vocational schools. The supply of educated workers expanded sufficiently to prevent the Canadian wage gap from widening to U.S. proportions. The lesson is clear and encouraging: Education promotes equality.

In the United States, the added supply of educated workers will come, in large part, from community colleges. Four-year colleges and universities have bigger enrollments, and corporate training is becoming increasingly important. But community colleges are where people like Ken Bohla go—people who waver about going to college, can't afford university tuition, want a marketable skill as well as an education, or need remedial English or math. Over the past decade, enrollment in community colleges has grown by 24%, nearly twice the rate of increased enrollment in four-year colleges. Roughly four of every ten students enrolled in college today are attending a community college.

Demographics will help. In the next few years, large numbers of the children of the baby boomers will finish high school. As a growing fraction of these high school graduates goes to college, they will increase the pool of potential college students and swell the ranks of young educated workers. Over the past decade, the number of 18-year-olds has declined by 7%; over the next decade, it will swell by 17%.

Just as important, more older workers will return to school or get trained on the job by their employers. At Cleveland's Tri-C, 41% of the students taking courses that count toward degrees are older than age 30. Cornelia Wade, 47 years old, was stuck in $6-an-hour jobs until she enrolled. "I just got tired of getting these little jobs that don't pay much money," she says. The mother of nine received her associate degree in the spring of 1996, and immediately signed up at a local hospital's two-year nursing school.

Older students like Wade do well at community colleges. Adults in their late twenties and early thirties who enroll in community colleges get an even larger payoff—8% to 10% higher wages—than those who enroll immediately after high school. Veteran steelworkers in their thirties who lost their jobs in the mid-1980s and participated in a program for dislocated workers at the Community College of Allegheny County, in Pittsburgh, ended up making between 6% and 7% more a year than those who hadn't entered the program.

Randy Kohrs is a community college success story. In June 1991, the video store that Kohrs had been managing in Cedar Rapids, Iowa, closed. With only a high school diploma, Kohrs, then 37 years old, couldn't find work that paid more than minimum wage. A string of jobs had carried him and his growing family to a succession of Iowa towns, but each job was a dead end and left the family in a deeper hole of debt. The Kohrs lost their house to the bank. Their teenage son attempted suicide. Kohrs still winces as he recalls trying to get a job managing a Cedar Rapids tuxedo-rental shop. "You have qualifications unsurpassed. What degree do you have?" he remembers the interviewer asking. "I don't have any degree. I've got 20 years of management experience," Kohrs replied. "If you don't have a degree, we won't hire you," the interviewer told him.

One night, Kohrs's wife suggested that he should go back to school. "I'm too old. Too dumb," he protested. He says he never intended to actually enroll when he finally went to inquire at Kirkwood Community College in Cedar Rapids. But, as Nancy Kohrs puts it, "He didn't have many options." A Kirkwood counselor urged that he take a standard aptitude test. The results: The gregarious Kohrs was cut out to be a priest or to work in the health-care field. It was a bit late to contemplate the priesthood, Kohrs says with a hint of a smile. Health care seemed a stretch, but he recalled how much he enjoyed the public contact at the various jobs he had held. Kirkwood offered eight programs in health-related fields. Checking the job prospects with area hospitals offered him some encouragement. He decided to pursue a two-year program in respiratory therapy—assisting patients who use ventilators, treating respiratory diseases, and administering any medication that is inhaled.

The problem was money. "I didn't have any," Kohrs says. Tuition ran about $900 a semester, plus $250 or so for books. Enter Kirkwood's "dislocated workers" office, a three-person staff that administers federal programs aimed at helping people like Kohrs. The staff helped Kohrs assemble a package of federal grants and about $10,000 in loans to pay the Kirkwood tab and support his family. A federal program even reimbursed Kohrs $150 a month for his daughter's extended-day program at elementary school.

Kohrs began college classes in the fall of 1991. He took the required English, humanities, and similar courses for the first two semesters because the respiratory therapy courses didn't begin until summer. "Socrates! Plato!" Kohrs exclaims, shaking his head at the memory. "Composition I was a nightmare. I could write a good story, but I was terrible with punctuation." He wrote his essays by hand, and his wife edited and typed them. To make her husband's schooling possible, Nancy Kohrs worked as a car-dealership cashier by day, and took a second job, three nights a week, at a Wal-Mart store. On Saturdays, she worked at the dealership in the morning and at Wal-Mart in the afternoon. "For two years, I didn't see a whole lot of Randy," she says. "And my daughter really missed her mommy. I just explained that it wasn't going to go on forever."

It didn't. Kohrs graduated from Kirkwood in 1994 and immediately landed a full-time job at the University of Iowa hospital, in nearby Iowa City. Despite recurring rounds of downsizing at Iowa hospitals, Kohrs says he feels secure and satisfied. He started at $26,000 a year—about twice his old pay level—and is now earning $28,475. Unlike his last job, this one includes health insurance.

Nancy Kohrs works just one job now, earning about $16,500 at a different dealership. The couple has replaced their 1980 Chrysler LeBaron with a 1994 Pontiac Grand Am. They purchased a new $32,000 three-bedroom mobile home that sits in a well-kept park with a swimming pool, a basketball court, and yards big enough for gas grills and lawn furniture. The Kohrs are pleased that they now have enough money to buy their daughter $27 shorts and $15 kneepads for cheerleading. To celebrate their son's 21st birthday, Randy and Nancy Kohrs took him to Las Vegas. "To us, that's life. That's really making it," Kohrs says with obvious satisfaction.

Randy Kohrs isn't exceptional. Although Kirkwood doesn't systematically track its graduates, several of the other twenty members of his

graduating class say they are doing equally well as respiratory thera-
pists. A 1994 survey of community colleges by the U.S. Department of
Labor and the American Association of Community Colleges found
that, nationally, graduates of two-year respiratory therapy programs
had little trouble getting work and were earning an average starting
salary of $25,000 a year.

Academic research supports the anecdotal evidence that community
college education pays off. In the most thorough examination, published in 1995 in the *American Economic Review,* the nation's premier
economic journal, Thomas Kane and Cecelia Elena Rouse compared
the experiences of men and women who graduated from high school in
1972 (the same year as Randy Kohrs). Looking at students who are
alike in most respects—sex, race, family income, test scores—but not
in their education, Kane and Rouse found that each year's worth of college course work, whether at a community college or a four-year
school, added between 4% and 6% to a worker's subsequent annual
earnings in the 1980s. A year's worth of college was just as valuable for
those who didn't finish an associate degree as for those who did, and
more than paid for itself over the student's working life. This finding is
particularly significant because most community college students don't
complete the degree requirements. Of the students who enrolled at
Cleveland's Tri-C in the fall of 1988, only one in ten had graduated by
the spring of 1995, a result that would seem disappointing in any other
light.

Brian Surette, a young Federal Reserve Board economist, drew even
more encouraging conclusions when he used different techniques to
examine similar data for men. A man who earns one year of community
college credits, Surette estimated, earns 9.6% higher wages than a man
who didn't go beyond high school; a second year of credits adds another 7.5%. Completing an associate degree brings 8.6% more.

The quality of community colleges in the United States is uneven,
but the best of them show how American workers can be educated for
solidly middle-class jobs. In Cleveland, a city struggling with economic
change, Tri-C shows the impact a successful community college can
have.

Cuyahoga Community College, Cleveland's first state-supported
college of any sort, opened in a century-old elementary school building in September 1963, two years after the Ohio legislature authorized

counties to establish community colleges, and decades after community colleges had sprouted in California, Michigan, Missouri, and elsewhere. Although it had little initial support from the Cleveland establishment, opening-day enrollment was substantial: 3,039 students. "It was the community college, which painted its ivory tower a rainbow of colors, that demolished the notion that a college education was only for the affluent," the *Cleveland Plain Dealer* wrote years later.

Today, Tri-C is as much a fixture in Cleveland as the Cleveland Indians, who play baseball in a new stadium directly across the street from the college's administrative offices. (Ever enterprising, the college charges Indians fans, the college president included, $10 per car to park on its property during the games. The money goes for scholarships.) In the fall of 1996, 21,800 students were enrolled in Tri-C courses that count toward degrees; two-thirds of them were studying part-time. Another 10,400 students were enrolled in not-for-credit courses that range from how-to sessions on Windows 95 to management training workshops.

One tangible sign of the community's support is repeated voter approval of the small property-tax levy that accounts for about 40% of the college's $100-million-a-year operating budget. (The rest comes from student fees and the state government.) Even amid today's anti-tax fervor, county voters, in November 1996, approved another tax increase by a 3-to-2 margin—the third such vote since 1990.

It's hard to find the heart of Tri-C. The college is divided among three main campuses: one across the street from a housing project in Cleveland's inner city; a second in Cleveland's eastern suburbs; and a third, as big as the other two combined, in Cleveland's western suburbs. College administrators work out of a separate building (across from the ballpark), and the college has teaching outposts at sites ranging from a downtown storefront to a Ford Motor Company factory in nearby Walton Hills. At these various locations—and via cable television, as well—the college bundles together disparate programs aimed at students who have almost nothing in common except their determination to make more money.

A community college's mission, in part, is to rescue social castaways—people who otherwise would never get jobs that pay middle-class wages. Tri-C's president, Jerry Sue Thornton, describes community colleges as "dream catchers," referring to the bits of netting and feathers that some

Native Americans hang over a sleeping baby to capture good dreams and allow bad ones to escape.

At least one politician appreciates that mission: President Clinton. "I want to make two years of education after high school as universal in America as a high school diploma is today," he told 15,000 people gathered on Tri-C's western campus on a rainy day in November 1996. The President was promoting a federal tuition tax break tailored to encourage enrollment at community colleges. Congress approved the Clinton tax credit in 1997.

Despite the enthusiasm for community colleges at the White House and among local employers, particularly those in need of technically skilled workers, Tri-C is occasionally ridiculed as "Tri-High." It is a not-so-subtle reference to the fact that a whopping 60% to 70% of those who enroll are required to take remedial—known these days as "developmental"—English or math classes before enrolling in college-level courses that count toward a degree. This reflects both the appalling shortcomings of American high schools and the ambitions of community colleges.

Community colleges are organized and managed to cope with students who, for whatever reason, need to brush up on their basic academic skills. Tri-C offers three levels of remedial courses in English and math, as well as tutoring-on-demand until 10:00 P.M.; other community colleges have similar arrangements. Although they enroll almost anyone who has a high school diploma, rigorous community colleges such as Tri-C require that students finish remedial-level work before enrolling in occupational programs. Ken Bohla, the Guyana-born machinist, took all the remedial English and math classes that Tri-C offers, and still had to take a three-hour test before he was admitted to the machinist training program.

Foreign educators who visit community colleges are as entranced by this American institution as their predecessors were by high schools at the Paris exhibition in 1900. One issue comes up routinely, says Laurel McFarland, a U.S. economist who consults on education and training issues for the European Commission. "They find it fascinating that enrollments fluctuate with demand," she says. Europeans rely much more on bureaucrats to allocate classroom seats.

One of the secrets behind the success of community colleges is their exquisite sensitivity to the local labor market. The best schools constantly revamp their curricula in response to, and even in anticipation of, employer demands. "Employers go into the labor market looking for skills. Both students and the community college pick up the signals," McFarland says. "Community colleges are the most flexible of any of the institutions of higher education. If they have classes that don't have students who want to take them, they drop them."

Community colleges haven't always been so focused on preparing students for the job market. They have been struggling for decades to resolve an identity crisis like the one that plagued high schools early in the twentieth century: Are they preparing students to transfer to four-year colleges, or are they preparing them to get good jobs?

The community college movement traces its roots to the founding of Joliet (Illinois) Junior College, in 1901, by a high school principal who was influenced by William Rainy Harper, the president of the elite University of Chicago. Around the turn of the century, Harper divided the four-year program at the University of Chicago into a "junior college" and a "senior college." He persuaded the faculty to grant an "associate degree" after completion of the two junior college years, hoping that less able students would leave at that point. He dreamed that universities could someday abandon junior college courses altogether, transferring them to high schools or independent junior colleges. Universities could then concentrate on teaching the brightest students and on doing research.

In the 1930s, however, junior colleges began to develop a distinct two-track curriculum—one for those who would go on to four-year colleges, and another for those who wouldn't. The approach survives today. Community colleges award one kind of degree to students who choose the academic track, and another to those who are on the occupational track.

Well into the 1940s, junior colleges still saw themselves, and were seen by others, primarily as college preparatory schools, even though many of their students never actually went on to complete four-year degrees. "It is very difficult to enroll students in a curriculum upon the gates of which are inscribed the motto, 'Abandon all hope, ye who enter here,'" said Walter Crosby Eels, executive secretary of the American Association of Junior Colleges from 1938 to 1945. Many students who would profit from a junior college education probably should never consider attending a university, he said, but "they will refuse to submit to any doctrine of academic predeterminism which forever forbids possible entrance to education paradise."

In the late 1940s, a commission appointed by President Harry Truman (using language uncannily echoed by President Clinton), declared that "the time has come to make education through the fourteenth grade available in the same way high school education is now available." After comparing test scores of college freshmen with the "mental ability" of the population at large, the commission concluded that "at least" half the population had the capacity to complete fourteen years of school—significantly shy of President Clinton's universal goal. At that time, only 16% of young Americans even began college, compared to nearly two-thirds of high school graduates today. One third of Americans between 25 and 34 years of age today have completed at least an associate degree (the equivalent of graduating from fourteenth grade), and another 20% have taken some college courses.

In 1948, the Truman Commission strongly endorsed the notion that the two-year degree would be "terminal" for many students, as the educational jargon of the time indelicately put it. It recommended that the term "junior college" be replaced by "community college" to emphasize that many students wouldn't proceed to four-year colleges, and to underscore the mission of an "institution designed to serve chiefly local community education needs." The term eventually stuck, but the tension over the primary mission of the institution has never been fully resolved. Even though a minority of their students go on to get four-year degrees, community colleges loudly advertise themselves as a cheap way for students to do the first two years of college before transferring. Tri-C publications invariably picture those who have transferred to four-year schools on the cover, though the college acknowledges that only 12% of students who enrolled in the fall of 1991 had transferred by the spring of 1995.

As college enrollments stagnated in the 1970s and colleges of all kinds recruited growing numbers of older and part-time students, community colleges made a distinct and lasting shift toward preparing students for jobs, rather than for four-year college. At the beginning of the 1970s, 43% of the associate degrees were in occupational fields. The rest were in arts and sciences or in general studies, which are more easily transferred to four-year colleges. By the end of the 1970s, 63% of the degrees were in occupational fields, such as nursing. Today, the statistic is around 70%.

Cleveland has seen the ups and downs of U.S. manufacturing, the deterioration of its city public schools, the invasion of computer technology at almost every workplace, and a growing public realization that education provides more lasting security than a job with a brand-name company. Tri-C has evolved in response.

Demand for skilled factory workers and technicians outstrips the available workforce in Cleveland, so Tri-C has been beefing up its manufacturing offerings. That strategy wouldn't make sense for every community college, but it makes sense in Cleveland. One recent Sunday morning, Tri-C assistant vice president Dallas Garrett counted 419 ads in the local paper for manufacturing positions for which Tri-C alumni might qualify—for example, quality-assurance technician, machine operator, welder. On a flip chart in his office, he matched the openings to Tri-C programs, using one color for those that the college already offers, another for those he wants to add. Where the college jargon doesn't match the want-ad lingo, Garrett plans to change the college label. "We've got to start using the titles that the want ads use, so that students know what we're talking about," he says.

Walter Hytell knew exactly what Tri-C was talking about. For sixteen years, he worked as a $10-an-hour machinist, using old-style, manually controlled machine tools. He knew his job would not last through his worklife. "Every ad and every 50-cent tour of any shop, I saw they had 'computer numerically controlled' equipment. No cranks. No handles. Everybody was pushing buttons," he says. At one shop, he thought he had a promise to be trained on the new machines, but the company hired outsiders who already had the necessary know-how. Another company said it was planning to buy new machines, and he took a couple of night courses to get ready, but the machinery never arrived. He answered ads from firms using modern equipment, but each one demanded experience. So, in September 1994, Hytell, then 39 years old, enrolled in the Tri-C program that pays students to operate machines while they learn them—the same program that had attracted Ken Bohla.

A freckled man with a high forehead, a trim mustache, and graceful fingers, Hytell had hoped to be a professional violinist before a hand injury interfered. He went to work in a factory in 1978 after he married. Unlike many of the other students in the Tri-C manufacturing program, Hytell wasn't laid off. He quit to get training that he believed was necessary to get a secure, well-paying job. While he was in school, he and his wife, a Tri-C-trained nursery-school teacher, supported four children on $21,000, barely above the government poverty line. Somehow they managed to come up with $3,200 for Catholic school tuition. Shortly after Easter 1997, Hytell landed the job he had long been hoping for: operating and programming a computer-controlled lathe for a new Valley View, Ohio, DuPont factory that makes parts for the aerospace industry. He started as a $12-an-hour temporary worker, was given better health insurance benefits than he had ever had before, and was expecting to be earning close to $13 an hour by the end of 1997.

Between the classroom courses he took toward an associate degree, Hytell went daily to the small Tri-C machine shop for what the college calls a "practicum." The shop, surrounded by floor-to-ceiling windows as if it were an exhibit in a world's fair, has one of each kind of modern basic machine tool. Several of them are directly controlled by a computer terminal that isn't much different from the average desktop PC. None of the equipment is more than four years old. Graduates say the equipment at Tri-C is newer than the machines they work on at their new jobs. The shop's products range from one-of-a-kind displays for Cleveland's new science museum to an initial production run of a paint-spray nozzle that a local manufacturer is trying to perfect. In one corner, one of the $7.15-an-hour apprentices operates a laser that scans a solid metal object and creates a precise electronic blueprint on the computer screen in front of him.

"The students actually make these parts," says Charles Barth, director of the Tri-C Manufacturing Learning Center, fingering stainless steel rings that the shop is making for a local company. "We are paying the students. Because they are learning, the labor efficiency isn't great. We get government subsidies to offset this." In addition to its paying customers, the center is supported by federal, state, and local grants and by a local foundation.

Barth, a Cleveland-born metallurgist who spent decades as a corporate R&D executive, sketches his view of the local factory labor market on the whiteboard in his cubicle, which overlooks the factory floor. At the top are jobs that pay $18 an hour—skilled machine operators, technicians, and such. These jobs are likely to require an associate degree and as many as 1,800 hours in the Tri-C shop, a curriculum that probably will take students three or four years to complete. Next come the $14-an-hour jobs, which require half as much classroom time and perhaps only 800 hours in the shop. Because a lot of students will leave the program at this stage, the college awards a vocational certificate, both as a reward to the student and a credential for employers. At the bottom are jobs that pay $8 to $10 an hour, jobs that are a step up for unskilled high school dropouts and for recently released prisoners who come to Tri-C for six months of state-funded remedial education and training in basic machine skills.

Tri-C's reach extends beyond the boundaries of its three campuses into the factories and offices around the county. At a 40-year-old Ford metal-stamping plant, Tri-C occupies a room with bright yellow walls, black linoleum floors, and twenty personal computers. Only the plant's 1,800 union workers and their spouses are welcome. Uwe Brausewetter, a tall, husky man with reddish-brown hair and a pocketful of pens in his coveralls, is a regular customer. The 43-year-old worker followed his father to the Ford factory after graduating from high school, and is now an apprentice tool-and-die maker. "I've been here off and on since '72—more off than on," he says. "I've learned that education isn't something they can take away from you when you get laid off. If something happens to this plant, I can walk into some other plant and get a job."

Under contract to a joint Ford–United Auto Workers education fund, Tri-C operates the Education Center forty-four hours a week. It opens at 7:00 A.M. daily and stays open until midnight on Wednesday nights. Nearly half the Ford factory's workers have participated. They come before or after work, or on their twenty-four-minute breaks, but always on their own time. Retired teachers serve as counselors, but all the instruction is done via self-paced computer courses. Formal courses that meet at preset hours are almost impossible for workers who put in heavy overtime and who sometimes move from one shift to another with little notice. Little of the course work in the Education Center is college-level; many of the gray-haired students are working on their high school equivalency certificates. But then, most of the students aren't looking for a degree; they want skills they can use.

Brausewetter sought help with the drafting he had to learn for his apprenticeship. He brushed up on his math before an assignment as a "preceptor" (lead worker) when Ford introduced statistical techniques to monitor assembly-line quality. He has now mastered WordPerfect and a popular computer-graphics program, and has gone from two-finger typing to touch typing at 30 or 40 words a minute.

A modern factory worker, even one in an old metal-stamping plant, is never far from a computer these days. Terry Haus, a soft-spoken 31-year-old with the paunch of a middle-aged man, had never used a computer before he was hired at the plant in 1994. He was stunned the first time he attended a weekly meeting of what's known in today's factory as "a natural work group" and was handed a quarter-inch stack of computer-generated charts tracking the output, efficiency, and safety of his part of the factory. "It was incomprehensible," he says. He promptly reported to the Education Center to learn how to use a computer and read the charts.

The eagerness of community colleges to court local employers is palpable. Miami-Dade Community College, in Florida, began a mortuary science program at the request of the Florida Funeral Directors. In 1996, Huntsville Community College, in Alabama, opened a satellite campus in a renovated Chrysler Corporation factory, to train workers for nearby firms. Greenville Technical College, in North Carolina, assigns a full-time faculty member to help a local General Electric facility with its training needs. Kirkwood Community College, in Iowa, allowed an insurance company to build a 55,000-square-foot corporate computer center on its campus; about a fourth of the space is for a computer-training facility operated by the college. Chicago's Harold Washington Community College offers courses to U.S. military personnel stationed in the Sinai. Satellite hookups allow almost instantaneous video, audio, and fax communication between the Midwest and the Middle East.

What business wants, community colleges teach. NYNEX Corporation, the New York telephone company that recently became part of Bell Atlantic Corporation, had joined with the Communications Workers of America in persuading community colleges to create a new associate degree that would train longtime telecommunications workers for an industry that is changing rapidly. More than 1,000 Bell Atlantic employees, at twenty-five community colleges in the Northeast, are now going to school one eight-hour day each week—on company time. Earning a degree takes four years. The company pays for tuition and books, and gives each student a laptop computer.

Fannie Mae, the government-sponsored mortgage company, turned to community colleges for help in increasing the number of minority mortgage lenders. Why community colleges? They already draw heavy enrollment among minorities and immigrants, and they move fast, says Harriet Ivey of the Fannie Mae Foundation. "When a corporation wants to start something, it doesn't like being told that it's going to take three years to get going," she says.

Largely as a marketing gimmick, but also to underscore their commitment to preparing students for work, several community colleges now guarantee that their graduates can do the jobs for which they are certified. If they can't, the colleges promise to retrain the students at no cost. It's an approach that clearly differentiates community colleges from high schools, in employers' eyes. Reporting on a series of focus groups conducted with employers in eight communities, University of Pennsylvania researchers said: "Put off by the young, saddened by their local high schools but not much interested in changing them, most of the employers with whom we talked had simply shifted their attention to the next age cohort, focusing on those in their early- and mid-twenties and concentrating on the educational institutions they attend. The firms and businesses represented in our focus groups did know about their local community colleges [and] had a good sense of what they offered and who to talk to if one needed training for current employees or wanted to tap a supply of new workers."

Employers need workers who can read and add, but they increasingly need workers who can work in self-managed teams. Community colleges are altering their curricula accordingly. In Chattanooga, Tennessee, a community college is revamping some of its math classes to emphasize problem solving and teamwork, as opposed to straightforward calculations, because those are the skills that DuPont and other big local employers prize. When DuPont's nylon factory hired 300 machine operators in the mid-1990s, it required applicants who passed a written test to spend nine hours, over three nights, working together in small groups to solve prescripted problems. (An example: "You're working on the night shift unsupervised. You have to keep production going. You need supplies, but there's a rabid fox in the warehouse. What do you do?") An eight-person team of DuPont employees observed and selected those applicants who demonstrated the best ability at communications, leadership, and working as a team. About fifty of the 300 hired, it turned out, were community-college graduates.

General Motors first turned to community colleges nearly twenty years ago to train auto mechanics for its dealerships. In 1979, GM installed computerized fueling systems in its cars for the first time, and knew that the automobile was destined to get increasingly electronic. But few experienced mechanics knew anything about electronics.

After thinking about expanding its own training facilities or contracting with private training companies, GM tried a mechanics' training program at Delta College, a community college near Saginaw, Michigan. It seemed to work, so GM tried the program at a community college in Dallas and another in Chicago. "In 1979, we said we're going to train a technician and he has to have a college degree. People laughed at us," says John Choulochas, who coordinates the program for GM. Today, GM-sponsored programs at Tri-C and fifty-two other community colleges annually graduate about 750 new auto technicians, as they're now known, for GM dealerships. Technicians earn $20,000 to $25,000 initially, and substantially more after a few years' experience. Ford, Chrysler, and Toyota now have similar programs.

In the GM version, students must be sponsored by a local dealership, which promises them a job if they complete the program. For two years, students alternate between the dealership and the college, working for eight weeks and then studying for eight weeks. Students pay the tuition, though dealerships sometimes help out. The college pays for faculty and facilities, including service bays. GM provides new cars and other state-of-the-art equipment, as well as periodic updating sessions for the instructors.

The training area at Catonsville Community College, outside Baltimore, Maryland, could easily pass for a prosperous suburban auto dealership. It has hydraulic lifts, banners with corporate logos, computerized diagnostic equipment, and blue-uniformed mechanics. The only clue that it isn't a business is the group of small classrooms off to one side, each with a table and twenty or more chairs, a blackboard, and a garage door that allows a car to squeeze into the room.

In the beginning, GM allowed technicians-in-training to take only courses like "Servicing Automotive Electrical and Electronic Systems." They could skip "English 102: Writing About Literature." GM now insists that students take the liberal arts courses and finish an associate degree. GM's John Choulochas says the goal is to produce technicians who are capable of learning more in the future—perhaps in a classroom, perhaps by viewing a CD-ROM sent to their dealership. "We understand that training will have to go on over their lifetime. We need higher reading skills. We need to have people who have good, solid reasoning . . . and have solid experience with the car," he says.

At Covington Buick, in Silver Spring, Maryland, veteran service manager Bill Belew no longer hires technicians right out of high school as he once did. Four of his thirteen technicians are graduates of the GM program at Catonsville Community College; he is sponsoring a fifth, and he is looking for another candidate to put through the program. After some bad early experiences—"a near 100% failure rate," as he puts it—he is now more careful about interviewing prospective participants and checking references, and more successful with his choices. In all, GM says, 80% of the participants graduate, and more than 80% of the graduates remain with the sponsoring dealership for a year and a half.

Covington Buick's burly, bearded transmission man, Mike Snyder, a Catonsville alumnus, doesn't look like a college boy. His beefy hands are stained with grease; he wears a blue workshirt with "Mike" embroidered in script on the front. Standing beneath a disassembled Buick, with the pieces of its faulty transmission in his hands, Snyder explains how the transmission has evolved from hydraulics to electronics. "The computer tells it when to shift," he says. The trick for the technician confronting a transmission problem is to figure out when the computer is at fault and when the transmission is.

Snyder worked for another auto repair shop for about three years while he was in high school, and considered looking for an auto mechanic's job after his graduation in 1988. Then a high school teacher mentioned the GM program at Catonsville. "Once I heard about the automotive college," as he calls it, "it made my decision easier." Snyder isn't convinced that the liberal arts courses that GM and the college required did him much good. "I took appreciation of art. I didn't see any purpose for it," he says. But that appears to be his only complaint. At age twenty-six, he is earning $20 an hour—better than $35,000 a year, and more than some four-year college graduates earn—and owns a three-bedroom house. "He's going to make someone a great husband," his boss says with a fatherly chuckle.

Creating a successful training program is easier when a corporate giant provides the equipment, teaches the instructors, and finds the graduates jobs. The tougher task is to alter an old program so that students can find good jobs in a changing market. Denver's Front Range

Community College has managed to do the latter. In 1987, the college, which is near the shuttered Rocky Flats nuclear–weapons plant, realized that federal environmental regulations were creating a demand for people trained in dealing with hazardous materials. In particularly short supply were technicians who knew how to sample groundwater in tests for pollution. When Front Range launched its program in the fall of 1988, it hoped for fifty students. "We had 333 walk in the door," says David Boon, the administrator.

Bill Brennerman, now an environmental scientist with the city and county of Denver, was twenty-eight years old in 1988. He had a bachelor's degree in forest management and a few years of experience on summer fire-fighting crews, but he couldn't find a permanent job. After reading about the Front Range program in the local newspaper, he enrolled, added an associate degree to his bachelor's, and immediately got a job supervising field crews who dug ground-monitoring wells at Rocky Flats. "The community college training was hands-on," he says, "like how to install and sample monitoring wells. Most people didn't have those skills. It gave me a big advantage: I was able to show up the first day of work knowing what to do." About a fifth of the students who have been through the Front Range program already have a four-year college degree, but half have only a high school diploma.

Until three years ago, Boon says, the Front Range program had never advertised or even had a marketing plan. But the market for environmental technicians in Denver isn't as strong as it once was, and the jobs that are available are changing. The demand for technicians to investigate hazardous waste sites is giving way to a demand for technicians to supervise cleanup. So Front Range is now altering its curriculum. An advisory panel of local industry executives and government officials, which advises Front Range, is meeting more often and is helping to structure a two-year degree that will train students to manage small cleanup programs, combining both engineering and construction skills.

The wage gap between more educated and less educated U.S. workers won't disappear. But with successes like those at Front Range and Tri-C, it will diminish. The market has sent a clear signal to American workers: Education pays. Community colleges work. People are responding by going to school. In the decades to come, many more Americans will share in the nation's prosperity as a result.

12

Making It Simple

How technology will make life better for less skilled workers.

When the U.S. Army was developing its latest computerized tank, the M1A2, in the 1980s, some generals fretted that they would have to recruit better educated tank crews. They predicted that the tank's electronic systems would be so complex that high-school-educated soldiers would be intimidated by them. But, partly through the urging of a group of research psychologists, the Army shifted its thinking and used the tank's sophisticated computer software to make the vehicle easier for ordinary soldiers to navigate and hunt for enemies. The Army is now fielding about 120 of the M1A2s each year. The tanks are so simple to operate that even crew members who scored poorly on Army aptitude tests rank among the Army's most proficient tankers. "If you can do well in a video arcade, you can do well in an M1A2," says Colonel Richard Geier, director of the Armor School at Fort Knox, Kentucky.

The Army has learned a crucial lesson about technology that is beginning to spread broadly through the economy: Complex computer technology can and should be easy to operate. With ever more powerful computer chips capable of handling complicated instructions, the most sophisticated machines ought to be the simplest to use. Craig Fields, who heads the Pentagon's Defense Science Board, which reviews technology issues, says a telecommunications system is a failure if it needs a thick operating manual. A tank's complex computer shouldn't burden a soldier, any more than a Dodge Caravan's sophisticated transmission should concern a parent driving kids to soccer practice. Talented engineers can design into a system's software many of the skills that humans once needed in order to operate machines. "True excellence in design is when you've taken something very complex and made it very simple," says Joe Belfiore, a Microsoft manager who's trying to apply that principle to the company's latest software.

Making technology simpler to use opens jobs to workers with lesser skills, and gives them a chance to move ahead. The effects are profound. Community colleges are expanding the *supply* of educated workers, and that is helping to reduce the gap in wages between those with more education and those with less.

There's another important reason for the wage gap's narrowing. As technology becomes simpler to use, employer *demand* for ever more skilled workers will ease. A wider range of workers will be able to fill jobs that involve computers, because those systems won't require as much special training as they once did. Better educated and technologically adept workers will continue to prosper. But a broader selection of jobs that once required advanced degrees will become available to those with more modest skills.

Over the past twenty-five years, workers with special skills and four-year college diplomas have benefited overwhelmingly from the computerization of the workplace. They have had the ability and training to run dauntingly complex equipment. But, as the past reminds us, this isn't always the way technology affects workers.

In the early part of the twentieth century, mass-production technology was a boon to unschooled immigrants and farm workers, who flocked to factories for high-paying jobs assembling autos and appliances. Skilled artisans were the losers back then. Similarly, in the offices of that era, demand slackened for the small number of highly paid bookkeepers who could calculate large sums in their heads. High schools were churning out trained workers who could do secretarial and bookkeeping jobs, and typewriters, adding machines, and other new machines made office jobs easier to perform. In that era, as in the one that's starting now, new technology made work simpler for many people, and gave those with lesser skills a chance to get better paying jobs.

The move toward simplicity in the 1990s is a reaction against the past twenty years of computer design, which have been guided by the principle of "More is better." That principle has produced machines that are stuffed with features—and frustrating to use. Who hasn't watched in horror as a computer screen freezes or mutates into gibberish because an elbow inadvertently grazed against a keyboard? Walter S. Mossberg, *The Wall Street Journal's* computer columnist, describes personal computers as "magic boxes, chameleon machines" that are supposed to transform into fancy typewriters, videogame players, architectural design boards, financial analysts, telephone answering machines, and more. By trying to do so many different things, computer systems don't do any of them well enough; instead, they become a jumble of features. In 1992, for instance, Microsoft's Word software had 311 commands that a user controlled to write or edit; by 1997, Word had 1,033 commands. "You never know if your machine will run right," Mossberg says. "You never know if new software will disable the rest of your machine."

Sensing the frustration among consumers, manufacturers now are bringing to market simpler devices that are supposed to do one or two things well. Several computer makers are pushing so-called network computers, which sell for half the price of personal computers, and run only software programs stored on computer networks. Simple handheld computer devices that can retrieve schedules, names, and addresses from desktop machines are also gaining a following. Even VCR clocks, whose blinking 12:00 epitomizes needless complexity in programming, have been simplified. Some Sony VCRs automatically reset their clocks after power outages, and also change the hour to account for Daylight Saving Time. Lots of even easier-to-use products are in development, including pocket computers to store notes and telephone numbers, and animated software to search the Internet.

The leaders in simplifying technology work in fields that depend on employees who have below-average skills. Faced with deteriorating math skills among job applicants, McDonald's deployed cash registers that automatically ring up prices and tabulate change. The same is true at grocery-store checkouts, where cashiers need only pass bar-coded packages over laser scanners.

Engineers working with the disabled have pushed the development of one of the most significant technologies of the next few decades:

computers that respond to human speech. As that technology spreads across the economy, verbal commands will replace keyboards and computer mice as the primary way of working with computers. "You can muse out loud" to your computer, says Janet Baker, president of Dragon Systems Inc., a company outside Boston that designs speech-recognition systems.

The Army moved early to simplify technology because it had no choice. In the late 1970s and early 1980s, the Army was planning a new generation of tanks and other weapons systems, but was attracting abysmal recruits. "We're taking guys who really can't read or write and putting them into a tank, a $2 million piece of equipment," complained a sergeant in an armored unit during that era. "There's a big, fat manual for operating it. But what good is that to an illiterate?" Such military reformers as then-Senator Gary Hart and writer James Fallows warned the Pentagon against relying on high-tech weapons, in part because they feared that many soldiers weren't educated enough to run the computer controls.

The Army learned the power of technological simplicity in the mid-1980s, as the first M1 Abrams tanks rolled across the test ranges of California and West Germany. The M1 replaced the 1960s-vintage M60 Patton series of tanks. Compared to the Abrams, the Patton was a clunker, especially in calculating distances to enemy targets, a critical step in aiming a tank's cannon. Patton gunners had to mechanically crank together two images until they overlapped to give a clear view of a target—like hand-adjusting old-fashioned 35-millimeter cameras. In the 1970s, the Army finally replaced the mechanical rangefinder in the Patton with a laser device. But the problem was, it took an M60 Patton crew twenty-three steps to turn on the finicky laser. In the 1980s, the M1 Abrams was outfitted with a new laser rangefinder, which took just three steps: turn on, point, and click a button to get distance readings.

The Army discovered that the simplicity of the M1's laser rangefinder, and other new systems, equalized the skill of gunners, regardless of their education and native talents. The Army divides soldiers into five categories of intelligence, depending on how they score on aptitude tests. Category 1 is at the top, and category 4 is at the bottom for those who are accepted into service. (The Army doesn't recruit those classified as category 5.) Category-4 soldiers score the equivalent of between 550 and 724 on combined Scholastic Aptitude Tests, out of a maximum of 1,600 points. M1 category-4 crews outperformed M60 category-4 crews by 85% because the M1's technology was so superior, according to a review of 1,131 tank crews at an Army firing range in Grafenwohr, Germany, in 1984. Overall, M1 crews from all categories performed 46.7% better than those in M60s.

"Any dummy could operate the M1," explains Lon E. Maggart, the blunt former commanding general of Fort Knox, the Army's armored vehicle training center. "Your lowest-level soldier could operate this [M1] tank more efficiently than higher-level soldiers on old tanks. The Army made the tank so sophisticated that you just had to push a button."

An M1A2—"the A-Deuce," tankers call it—was introduced in 1992 to replace the M1 and an improved model, the M1A1. The A-Deuce is a 70-ton, turbine-powered killing machine that can blow up a house two miles away, and then slurp ten gallons of fuel driving to the remains. Watching tanks roar through the desert is like watching tyrannosaurs rampaging in *The Lost World*. But the Army's development of the A-Deuce illustrates how complex systems throughout the economy—utility control panels, milling machines, medical screening systems—can be simplified for use by ordinary Americans who receive a little training.

The challenges facing tank recruits are similar to those faced by young, high-school-educated workers elsewhere in society. Even though educational standards have improved in the Army—no one talks of illiterate tankers anymore—recruits usually have high school diplomas, at best. In the civilian world, those are precisely the kinds of workers who have been bloodied by the economy since 1973. Just as companies now expect more out of their hirees, the Army is ratcheting up demands on recruits, too. In both cases, young workers are expected to think for themselves, innovate, and handle technically daunting equipment. American companies are in economic combat with competitors at home and abroad; the U.S. Army trains as though it will always be outnumbered by any enemy. Whether managers are tank commanders or department supervisors, they count on technology to give them an edge.

The Army thinks more deeply than most businesses about how to use technology to leverage the skills of its workers. Army weapons developers are more likely than civilians to pay attention to the rules of good software design: quickly make prototypes, test them thoroughly on the people who will use the systems, listen to their complaints, and modify the systems. Repeat the process; then do it again.

Recruits report for tank training to Fort Knox, a sprawling complex of motor pools, forested gunnery ranges, and motel-style housing 30 miles from Louisville. (The Treasury rents land on the base to store its gold in a 1930s-era white bunker surrounded by rows of security fences.) Outside a motor pool, new recruits swarm over 1980s-era M1 tanks, learning how to use night-vision systems. They work in groups of three; some read manuals, others finger the equipment. Private Lionel Holguin, an easygoing soldier from Intoio, California, is typical. After graduating from high school, he tried his hand at cleaning pools, waiting tables, and working on construction. "I wasn't going anywhere," he says, so he joined the Army. This is his first day working with a tank. "I fell in love with it," gushes the twenty-four-year-old recruit.

The A-Deuce is the Army's leap into the digital age. On the outside, the M1 and A-Deuce look similar; indeed, the A-Deuce is simply a renovated version of the older M1 Abrams tank. Starting in the early 1990s, the Army began to tear apart the inside of 120 M1 tanks a year, add computer and communications equipment, and rename the tanks M1A2s. Computer screens, software, and a digital communications backbone separate the A-Deuce from its predecessors. The $5 million A-Deuce uses computers to navigate featureless terrain, such as deserts; hunt and shoot the enemy; and transmit maps and reports among tank units. The tank is now a model of how technology should work, but it took some far-sighted advocates to push the service in the right direction. Like other organizations that make computer-rich systems, the Army initially was more interested in adding gee-whiz features than in making sure the A-Deuce worked as promised when soldiers hopped into the turret.

Kathleen Quinkert, a quiet, serious Army research psychologist assigned to Fort Knox, prodded the Army to keep soldiers' needs in mind. Ms. Quinkert's group, the Army Research Institute for the Behavioral and Social Sciences, is a collection of 125 psychologists and other social scientists who are assigned to Army bases. The research group has played a greater role in equipment design since a series of weapons-development disasters in the 1980s humiliated the Pentagon. The Sergeant York antiaircraft system, dubbed "a rat's nest of complexity" by military novelist Tom Clancy, failed so miserably, for instance, that most ended up as Air Force practice targets.

Quinkert's specialty is studying the interaction of people and machines. She realized that the Army's early plan to equip the A-Deuce with a helicopter-style controller, stuffed with more than a dozen buttons, would be disastrous. "In a tank, you're bouncing all over the place," she says. "You don't do that on a helicopter." Instead, she used a Macintosh computer to design a joystick-style controller with only three buttons. Then she sold her idea to the Army's tank designers near Detroit. "We had them think of the tank as a system, not a bazillion buttons," she says. "We wanted a joystick that could shoot, designate [enemy targets], run IVIS [communications systems], and 'lase' targets. I hadn't ridden in too many tanks, but I had talked to soldiers who had, and that was more than the contractors had done."

She and the Army Research Institute's seven other psychologists at Fort Knox stressed the importance of keeping in mind the users—high school grads who are being trained as warriors. "We're dealing with humans whose mission is to demolish things," says the forty-four-year-old psychologist. "They're not typists." So she argued strenuously against systems that required tankers to use their controllers to tap out reports.

She adapted Fort Knox's tank simulators to test her work. Simulators are fancy video games; tankers sit in plywood shells designed to look like the inside of the tank. They practice driving, or firing tank guns, by working the controls and watching the results on computer-screen depictions of the battlefield. Fort Knox generally uses simulators to train crews to face battlelike conditions, but Quinkert realized simulators could also test M1A2 systems before they were deployed.

In 1990, she sent forty teams of tank commanders and gunners to the simulators. Half of the teams used the A-Deuce's proposed hunting system, which gives a commander and a gunner separate screens to search for enemy targets; the other half used a conventional M1 system, in which a commander has to share a single screen with the gunner. Commanders in A-Deuce mock-ups were able to spot targets more quickly than commanders of the older tanks were. But nearly 75% of the A-Deuce commanders wanted the control handle redesigned again to make it still easier to use. After running two of these tank-simulator tests, the Army made a number of changes. Buttons were repositioned on the handle, and laser readings that give precise enemy target locations were automatically included in e-mailed requests for artillery barrages.

Several years later, Fort Knox's brass, as innovative at getting money out of the Pentagon as in designing weaponry, used the simulators in a different way. When the Army was considering eliminating a computerized navigation system on the A-Deuce to save money, senior officers at Fort Knox invited Pentagon aides to drive conventional M1 tanks through Kentucky's forested tank ranges. With their steering guided by paper maps, the Pentagon staffers got hopelessly lost and wasted valuable fuel. Then Fort Knox put the aides in a tank simulator, which included a mock-up of the A-Deuce's new computerized navigation system, and had them drive through a simulated version of the tank range. In the A-Deuce, drivers navigate by referring to a computer image of a circle with a number superimposed on it. To steer along a 45-degree azimuth, all a driver must do is make sure that the circle reads 45. If the heading suddenly says 48 degrees, the driver compensates by moving the steering column, which looks like a motorcycle handlebar, until the heading reads 45 degrees again. The technology was so simple that even the Pentagon aides couldn't get lost. The funding was saved, and the navigation system is now touted as one of the A-Deuce's most important features.

Fort Knox also began insisting on what it calls user juries—groups of officers and enlistees who try out new systems before they are deployed, and then suggest changes in design. A user jury wasn't impressed with an advanced mapping and communications system the Army wants to add to future M1A2s. The jury found that the system took fifty movements of a thumb-controlled cursor to send a message—far too complicated for battle conditions. Fort Knox forced the contractor to reduce the count to fewer than ten movements, make the computer-screen icons larger, and redesign the markings used to indicate a chemical or biological attack so they're easier to spot on a colored-map background.

In the same way that factories are boosting productivity by giving workers more responsibility, the A-Deuce requires more from each of the tank's four crew members because the technology is designed to help them do their jobs better. Staff Sergeant Stephen Otamura, a veteran of the Persian Gulf War, trains M1 tankers to learn the new A-Deuce systems. The thirty-six-year-old tank commander calls himself a "typical skateboard kid" from southern California, but he's far from typical. His Japanese American parents were interned during World War II, but that didn't diminish his desire to join the Army rather than work in the family pharmacy.

During the 1991 Gulf War, Otamura fought in what became known as the Battle of 73 Easting, the most significant tank engagement since the Arab–Israeli War of 1973. He commanded one of about seventeen tanks and a few dozen armored personnel carriers that were speeding through the desert when they came upon a large encampment of Iraqi tanks and other armored vehicles. The M1s' thermal sensors, which produce images of enemy vehicles from the heat they generate, spotted the Iraqis before the Iraqis could see them. The Americans destroyed about 100 Iraqi tanks and thirty armored personnel carriers in twenty-three minutes without suffering a single U.S. casualty.

At Fort Knox, Otamura climbs into the turret of an A-Deuce, which wasn't ready in time for the Gulf War, and shows its advantages over the tank he commanded during the Battle of 73 Easting. Computer technology has augmented the role of each crew member. During the Gulf War, the M1's gunner usually acted as an appendage of the commander, who in turn searched out targets, locked on them, and told the gunner when to fire. In the A-Deuce, the commander and gunner have separate screens on which thermal sensors project eerie green silhouettes of enemy targets. The two men work as a team: The gunner destroys one target while the commander searches for the next one and locks in that position. The tank cannon then automatically rotates in the general direction of the second target. While the gunner refines the aim, his commander searches for a third enemy position.

"The two-site system takes the leash off gunners," says Otamura. "The tank commander isn't looking over the gunner's shoulder." With the commander and gunner working in what the Army calls a "hunter–killer" combination, the tank's lethal power is multiplied.

The A-Deuce's simplification, while substantial, didn't go as far as it should have. Otamura and other veterans complain that the tank's map and communications systems overload crews with information. The communications screen shows an orange map grid dotted with icons representing friendly tanks, enemy tanks, minefields, and other information gleaned by intelligence and routed to tank companies. But the system takes too long to fill out reports—commanders have to click a thumb cursor a dozen times to send electronic reports when they encounter the enemy. And it doesn't alert commanders when incoming reports are urgent. The results can be disastrous—reminding the Army again about the importance of simplifying computer design.

Even a tanker as proficient as Otamura got so hung up filing and reading reports during war games that his M1A2 unit was blasted away by older tanks that relied on old-fashioned radios. For now, the Army tells tankers to use the A-Deuce's jazzy communications system to keep in touch while driving to and from the battle, but to forget it during battle. "Once contact comes, you fight like a tank," says Otamura—which means ditch the e-mail and bark orders by radio.

Army psychologists uncovered the communications problem during early simulator tests of forty-eight tank crews. A-Deuce commanders, hobbled by the communications system, were sending nine reports during each simulated battle, compared to one or two for commanders of older tanks. That slowed their response and further bogged down the communications system. But little was done to fix the problem early, because it would have required expensive overhaul of the tank's communications architecture. That's being left for future A-Deuces.

The Army wants to add a number of features to the MIA2 over the next few years: computer screens with three-dimensional images, and colored computer images that mark whether nearby tanks are friends or foes. All the enhancements will require better communications among tanks and other weapons systems, and all must be designed so that soldiers can operate them simply.

Making systems simpler often means reducing choices. So, rather than filling a tank's computer screens with a dozen possible reports that commanders can send, designers and user juries are trying to figure out which reports are crucial to success on the battlefield. Those will be featured prominently on computer screens and automated as much as possible. Designers also plan to replace cursor controls, which are hard to manipulate during battle, with fist-sized buttons that tankers can whack to send reports. Eventually, the Army wants to shift to voice commands. "The notion is you could talk to the machine and do away with button-mashing and cursor-moving," says Colonel John Kalb, who is working on A-Deuce upgrades.

The Army's efforts to simplify technology are echoed by work in the civilian world. Computer researchers and commercial companies say that easier-to-use technology can reduce the cost of training workers, and can help employees who have average education to use complex systems. "Our goal is minimal training," says Peter Kelly, a computer manager at First Union Corporation, the large financial services firm. "We want to go from a day's worth of training [on new software] to fifteen minutes' worth." That requires software that's simpler to learn and use—a goal shared by the Army and civilian employers.

Commercial companies are just learning how to use Army techniques to solve their problems. Unfortunately, the cleavage of society into separate military and civilian spheres has become so deep that few commercial firms now know much about the Army's successes. Barry Wolcott, who served as an Army physician for twenty-seven years, has been able to overcome that division. He adapted the Army's method of breaking complex subjects into smaller, manageable tasks to develop software that lets nurses screen calls from patients to health care networks. Consulting desktop computers, the nurses decide who should get rushed to an emergency room, who can wait to see a physician, and who just needs an aspirin and rest—decisions once handled by physicians. In 1997, about thirty-five million Americans had access to these phone services, up from fewer than two million in 1990.

Wolcott explored the techniques when he was an internist at Brooke Army Medical Center, in San Antonio, in the 1970s. Providing a consistent level of care for the 180,000 patients the clinic saw each year was difficult because the Army doctors usually quit when their tours were over. Wolcott assembled formulas that Army medical corpsmen, who had three or four months of medical training, could use to do screening for the clinic. Those screening formulas were later inscribed in software and expanded.

Now, if an adult suffering from lower-back pain calls a phone center run by Wolcott's firm, Access Health Inc., in Broomfield, Colorado, a nurse asks a series of computer-prompted questions that mimic how a doctor would handle such calls. Did the pain develop after a car accident? If the patient answers yes, the computer suggests a follow-up question: Has there been a loss of motor function or numbness? Another yes, and the caller is switched to a doctor. If the patient answers no to these and other questions, the nurse gives advice on treating the pain at home. The computer translates questions from medical language into terms patients can understand. For instance, the clinical question: "Did a health care provider diagnose the pain as representing cardiac ischemia?" becomes "Did the provider say that you had narrow heart arteries? Not enough blood getting to the heart?"

Wall Street Journal reporter George Anders described a phone bank run by Access Health in a Denver suburb where ninety nurses, working in shifts, answer 500,000 calls a year. "As nurses in blue jeans and ski sweaters report to work, they enter a honeycomb of beige cubicles that look much like an airline reservations operation," Anders reported.

"From each desk, nurses can hear their neighbors' voices blending in an eerie medical medley. 'Hi, this is Debbie, one of the nurses.' . . . 'If you press down gently, how much does it hurt?'. . . 'Have you taken his temperature?'" Nurses are paid as much as $20 an hour, which matches the going rate at local hospitals, and they rely on their previous experience, as well as the computerized questions. Critics complain that the practice can be harmful, especially if the nurses don't quickly spot life-threatening problems, but call-center managers say they regularly improve the software and nurse training so that emergencies are quickly detected.

The technology used at call centers is an offshoot of expert systems—an earlier, failed attempt at technology simplification. In the mid-1980s, computer entrepreneurs boasted that they could write software that could handle the jobs done by experts in fields as diverse as manufacturing and medical analysis. So-called knowledge engineers interviewed experts and followed them around their workplaces to try to capture their expertise in simple rules that could be written in software. The experts were usually happy to comply; they felt they could gain a kind of immortality through software patterned on their knowledge. And companies figured they could use the software to boost the skills of other employees.

But expert systems companies chose tasks that were far too difficult to replicate through simple rules—diagnosing cancer, planning financial estates, plotting space shuttle missions. Most of the programs flopped, and a slew of software companies went broke. Now, companies that use expert systems technology flee from the label; they prefer to call themselves "knowledge-based agents." Still, the technology is generally the same: Pick the brains of experts and codify what they do in rules. But the tasks selected for emulation are far simpler, allowing less educated workers to be hired for jobs they wouldn't have been capable of doing before.

Carnegie Group Inc., in Pittsburgh, once dreamed of developing expert systems to pick stocks and analyze mergers and acquisitions; now it develops knowledge-based agents to sell phones for home offices. At a calling center of U S West Communications Inc., in Phoenix, 180 telephone sales reps—grandly called consultants—check Carnegie-developed software before asking customers a series of questions. Is your phone usually busy? Is there a teenager in the house? How large is your monthly phone bill? How frequently do you fax? Then the software suggests solutions: A customized ringing for different family members, call-waiting, a second phone line. Today's expert systems lack the pizzazz of the 1980s, but they're far more practical and they let people with less education get jobs once reserved for technicians. "We want sales people, not techies," says Brad Derthick, a U S West marketing executive. Home-office sales reps can make $55,000 a year, he estimates, about $10,000 more than other U S West sales reps who don't yet have Carnegie's sales software.

Other companies and laboratories are taking different tacks in simplifying technology. Xerox's Palo Alto Research Center, known as Xerox PARC, invented many of the technologies that made computers easier to use in the 1980s, including the computer mouse, the computer icon, and the pull-down menus. (Apple Computer and other companies brought the products to the market first.) Those technologies enabled computer novices to run machines without memorizing obscure commands. Now, Xerox PARC researchers derisively call that computing style WIMP technology—windows, icon, menu, and pointers—and say it is overloaded by programs that have hundreds more files and billions more pieces of information than envisioned in the 1980s.

Xerox PARC is working on different ways to operate computers simply. In an office overflowing with computer magazines and piles of technical papers, Xerox PARC's chief technologist, Mark Weiser, pulls out of his pocket a keychain computer that stores the names of contacts and other information. "The measure of the future of computing is whether you can hold a computer in your hand," he says. Over the next few decades, he predicts, tiny computers will become so ubiquitous that each will be outfitted for a special purpose. Computers mounted on office walls could find missing pieces of paper in offices as messy as his by searching for invisible bar codes printed on the paper. Computers mounted on refrigerators and linked by the Internet to computers mounted at supermarket dairy sections could remind shoppers when they need milk. Like the Army's tank designers, Weiser says single-function buttons hold promise; they could reduce the time users have to hassle with a computer mouse and cursor. He pulls out a mock-up of a computer screen ringed by buttons that could be programmed to do different things—for instance, call up spreadsheets or e-mail documents. "We're moving into a simplification era," he says.

Down the hill from Weiser's office, Ramana Rao shows new ways of searching hundreds of computer files, especially those gleaned from the Internet. Rao is chief technology officer of InXight Software Inc., a Xerox PARC spin-off. He and his colleagues have invented computer-screen tools that are animated and appear three-dimensional; they let computer users know at a glance the content of large inventories of records.

Think about searching a computer company's website to learn about a particular software product. At present, that would require clicking through endless computer screens of information without any assurance the information is even there. Rao's tool gives a fish-eye view of the website. In the center is a small box representing the home page; connected to that, like branches on a tree, are the website's main subject areas: sales, software, personnel, hardware. By clicking onto the part of the tree that represents software, all the branches containing different software products move toward the user and get larger in size. Ultimately, the box representing the sought-after software program is uncovered. Rao calls this technique "zoom and bloom": The user zooms onto one of the branches, and the information contained there blooms. In InXight's current version, the animated tree can represent as many as 8,000 items on a single screen.

Microsoft lauds InXight's work, but the giant software company has a special problem in trying to make its products simpler. Microsoft has such a huge share of the personal computer market that its customers range from novice to expert, and each category of user has very different needs. When the Army tries to simplify software, it purposefully limits choices and figures out precisely what its soldiers need to do. Microsoft's customer base is too wide for that approach. Instead, says Joe Belfiore, the Microsoft software manager, the company is planning to use its newest software to help users make their own choices, and to customize users' screens so they aren't so complex and daunting.

The next version of Windows, the personal computer operating system, will include what Microsoft calls a software wizard. The software will track which programs a user turns to frequently, and which ones are rarely used. Then it will suggest getting rid of rarely used files, or at least storing them deeper in the Windows menu. Only the programs that the user regularly consults would pop up on the initial Windows menu. "It's really easy to get into a situation where there's lots of junk in your computer," he says. "It's hard to get out of it."

Perhaps the most promising way to simplify technology is to teach computers to better understand human speech. Speech recognition technology gobbles an awesome amount of computer processing power, but it has improved dramatically as computing power has escalated and prices have fallen. Michael Dertrouzos, head of MIT's Laboratory for Computer Science, says that speech will reduce the need for computer keyboards and computer mice. "Most people will interact with computers in a normal, natural way," he predicts.

There are two different kinds of speech recognition, both of which will have broad effects over the next two decades. The first kind, led by Dragon Systems, a software maker, requires a user to train the computer to recognize his or her voice by talking into the system for a half-hour. The voice recognition software compares an individual's speech patterns with different models of how other people talk, and then figures out which word the speaker actually said—not an easy task when "I can" sounds something like "icon." After more than a decade of experimentation, Dragon has developed software, which costs between $150 to $700, that can transcribe people's speech as fast as they can talk. Speakers don't have to pause between words—the bane of earlier speech-recognition systems—or use specialized language. "It can be a great leveler," says Janet Baker, the company's president. "All you have to do is talk to get what you want from a computer."

The Dragon system does have a big drawback: A speaker can use only the single computer that has been trained to his or her voice. But as is often the case in speech-recognition technology, engineers working with the handicapped are pushing the technology further ahead. At Stanford University, Neil Scott, a senior research engineer, is using the Dragon technology to develop a personal communicator. After a speaker trains the communicator to recognize his voice, the communicator can operate a variety of different machines—in the same way that a single remote control panel can work a television set and a VCR. Although the technology was developed with the handicapped in mind, Scott says, it has broad applicability. "If you give a nondisabled person the same tools, you can increase his throughput [working with a computer] by 20%," he calculates.

The second branch of speech recognition develops systems that try to recognize English, regardless of who is speaking. These systems aren't trained to recognize an individual's voice, so the vocabularies of so-called speaker-independent systems usually number fewer than 10,000 words. Given that limitation, developers carefully pick areas where the variation in words isn't too great. For instance, MIT is developing an airline-reservation system that's supposed to recognize callers regardless of accent. Nearly all callers want to know the same information—where the flight is going, when it arrives, whether they can book a rental car, and so on. The system can home in on a key word like "rental," and assume the caller is asking about cars to rent. That further narrows the number of words the caller is probably going to use, and makes it more likely the system will recognize the right one.

Charles Schwab Corporation now uses a voice recognizer to give stock prices over the phone. The system uses complicated statistical models to recognize 14,000 different stocks and mutual funds. Dertrouzos, the MIT computer lab chief, predicts that, within five to seven years, systems that recognize voices, regardless of accent, will cost as little as $200, making computer technology fundamentally simpler to use. The technology will eliminate the jobs of many who now answer routine calls at airline reservation centers and similar places, but it will make available many more jobs for those who now can't master difficult-to-use computers.

The Army is playing a lead role. Lon Maggart, the former commanding general at Fort Knox, who pushed technology simplification in the military, wants to adapt voice recognition systems for tanks, so ordinary soldiers can do some maintenance jobs reserved for highly trained mechanics. He is now a program director for advanced learning environments at the Research Triangle Institute near Durham, North Carolina. One of the projects he oversees shows how a maintenance system using speech recognition would work. The computer conversations don't come close to the skill of HAL, the malevolent computer in *2001* which could lip-read, but they give a flavor of the future. A tank–tanker conversation goes like this:

TANK MAINTENANCE SYSTEM: "How may I help you?"
TANKER: "The commander cannot fire the laser rangefinder."
TANK: "Conduct test 1450."
TANKER: "Help me do it."
TANK: "Lock the gun travel lock."
TANKER: "OK."

TANK: "Turn the laser rangefinder [to] safe."
And so on.

"The Army's view is well ahead of the civilian world," says Maggart. "We have complex pieces of gear, and we have to make them perform complex functions in a simple way." That will become the motto of many commercial ventures over the next decade or two. The winners: Americans who have been stuck in dead-end jobs because they couldn't master the latest technology.

13

The Balance of Trade

*How foreign trade and investment will benefit the
American middle class.*

As Interstate 85 climbs through the foothills of the Piedmont Mountains in South Carolina, it becomes a passage into America's global
future. Only a generation ago, the road could have been called the Textile Turnpike. It linked cotton mill after dusty cotton mill—unhappy
places that paid subsistence wages, chased away unions, and lobbied
to close U.S. borders to foreign competitors. Now, locals call I-85 "the
Autobahn." About 250 foreign firms, many of them German, have set
up factories and offices along a thirty-mile stretch of the highway that
connects the state's northern border to Spartanburg and Greenville.
Just off I-85, Groupe Michelin of France churns out tires; they are delivered to the gleaming white campus of BMW AG of Germany, where
American workers mount them on sporty BMW Z3 roadsters. Nearby,
Hoechst AG of Germany produces polyester fiber, Sulzer AG of
Switzerland repairs textile machinery, Karl Menzel Maschinenfabrik of
Germany makes plastics machinery, and Adidas AG of Germany ships
sneakers.

Two graffiti-scarred slabs of the Berlin Wall stand in front of the Menzel factory. From the highway, they look like tombstones—and, in a
way, they are. They commemorate the death of the Cold War and the
demise of South Carolina's inward-looking textile economy.

This chapter and the next two explore the effects of globalization on the American middle class. Along with technology and education, globalization is the third major force shaping the future of the middle class, and the most politically explosive one. Politicians as diverse as conservative Republican Pat Buchanan and House Minority Leader Richard Gephardt, a liberal Democrat, campaign to restrict trade and overseas investment, based on wrongheaded calculations that the American middle class suffers when the United States expands its global ties. Just the opposite is true. This chapter weighs the impact of expanded global trade and investment in South Carolina, a state that once was devastated by international trade but now greatly benefits, on balance, from globalization. Chapter 14 tells how imports improve living standards in every country that welcomes them. Chapter 15 shows why trade with poor countries won't kill jobs and undermine wages here, even when software companies in India, which pay their workers one-tenth the salaries of Americans, compete with U.S. firms.

Global integration will be tumultuous for the United States, as the various regions of the country try to adapt to international competition. Trade is an engine of efficiency that powers regions agile enough to compete. It destroys the leaden-footed, and remorselessly divides the United States into economic winners and losers. Writer William Greider, a passionate critic of globalization, complains of the "manic logic of global capitalism." He compares globalization to a machine tumbling out of control, and predicts a monumental crack-up that will dump the world into depression as companies produce far more goods than the world's consumers can buy. But Greider and other doomsayers are wrong. The marvel of trade-based capitalism is its relentless rationality. Trade and investment distribute innovation and capital throughout the world and favor those regions that use them well. That's a huge plus for the United States, which is more flexible and inventive than many other countries. Globalization will produce far more prosperity than misery for Americans.

If any area should show evidence of the devastation of trade, it's the Piedmont region, which South Carolinians call "upcountry" or "upstate." For generations, upcountry South Carolina was an impoverished land of struggling farmers and mill hands, moonshiners and sewing-machine operators. Global trade and investment tossed many textile and apparel hands out of work. Some lost their homes and were forced to pawn their furniture to survive. But globalization has helped many more upcountry people than it has hurt. Too often, the press focuses solely on the losers or the winners, and gives a distorted view of the effects of globalization. Upcountry South Carolina shows why the United States is a big winner from global trade and investment, and why it will flourish because of them in the coming years.

Along I-85, wages are rising, schools are improving, and businesses are expanding. Incomes in Spartanburg and Greenville, which have lagged the nation at least since the Civil War, are catching up to the national average. Towns that once were suspicious of foreigners now sport European-style cafés and Oktoberfests. People whose future seemed drab and circumscribed now celebrate opportunities.

But the changes that came to the Piedmont region also show how brutal globalization can be. South Carolina has benefited as a whole from global trade, but many businesses can't match the low-priced foreign competition. Mills and factories have closed. Since 1986, about 16,000 South Carolina apparel workers have lost their jobs; that loss of one in three garment jobs represents a steeper rate than apparel workers have suffered nationally. Jobs as cutters and sewers once provided the first step into the middle class for South Carolinians who labored in the cotton fields. But garment work is especially vulnerable to foreign competition. Sewing-machine operators make only $7.40 an hour in South Carolina, but that's five to ten times the wages of Mexicans or Asians doing essentially the same work.

"A shirt is made in the same way it was made at the turn of the century," says Erwin Maddrey, president of Delta Woodside Industries, Inc., a textile and apparel maker based in Greenville that has moved its T-shirt and sportswear production to Costa Rica and Honduras. "The factory may be air-conditioned and the machines may move a little faster, but it's still a person behind the machine. That's the part that goes to the Caribbean."

But layoffs are only one face of globalization. A full accounting shows that upcountry South Carolina benefits greatly as the U.S. economy grows more tightly connected to the rest of the world through trade, investment, and immigration. Between 1988 and 1994, South Carolina textile and apparel firms eliminated 26,000 jobs, most of which were paying well below the state manufacturing average of $10 an hour in

1994. During the same time, foreign-owned firms in South Carolina directly added 20,600 jobs, most of them paying well above the state average. Suppliers to the foreign firms added thousands more jobs, as did restaurants, retailers, and other service companies that sprang up with the new prosperity. The new jobs outnumbered the jobs lost when the textile and apparel factories shut down. Employment statewide grew by 163,000 jobs, a 9% increase.

As foreign investment poured into the state, exports boomed. Since 1987, South Carolina's exports have tripled, setting a much faster pace than the national average. Mark Zandi, the chief economist for Regional Financial Associates, a consulting firm outside Philadelphia, finds faster job growth in states whose export growth exceeds the national average. Payrolls grew 25% faster in South Carolina than in the rest of the nation between 1987 and 1996; Zandi attributes half that growth to the state's export boom. "The more global a regional economy, the more likely it will perform well and outperform the nation," he says.

The new jobs tied to trade and exports pay much better than the ones they replaced. In plants that export, pay is about 10% more than for comparable jobs in plants that don't export, and jobs in facilities owned by foreign companies pay about 14% more than jobs in U.S.-owned firms. The reason? Exporters and foreign-owned firms are concentrated in higher-paying industries. They're also leaders in their fields and can afford to pay more to hire the workers they want.

But exports and investment tell only half the story. Americans also gain from imports, despite their reputation as job killers. As the next chapter details, imports lower the prices of the sweaters, televisions, and sewing machines bought by consumers; lower prices improve living standards as surely as pay hikes would. Despite all the grief that imports cause some U.S. firms, foreign competition also forces American companies to hone their business practices and boost productivity. The textile makers of upstate South Carolina blamed all their woes on imports. In a tale that the textile makers are loath to tell, textile firms also turned to imported machinery in the 1980s to save their businesses. Those that survive the import gauntlet are better positioned to compete internationally; they thrive in a global marketplace that has expanded by billions of consumers since the end of the Cold War and the easing of protectionism abroad. "We are in the midst of one of history's greatest expansions of market capitalism ever," says Harvard economist Jeffrey D. Sachs. "If we play our cards right, we're at the beginning of a period of significant long-term prosperity."

After analyzing the economies of 118 countries, Sachs and his Harvard colleague, Andrew Warner, found that countries that pursued open-trade policies grew much faster, on average, than those that shut their borders. Between 1970 and 1989, the authors calculated, such open economies as Singapore and Thailand grew six times as fast as Egypt, Iran, and other closed economies. Their conclusion: "We find no cases to support the frequent worry that a country might open [itself to trade] and yet fail to grow."

Economists Jeffrey A. Frankel and David Romer of the University of California at Berkeley studied the economies of ninety-eight countries over a thirty-year period. They found that incomes rose faster in trading nations—and it didn't matter whether trade rose through exports or imports. Exports boosted incomes through improved jobs, says Frankel, who later became an economic adviser to President Clinton. Increased imports were also a boon, he says, because competition exposes domestic firms to new technology and management techniques from around the world. Over the long run, these productivity enhancements lift worker incomes throughout the economy.

Novelist Dorothy Allison grew up in Greenville before its transformation into a global outpost. Back then, it was tightly segregated by race, and youngsters of both races were poorly educated. "Greenville, South Carolina, in 1955 was the most beautiful place in the world," she wrote in her chilling and evocative account of life there, Bastard Out of Carolina. "Black walnut trees dropped their green-black fuzzy bulbs on Aunt Ruth's matted lawn past where their knotty roots rose out of the ground like the elbows and knees of dirty children suntanned dark and covered with scars. Weeping willows marched across the yard, following every wandering stream and ditch."

But for children on the cusp of adulthood, Greenville was a place of stunted hopes. "Growing up was like falling into a hole," she wrote, "The boys would quit school and sooner or later go to jail for something silly. I might not quit school, not while Mama had any say in the matter, but what difference would that make? What was I going to do in five years? Work in the textile mill? Join Mama at the diner? It all looked bleak to me. No wonder people got crazy as they grew up."

Today, Greenville is still beautiful but no longer languid. Reflecting-glass office buildings overlook the city of 58,000, which is chockablock with coffee houses and pricey foreign restaurants—Italian, Japanese, and "Mexican vegetarian." Main Street's only pawn shop is closing after fifty years of making loans to mill hands; a Thai furniture store that sells carved mahogany chests is expanding nearby. On the outskirts of town, a Japanese teahouse with a lovely rock garden caters to Japanese businessmen and skeptical natives. A local family peeks into the dining area, where tables seem to hover only inches above floor mats used for sitting. "Mother, there's space under the tables [for your legs]," explains an exasperated teenager, whose parents, unconvinced, park themselves at traditional tables and chairs.

Addy Sulley, who moved from Amsterdam to Greenville in the early 1980s to design textile machinery, now runs a Dutch-style tavern. Heavy German lagers and Belgian raspberry beers are on the menu at Addy's Café, but not Budweiser. "Horrible stuff," says Sulley. (Cosmopolitanism goes only so far in Greenville; liquor sales are banned on Sunday, so last call at Addy's is midnight on Saturday.) To make upstate more homey, expatriates have started rugby and soccer teams for adults, and German-, Japanese-, and French-language schools for foreign-born children. The expatriates' focus on education has rubbed off on the local schools, which for generations were among the nation's worst. Greenville's elementary schools have added intensive language programs in French and Spanish, and the middle schools now offer German and Japanese. South Side High School features an international baccalaureate degree; students immerse themselves in regional studies, sciences, and foreign languages. The high school dropout rate has been cut in half since 1984, and the fraction of Greenville graduates going on to college has increased by 20%.

Globally competitive companies search for educated workers who, in turn, demand more of their new towns. The newcomers become activists in the arts and education, says former South Carolina Governor Carroll Campbell. "That raises the whole community, which then becomes attractive to Wal-Marts and other big retailers. Pretty soon, you've elevated the local economy above the minimum wage." Bill

Page, a retired Greenville businessman, says that lobbying from foreign firms and exporters helped win passage of a sales tax increase to pay for increased education spending. "This part of the state was once an exporter of brain power," he says, because teenagers deserted the area in search of better jobs. "Now it's not hard to import brains. The influx of job opportunity has been a great thing." Indeed, in 1997, unemployment in the upstate region hovered around 3%—full employment.

China, Malaysia, and other Asian nations have made headlines for attracting foreign investment, and will do so again after the financial crisis in Asia ebbs. But the United States is the destination for far more foreign investment than any other country. Investments in the United States are considered the safest in the world, and America's steadily growing markets offer investors an attractive return on their money. Overall, the United States received $84.6 billion in foreign investment in 1996—twice as much as China, and nearly as much as all Asia.

South Carolina is one of America's most powerful magnets for foreign investment. With a population of only 3.5 million, South Carolina snags about $2 billion a year in foreign investment—roughly as much as India, which has a population of 950 million. Much of that investment builds factories in Greenville or Spartanburg counties, where 600,000 people live and where BMW, Adidas, Fuji, and Hitachi are expanding operations. Those foreign companies, in turn, have sparked an export drive by selling a big slice of their production abroad and helping domestic firms to expand their overseas sales.

South Carolina has recognized the power of trade and investment since the early 1970s, when then-Governor John West began wooing European firms. But BMW's decision, in 1992, to build its first foreign plant in Spartanburg, which is next door to Greenville, was the capstone of South Carolina's foreign strategy. Carroll Campbell, the governor in 1992, wooed BMW with the ardor of Cyrano and the strategy of Rommel. Campbell negotiated in secret, quietly stopping off to meet company officials in Germany on the way back from a trip to Israel. He appointed as negotiator a retired German executive who had moved to Spartanburg many years earlier and could testify to its virtues.

As part of a $130 million package of incentives, the state purchased the land BMW wanted, rented the 1,000-acre parcel to the company for $1, widened nearby highways, and awarded the company employee tax credits. The state also used its community college system to train new employees for free, a perk that is offered to any company that relocates in the state. Once BMW agreed to open the factory, the state winnowed through the 85,000 applications that flooded BMW for 2,000 jobs, highlighted promising resumes, and even raised $3 million from private businesses to help BMW train supervisors in Germany. The state was criticized for corporate giveaways, but Campbell saw the aid package as a strategic investment. He believed that "BMW would be a magnet for a higher level of investment," and that BMW's tony image could help erase the state's lingering redneck reputation. Newspaper articles at the time joked that the letters BMW really meant: Can Bubba Make Wheels?

In Spartanburg, BMW now annually makes 50,000 Z3 roadsters, the sporty convertible that James Bond drove in the movie *GoldenEye*. Blue-collar pay at the plant is about $17.55 an hour—substantially higher than the state's average manufacturing wage of $10.35 an hour—and, with overtime, many workers earn $40,000 a year. On average, foreign-owned plants paid 14% more than their U.S. counterparts, according to a 1990 federal survey of 12,000 facilities. That's partly because foreign investors concentrate on higher-wage industries, and partly because they often build larger factories, where salaries tend to be higher. Whatever the reason, the growth of foreign investment has helped to reduce the income gap between workers in upstate South Carolina and the rest of the nation. In Greenville County, per-capita income is now roughly the same as the national average; in Spartanburg County, traditionally a poor cousin to Greenville, the local income has risen to about 86% of the national average. Overall, the income gap between the two counties and the rest of the United States has closed by about five percentage points since 1985.

For Ronald Anderson, a 40-year-old father of five, foreign investment has meant opportunity. After graduating from high school and trying his hand at bricklaying, Anderson worked for seventeen years at a factory that makes fibers for disposable diapers. He had worked his way into a supervisory job, but still earned just a bit more than $30,000 a year. He applied to BMW partly because of better pay, and partly because he was a car fanatic who admired BMW's handiwork. "If it had been Hyundai, I wouldn't have been so interested," he says.

A trim African American, Anderson says that he and his friends were skeptical about whether BMW would treat blacks fairly. Throughout the South, foreign firms have earned reputations for discriminating against black applicants—or hiring them and dumping them in dead-end jobs. That reputation is shared by many U.S.-owned firms too, of course. Textile mills, for instance, long were redoubts of white supremacy. In the 1920s, southern businessmen lured Northern mills to move south by advertising "cheap and contented, 99 percent pure, Anglo-Saxon labor." In the 1960s and 1970s, the mills were slow to desegregate. But race relations in upstate South Carolina these days are no worse, and probably a bit better, than elsewhere in the country. For its part, BMW hired a workforce representative of the local population: about 20% of the workers are black.

Anderson survived a series of BMW tests, including a grueling 90-minute simulation of the worst of assembly work, in which applicants had to tighten different-sized lugs at an ever faster pace. One of Anderson's friends found the work so distasteful that he struck his name from the applicants' list after he tightened the last lug. But Anderson stuck it out and was finally hired, the only one to land a job at BMW out of a band of thirteen friends who had applied. To his surprise, BMW made him a road tester; his job entailed driving freshly minted BMWs around the factory track at speeds topping 100 miles per hour. When he heard the news, Anderson says he shouted, "Yes!" and pumped his arm in the air in triumph.

"It's a lot different now than when I was growing up," he says. "Jobs were more limited then. If you weren't a doctor or lawyer, you'd stay in textiles. Now the choices are better."

John Thaiss comes from a more affluent background than Anderson, and had more career choices. At 29, with a master's degree in international business, he was sure he was headed out of the upstate region, like so many other bright, ambitious people before him. "I thought this place was dead," he says. Instead, he's leading a BMW team that is working out the many problems involved in manufacturing the latest Z3 model in Spartanburg. He has more responsibility than most young managers his age, except those in Silicon Valley. Much of his day involves chatting on the phone in German with his counterparts abroad. "If you speak their language, they open up to you," he says. "You're part of the network."

The BMW plant is a testament to flexible manufacturing; half the cars are headed for U.S. customers and half are exported to 100 different markets. BMW officials count seventy-four variations of roadsters that are built at Spartanburg. Teams of workers are trained to assemble cars with right-side steering columns, bound for Britain, and then to switch to roadsters with left-side steering columns, bound for Boston. The roadsters have different headlights and different trunks, and must meet different environmental tests and crash standards, depending on the country for which they're destined. To mass-produce so many roadster variations, BMW uses a mixture of automation and handwork. A robotic storage system pulls chassis on and off the assembly line, allowing workers with hand files to grind off tiny imperfections.

BMW's finicky requirements have forced its nearby suppliers to improve their standards, thereby lifting productivity in the upstate region. Spartanburg Steel Products Inc., which stamps out body parts for BMW and Toyota, runs adult education classes for its 650 employees, and has raised reading and math scores in the plant by four grades overall. That's necessary, says the company's president, Frederick Schoen, because workers must understand how to set up machinery quickly for smaller production runs, and to use sophisticated sensors for inspection of the results. "We used to say, 'Do what we say; don't ask why,' " he says. "Now, we want them to use their heads." The employees and the company benefit. Workers get productivity bonuses, averaging about $1 an hour on top of the $11-an-hour base pay, when they exceed production and quality goals. The company saves money: Rather than spend an estimated $21 million to buy huge new presses to stamp out steel parts for BMW, Spartanburg Steel's workers have become so productive they can bang out additional orders using existing machinery.

BMW's newly efficient suppliers now are testing export markets themselves, which will further boost work—and wages—for their employees. Spartanburg Steel is beginning to export auto parts to Toyota plants in Canada and Australia. Springfield Tool and Die Inc., a small machine shop down the road from BMW, is following the same course.

To supply BMW, Springfield had to buy $500,000 worth of computerized machine tools. The company now plans to use the new machinery to make steam-engine parts for General Electric plants outside the United States. "Once you've got the machinery, you have to keep it busy," says Springfield's ebullient plant manager, George Hills. He thumbs through work orders stacked on his desk. Some of the customers are old-line U.S. firms such as General Electric, but many are foreign firms that have built facilities in the United States. Springfield is building machine tools and parts for a carburetor maker from Germany, a pump maker from Sweden, and a car-door maker from Canada. As with the rest of upstate South Carolina, little Springfield Tool and Die, with forty employees, is going global.

The growth of today's global economy is often portrayed as unprecedented. But globalization actually represents a rerun of the trade and investment levels of nearly a century ago. Economist John Maynard Keynes's reminiscence, in 1919, of what the life of a London sophisticate was like on the eve of World War I, might easily describe a San Francisco computerphile today, so long as "modem" is substituted for "telephone." "The inhabitant of London could order by telephone, sipping his morning tea in bed, the various products of the whole earth, in such quantity as he might see fit, and reasonably expect their early delivery upon his doorstep," Keynes wrote. "He could at the same moment and by the same means adventure his wealth in the natural resources and new enterprises of any quarter of the world, and share, without exertion or even trouble, in their prospective fruits and advantages. . . . But, most important of all, he regarded this state of affairs as normal, certain, and permanent, except in the direction of further improvement, and any deviation from it as aberrant, scandalous, and avoidable."

World War I, and the decades of high tariffs that followed it, wrecked that era of globalization, which had been dominated by Britain's trade with its colonies and with the industrializing nations of the Americas. Barring a similar cataclysm at the start of the twenty-first century, global trade and investment are bound to finally leap ahead of the expansion at the turn of the twentieth century. How deeply will the United States become interwoven with the world's economy? Here's one hint. Globalization is often measured by the percentage of economic output accounted for by the export of manufactured goods. By that measure, America's exports in 1996 were only half as large as Britain's in 1913. The push toward global integration still has far to go.

For upcountry South Carolina, the turn toward a global economy also represents a return to the past. Before the Civil War, British oceangoing ships sailed deep into South Carolina's rivers to load cotton bound for Manchester mills. The South was the trading part of the nation; southerners regularly lambasted the "tariff gang" up north, who insisted on high levies to block imports and keep cotton prices low for New England mills.

But then mill owners began deserting the north, opening plants in the low-wage Piedmont region and bringing their protectionist politics with them. By 1901, the Southern Manufacturers Club, in Charlotte, North Carolina, was already debating "the Oriental question"—cheap cotton imports from China. Over the years, the textile lobby deserted the north, became firmly headquartered in the Carolinas, and succeeded in persuading Washington to erect high tariffs against imported fabric and clothing. The Kennedy Administration and its allies in Europe established a complex and temporary—or so it was planned—series of tariffs and quotas to keep out Asian imports. That regime is finally supposed to be abolished in 2005.

Even with trade barriers, textile and apparel imports from Asia expanded massively during the late 1970s and early 1980s, driving many U.S. companies out of business. But although imports are often blamed for wrecking the domestic economy in those years, the history of South Carolina's textile manufacturers tells a more complicated tale, full of twists and ironies. It's a history that has lessons for the rest of the country.

South Carolina's textile makers, it turns out, contributed greatly to their own problems by failing to modernize. When they finally realized their mistake, they turned to imports—specifically, imported looms and spinning equipment—to rescue their businesses. The person who spurred this import boom is one of the nation's most prominent protectionists, Roger Milliken, the billionaire owner of Milliken & Co., a Spartanburg textile empire. Despite his antitrade rhetoric, Milliken recognized, well before others in his industry and across the nation, that imports spur productivity. According to a study of ninety-four manufacturing industries, that productivity increase usually comes three years or so after the start of an import surge, especially in industries where the bulk of sales is concentrated in a few firms. In other words, those that manage to survive the competition prosper.

Now 81 years old, "Big Red" Milliken's hair has long since turned white; only a few reddish strands in his eyebrows hint at his nickname. He's tall and courtly, and he speaks with a trace of a New England accent, more than 40 years after moving his operations to Spartanburg in

1954. Milliken is justly proud of his 585-acre research center off I-85, adjacent to a peach orchard where Milliken & Co. horticulturists tend 500 different species of trees that are bar-coded to track their health. In front of the visitors' center, next to cascading fountains, is a large green shrub shaped like a gazelle. "Milliken has chosen the gazelle as the symbol of its quick response strategy, which is continually to adapt to our customers' ever changing needs," reads the label beneath the shrubbery. Inside the center are displays highlighting Milliken's prowess at using computer-controlled printing and weaving systems to produce intricately decorated carpets and fabrics. Roger Milliken and his family own the company, which has annual revenue of more than $2 billion, and which includes 55 U.S. mills and 15,000 employees. A white helicopter ferries him from plant to plant.

Trade policy is his passion. Ross Perot and Pat Buchanan are the public face of protectionism, but the publicity-shy Milliken quietly organizes and finances the antitrade forces. In 1993, he spent about $400,000 financing protectionist think tanks and conservatives in a losing fight against passage of the North American Free Trade Agreement (NAFTA) with Mexico and Canada. Undaunted, he promises well-funded fights to block NAFTA's expansion and liberalized trade with China. When it comes to trade, "We're the saps of the world," Milliken complains over a lunch of stuffed peppers at his company's cafeteria. "A certain amount of trade is good, but what we have now is barracuda trade."

His own history belies his words. He recognized far earlier than his competitors that U.S. textile-machinery makers were falling hopelessly behind international competitors—a situation that would raise Milliken's costs and eventually undermine his fabric-making operations. He turned to foreign textile-machinery makers and imported the best equipment he could find, even though that pushed U.S. suppliers further into the hole. Milliken's market power was so great that the firm could sometimes block U.S. competitors from getting the same equipment from abroad. "If new technology comes out, he can buy up all the output until he fills up his plants," says Jock Nash, head of Milliken's Washington office. "That also denies the technology to others."

Roger Milliken recalls taking a trip, in the mid-1970s, with the head of Draper Corporation, a U.S. firm that had dominated loom making in America for a century. A Swiss firm was introducing new technology that used tiny projectiles to shoot yarn across a loom at four times the speed of old-fashioned looms using wooden shuttles. Draper could have licensed the technology, but decided against it because the new looms cost five times as much as the old ones. Draper figured U.S. firms wouldn't pay the higher prices. "That was a terrible mistake," says Milliken, who bought the Swiss machines and, later, foreign looms that used jets of water and bursts of air for even faster weaving. Draper's business steadily dwindled to where it could sell only spare parts for old looms; in 1996, it was purchased by an Indonesian textile conglomerate.

As Milliken & Co. renovated its mills, it laid off workers there. Milliken is secretive about its operations, but since 1989 it appears to have added about 1,000 employees overall by picking up business as competitors failed and by expanding into new markets. Other textile mills weren't as fortunate: They laid off huge numbers of workers as they modernized their mills with foreign technology. Upstate South Carolina residents bitterly complained in the mid-1980s that the mill owners' strategy was: "Buy foreign and fire American." In Washington, the textile industry blamed the layoffs solely on foreign competition. Textile employment dropped to about 625,000 workers in 1997, a 12% decline from a decade earlier. Sympathetic lawmakers and administration policy makers regularly renewed tariffs and quotas that substantially raised the price of fabrics, carpets, and clothes for consumers.

The textile industry's big layoffs reflected a process far more complex than cheap textile imports. Textile makers were getting rid of antiquated machinery, consolidating mills, and using new, foreign technology. Together, these changes have boosted hourly loom production nearly threefold since 1987. "The image of the textile industry is that foreign competition is driving people out of business," says Erwin Maddrey, head of Delta Woodside, a Greenville textile maker. "Our industry got real negative; everything we did we blamed on foreign imports. . . . The correct answer to questions of layoffs is modernization."

The surge in imported machinery also prepared the way for other foreign investments upstate—a process that would lift the region's economy overall. Sulzer of Switzerland set up an office across from the Milliken campus, to service the advanced looms; Menzel of Germany began manufacturing big textile-winding machinery nearby; Hoechst of Germany produced polyester fibers that Milliken and others wove into fabrics. As other foreign manufacturers flocked to the region, they were

able to hire many of the workers laid off from textile and apparel operations. "Being from so far away, these companies don't know the locali-
ties in the U.S.," says former South Carolina Governor Richard Riley.
"Once they find a place that's responsive and works well, they congre-
gate. They rely on word of mouth." By the time BMW chose to build in
Spartanburg, it was the forty-sixth German company operating in the
county.

Milliken and the newcomers agree on one strategy: Keep unions out.
Textile makers moved south to escape unions, fought bitterly to bar
them from southern mills, and made sure that foreign firms—even
those that are unionized at home—understood that's the way business
is done upstate. BMW got the message. The carmaker, which has a
powerful union in Germany, circulated to upstate business leaders
plans that showed its intention to run a nonunion operation. (BMW
pays high wages for the area, but they're below those paid by plants organized by the United Auto Workers in the Midwest or by BMW's
union in Germany.) "We try to fit in where we go," says Robert Hitt, the
BMW spokesman. "That doesn't mean we're antiunion."

The foreign investment produced two results that Milliken couldn't
have foreseen. First, the new firms pay wages well above those at the
mills, to the dismay of textile executives who look to Roger Milliken for
leadership. "BMW comes in and attracts your better technicians," complains Mack Cates Jr., chairman of Arkwright Mills Inc., in Spartanburg. Replies BMW's feisty spokesman: "[Cates] ain't got the pick of the
litter anymore. The litter has changed. He'll have to train his people."

Second, the investment surge drove up South Carolina's trade deficit.
Foreign subsidiaries—whether U.S. companies in Europe, or European
companies in the United States—invariably import more than they export. According to Roger Milliken, South Carolina should have suffered
as a result. By his analysis, trade deficits are always bad; they slow
growth and rob jobs. "We cannot go on with an international deficit,"
he charges. But in fact, South Carolina benefited overall because the
firms that settled in South Carolina and imported goods from abroad
also created jobs. "The trade deficit is offset by inward [foreign] investment," says Syracuse University economist J. David Richardson. "That's
a virtuous trade deficit."

Globalization surely causes pain, too. The tiny hamlet of Iva, South
Carolina, about thirty miles south of bustling I-85, shows how brutal

the consequences of trade can be for workers whose companies can't compete. Iva (population 1,200) is a town with one traffic light, an abandoned red-brick cotton mill, and a restaurant named Duds that serves all-you-can-eat fried chicken for $5. After the cotton mill closed, around Christmas 1995, Iva's sole apparel maker, Iva Manufacturing Company, became its largest employer. But, nationwide, the apparel industry is fighting off bankruptcy. Many of its clients have taken their business to the Caribbean and Mexico, or sometimes to sweatshops in New York's Chinatown, where immigrants toil at wages well below the legal minimum. "We've lost lots of money," says Julian Maxwell, the soft-spoken president of Iva Manufacturing. "Our future? It's bleak."

Cora Thompson, a slender, thirty-year plant veteran, says garment work was a step up from her first job of picking cotton. Five years ago, Iva finally appointed her a supervisor. But with the cutbacks, she was soon forced to give up the promotion and go back to stitching pockets. "There wasn't enough work on the floor," she says, "so I had to take a seat again." She's remarkably free of rancor and is proud that she and her husband, who worked at the local mill before it closed, managed to put two kids through college despite their modest incomes. Still, the layoffs and cutbacks have taken their toll. Her husband finally found a job, but with a steep cut in salary. "It was hard on him," she says. "His back went out. I think it was just nerves." Her husband's tale is fairly typical of workers who are laid off in industries hammered by imports. Those workers remain unemployed for as much as four months longer than workers laid off from comparable industries unaffected by trade. Worse, their wages are 10% lower than other laid off workers two years after being let go.

In 1988, Iva had revenue of about $17 million, and employed 750 workers spread over seven plants within fifty miles of town. Maxwell and other top executives piloted the company's Beech Sundowner aircraft from plant to plant to check on blouse production for Sears, JCPenney, and Liz Claiborne. Now, Iva is down to two tiny plants, with a staff of 100. If all goes well, revenue will hit $1.5 million, and the company will break even. Maxwell blames trade deals for the decline, and he has a point: U.S. negotiators regularly offered to reduce tariffs and increase quotas on apparel imports to close trade deals with European and Latin American nations. In the 1980s, blouse production moved to the Caribbean after Congress approved tariff cuts as part of a plan to bolster the economies of Caribbean and Central American nations and to help them ward off guerrilla insurgencies. In 1994, garment production shifted again to Mexico as NAFTA eliminated import tariffs on garments and other U.S. goods in exchange for broad reductions in Mexican tariffs, and protection for U.S. investments south of the border.

To stay afloat, Iva has been desperate to cut costs. In 1994, the company dropped fringe benefits altogether: no health insurance for new hires, no profit sharing, and no paid vacations. Workers apply for unemployment insurance during plant shutdowns over the July 4th and Christmas holidays. Iva pays workers just 50 cents to $1 more than the minimum hourly wage; in early 1997, Iva's average manufacturing wage was about $6.10 an hour.

What's especially galling to Iva's managers is that they foresaw the impact of cheap competition and did their best to meet the challenge through technology. In 1988, the company spent $1 million on computer-controlled equipment to boost productivity, and gained national recognition in the garment business. *Bobbin*, the leading apparel-trade magazine, featured Iva's former owner, William Epstein, and his airplane on the cover. The headline was: "Iva's flight to the top." "Although some might see his actions as derring-do," the *Bobbin* writer enthused, "he knows his strategy isn't really a gamble at all—but the only way to stay on top in today's apparel industry."

Epstein, now 64 years old, strolls around the Iva plant, an aluminum-sided building audaciously named the "Hi-Tech Center." "My big investment was the biggest mistake I ever made," he says glumly, his New York accent undiminished by forty-four years in South Carolina. "The business continued to deteriorate." On the plant floor, computer equipment sits idle. "Robot Tex," a $150,000 machine the size of a credenza, was supposed to pick up fabric, lay it down with a liner, and then push the two through a machine that fused the materials together. But Robot Tex was never sensitive enough to pick up the sheer material.

Nearby is the factory's "Unit Production System," a motorized track system to carry garments from one manufacturing station to another. The system looks like a moving clothes rack that a dry cleaner might use to search for suits and dresses. Iva bought two of the systems—one from Sweden, the other from Spain—for a total of $200,000. But the technical support was so poor that Iva's engineer had to call the home countries for help with the computer controls. The Spanish machine's manual wasn't translated into English, so Iva kept a bilingual dictionary nearby. Iva finally turned off the apparel mover when it realized it would have to spend $90,000 to upgrade the computer controls.

Some technology performed better. Iva uses a computerized system to draw sewing patterns and to plot how best to place the patterns on layers of fabric to minimize waste. A large automated machine spreads fabric; several smaller ones sew pockets on blouses—a surprisingly difficult task. Epstein figures that Iva's technology binge increased productivity by 20%, but that wasn't enough to compete with low apparel prices from abroad.

In 1994, disgusted at the passage of NAFTA, Epstein sold the business to Julian Maxwell and his family for a pittance. Epstein leases the equipment and building to the new owners, and looks the other way when they're late on payments. Every so often, he'll auction excess sewing machines to raise cash. Why did Maxwell buy the place? "This is all I know," says Maxwell. "I'm 52 years old. I live three minutes away. My sons are still working here. This has been my whole life. Why did I buy it? Fear. What else did I know? What else could I do? I'm encouraging my sons to leave."

Iva's strategy, to the extent it has one, is to outlast competitors who are facing the same problems. Not all garment making can move abroad. High-fashion companies need quicker turnaround and smaller production runs than firms abroad can manage efficiently. Anyway, some of Iva's competitors that moved to Mexico are also having problems. One factory manager drives back and forth from South Carolina to Mexico, trolling for work. "He is trying to keep his factory going in Mexico," says Maxwell. "There, you have to pay the workers whether they're working or not."

These days, Iva sews bustiers for suppliers to Victoria's Secret, and collarless dress shirts for other catalog companies. But the industry overall is suffering. Since NAFTA went into effect in January 1994, the number of apparel jobs nationwide has shrunk by 16% to 807,000. That's the cost of open trade: Poor nations that pay lower wages will grab a larger share of the market for goods that have a high labor content. But the United States, with its lead in so many fields of technology, will gain a bigger share of fields where labor doesn't matter quite so much and innovation does.

Textile makers—with the notable exception of Roger Milliken—hold out the hope that NAFTA will ease the harm caused by trade, at least for textile workers. By eliminating tariffs with Mexico, garment making will shift to Mexico from China, India, and elsewhere in Asia, they argue. Because 80% of apparel imported from Mexico is assembled from U.S.-made fabric, they say, U.S. textile mills should benefit. There is some evidence that the theory is working. Exports to Mexico of fabric and sections of garments have nearly doubled since the passage of NAFTA. In Mexico, those goods are sewn into finished garments and sent back to the United States. Indeed, apparel imports from Mexico have tripled since NAFTA took effect, and apparel imports from Asia have been flat. Meanwhile, the rate of job losses in the textile industry has slowed recently, compared to the calamitous declines of the 1970s and 1980s.

J. David Richardson, the Syracuse University economist, and C. Fred Bergsten of the Institute for International Economics, a think tank in Washington, look more broadly at the job effects of trade. American exports are rising and will power a rise in manufacturing employment starting in the year 2000, they estimate. At that point, the rise in employment in exporting plants will more than offset the employment decline among plants that don't export. By 2017, the two economists predict, the number of manufacturing jobs will match the 1987 levels, rather than continue on a steady decline. Over that time period, service jobs surely will expand even faster, however, so factory workers will continue to represent a shrinking percentage of a growing workforce over the next few decades.

Pumping up the number of apparel jobs in the United States would require retaining high tariffs and tight quotas, which would add greatly to the cost of clothes. In effect, tariffs are just another form of sales tax. Eliminating clothing tariffs would save consumers $21 billion annually, according to one estimate by the Institute for International Economics. Looked at from another angle, consumers now spend $140,000 a year to save each domestic apparel job. The Congressional Budget Office, which places a more modest price tag on protection, still concludes that "it would generally be more efficient for the government to allow the jobs to disappear and compensate the workers who cannot find equivalent work."

Iva's Julian Maxwell knows the arguments against protection and, surprisingly perhaps, doesn't dispute the logic. "I have problems arguing my point," he says. "I don't want to say, 'Buy a blouse for $10 when you can buy one for $7 in Mexico,' just to keep me in business." He and his old boss, William Epstein, both drive foreign cars and say they shop for bargains, no matter where the products are made.

Upstate South Carolina's global links have brought it overall prosperity. Even textile and apparel workers who are laid off generally find other work. And the region's greater economic opportunities offer hope for their children. John Horton grew up north of Greenville in a mountainous area called Dark Corner, where the mountains turn purple-gray as the sun sets behind them, and where moonshiners once plied their trade. "At the age of eight, my sister was saying that who picked a row of cotton the fastest would get a cigarette at the end of the row," he wrote in a short account of growing up in the 1940s that he composed for a visiting reporter. "I won, but I didn't like the smoke." As an adult, he worked at a series of mill jobs in Tryon, North Carolina, a few miles across the state line, and spent his spare time fixing cars. "Restoring VW Beetles and working lots of overtime to send 2 girls to college," he wrote.

Growing up, his two daughters wondered whether they would have to leave the area to find the kind of jobs they wanted. Instead, the global economy brought the jobs to Greenville. Sandra, a quiet 34-year-old who talks of her mother's determination that her daughters should rise in the world, programs computers for a Dutch supermarket company with large operations in Greenville. Renetta, a vivacious 41-year-old, used to research the local economy for the Greenville Chamber of Commerce, as part of its efforts to woo foreign investment, and now writes for a local business newspaper. "I thought I'd have to leave to get a decent job," Renetta says. "It turned out that wasn't true; there have been reasonable opportunities."

The changes in Greenville still surprise her. She and her husband take their three-year-old son to a Montessori school, where he is taught by a young Indian woman who dresses in a sari. "Here it is, India coming to us," Renetta says. "Imagine that."

14

Imports: The Consumer's Friend

How consumers will gain from imports.

Imagine what life would be like for Americans if the United States were to turn back history and limit imports, as politicians as different as Pat Buchanan and Richard Gephardt sometimes propose.

There would be some winners: General Motors, Ford, and Chrysler could charge more for cars and might pay workers more if they didn't have to worry about Honda and Toyota. But most Americans would end up spending a lot more to buy a car, and probably a less reliable one; that would be as much a blow to their standard of living as a pay cut.

The shelves of the stores where the American middle class shops would look different, too. There would be more American-made television sets and sneakers, but the prices would be far higher, and American families would be forced to devote a bigger chunk of their paychecks to the necessities of life. Today, half the clothing for sale at a typical JCPenney store is made abroad. Racks of imported shirts, pants, and dresses help explain why the average four-person American household spends only about 4.5% of its budget on clothing today—two-thirds of the amount a four-person household spent in the early 1970s. More than 90% of the rubber and plastic footwear and 85% of the leather shoes and sneakers come from abroad. So do three-quarters of the household audio and video equipment that Americans buy each year, 60% of the musical instruments, and nearly 30% of the pharmaceuticals, according to estimates by Standard & Poor's/DRI.

Without imports, America would be battling inflation—a struggle that would saddle consumers with higher interest rates on car loans and mortgages. Imports of raw materials, parts, and finished goods from overseas recently have helped the United States grow without a widely forecast increase in inflation. Helped by a strong dollar and currency devaluations in Asia, falling import prices trimmed 0.3% off the Consumer Price Index in 1997, according to economist Joel Popkin, a former Bureau of Labor Statistics official; that's no trivial amount when prices are rising at less than 3.0% a year. The Federal Reserve's willingness to allow the economy to keep rolling along in 1997 partly reflected the effects of cheaper imports and the power of import competition to discourage domestic producers from raising prices.

Imports are the consumer's friend. They bring better goods, more choice, and lower prices. Competition from imports also stimulates American producers to make better products. American-built cars are more fuel-efficient and reliable today, in part, because Detroit responded to the import threat; American car buyers are better off.

When prices decline or products improve because of imports, American living standards rise just as much as they do when wages go up. That fact of economic life never gets the attention it deserves during the bitter and emotional political debates about trade and job-killing imports. Imports have risen to nearly 13% of all purchases of goods and services, compared to about 4% in 1960. Continued openness to foreign goods will be an important force in lifting American living standards in the next ten or twenty years—provided that scare-mongering politicians, misguided labor leaders, and business executives, who often pay lip service to competition but really fear it, don't prevail.

Imports are rarely celebrated; the response is just the opposite. They make Americans uneasy because they hurt the job prospects and wages of less skilled workers, although not as much as the exaggerated public debate sometimes suggests. America is hardly alone in ambivalence toward imports. The Japanese worry about the "hollowing out" of Japanese industry through imports, the French fear that imports will diminish their distinctive culture, and South Koreans believe that imports will undermine their sovereignty.

Nor is the fear of imports a new concern. As early as 1697, English merchant-politician John Pollexfen warned that unchecked imports would inevitably lead to economic ruin. "Those [goods] from India must otherwise be cheapest, and all people will go to the cheapest markets, which will affect the rents of land, and bring our working people to poverty, and force them to fly to foreign ports, or to be maintained by the parishes," he wrote. Fortunately, England ignored his warning, imported more and more, and enjoyed two centuries of prosperity before it slid into decline for other reasons.

It's hard for Americans to appreciate the benefits of imports because it's impossible to imagine life without them. There isn't any basis for comparison. In much the same way that anthropologists better understand our culture by comparing it to very different Asian or African societies, the experiences of consumers in other countries are instructive. Three nations offer particularly important lessons on the value of imports to consumers: Japan, a rich country that recently has changed its ways and begun to import more; New Zealand, a small agricultural economy that abruptly opened its once-protected markets; and Argentina, which fell from the top tier of economies partly because it curtailed imports.

In Japan, imports grew by 36% between 1992 and 1996—a stunning rise, given that economies that stagnate, as Japan's did for much of the 1990s, usually cut back on purchases of foreign wares. As the value of the yen rose against the dollar, it made imports cheaper to Japanese consumers and prompted Japanese manufacturers to move production offshore. Imported food, clothing, and other consumer items, once mainly high-priced luxuries, suddenly were more affordable. In just four years, Japan's meat imports rose to 2.2 million metric tons from 1.6 million. Imports of VCRs shot up to 4.6 million from fewer than 500,000. Discount stores that directly imported from overseas sprang up across Japan, offering stiff competition to higher-priced domestic goods for the first time in decades. The share of Tokyo family budgets devoted to food, clothing, and recreation shrank.

Tamiko and Kogo Usami benefited, just as millions of other Japanese families did. A surge in imports of consumer goods has given Japanese families a chance to enjoy a lifestyle that import-buying consumers in the United States take for granted. Their experiences show the way imports improve life. The Usamis live with Kogo's father and the youngest of their three children in the trendy Omotesando neighborhood on the west side of Tokyo. The Usamis' spacious four-story house resembles an American home, and is unusually large by Japanese middle-class standards. The living room is dominated by a large-screen television; an upright piano stands in one corner. The dining room is hemmed in by houseplants; another television sits on a side table. Off the living room is a quintessential Japanese *washitsu* room with straw *tatami* mats and a religious shrine.

Tamiko Usami opens her refrigerator and pulls out a head of American-grown broccoli, which costs less than domestic varieties. Imported steaks wrapped in paper rest on one shelf; the Usami family eats steak once every week or two now, instead of only a few times a year, as before. Cans of imported Heineken beer line another shelf. Bottles of French and Chilean wine stand in the door. "This wine is really good, and it's only 700 yen [about $5.60]," Tamiko says, pointing to the Chilean bottle. "Our lifestyle has really changed. So many things have become cheaper."

Her husband, Kogo, a branch manager for Tokyo Electric Power Company, in Saitama prefecture near Tokyo, recently bought Eddie Bauer sport shirts that were only about a third as expensive as typical Japanese brands. The couple's middle child, 20-year-old Makiko, a college student who lives on campus but still has a room in her parents' home, shops regularly at new imported-clothing stores in the neighborhood, browsing for bargain items from European fashion designers. She rushes to her room to collect and show off two of her recent finds: a white sweater, and a green-and-orange checked skirt, both made in France. "These kinds of stores are everywhere now," she says. Even the family dog, an Australian whippet named Henri, is imported. ("We call him that because he looks so noble," Makiko explains.)

Sometimes, the Usamis aren't even aware how imports have made their lives better. In 1996, Makiko spent roughly $200 on a Sony mini-component stereo for her room, a product that likely would have cost more than three times as much four years earlier. Although she had always assumed it was made in Japan, she checked the back panel recently, and found a "Made in Korea" label. Thanks in part to Japanese manufacturers who have shifted their factories to other parts of Asia, prices of stereos, televisions, and VCRs all have been cut in half, or more, over the past several years.

The Usamis, like their American counterparts, are sometimes ambivalent about imports. The family saved money when it traded its Toyota for a Ford station wagon, but Tamiko isn't happy with the service the U.S. automaker offers in Japan, which she says doesn't compare to the attention Japanese car companies lavish on their customers. "If something goes wrong, they'll fix it, but they never call us to ask how the car is doing," she says. "Japanese companies are more polite, and really take care of us."

As far as Tamiko is concerned, the import trend hasn't yet gone far enough. The Usamis lived in the United States briefly in the late 1980s, when Kogo was sent to Stanford University by his employer. That hooked the family on such American innovations as discount outlet stores and inexpensive appliances. "Living in California was wonderful—that's where we first became familiar with cheaper clothes and wine," Tamiko says. "Now, little by little, Japan is going the same direction."

What is happening "little by little" in Japan happened almost all at once in tiny New Zealand. In 1984, New Zealand, with fewer people than the state of Colorado, launched an experiment in free-market economics that makes Ronald Reagan look like a wimp.

New Zealand was ripe for radical change. In the four decades after World War II, its economy grew at half the pace of other developed countries, and its living standards lagged countries it once considered to be its peers. It seemed more like Eastern Europe than the West. "Daily life was a patchwork of controls, regulations, and state interventions," former finance minister Roger Douglas, architect of the reforms, wrote in his book, *Rogernomics*. "Hotels closed at 6 P.M. Only the government was allowed to broadcast television programs. If you wanted to bring in Italian tiles or German beers or an American car, you needed a government license. . . . Movies took nine to 18 months to arrive here. There were just two sorts of refrigerator—both made by the same manufacturer to the same specifications."

After the election of a new Labour government in 1984, New Zealand abruptly curtailed state subsidies, cut the income tax and partially substituted a sales tax, privatized state-owned industries, deregulated almost everything it could, and set strict inflation goals for the central bank. Before the reforms, New Zealand had the highest tariffs and the most restrictions on imports of any developed country. Although imports of raw materials and machinery were encouraged so that New Zealand businesses could make things to export, imports of consumer goods were discouraged and often required hard-to-get government licenses. The price of imported clothing was more than doubled by import restrictions. New Zealanders needed a government license to subscribe to an overseas journal.

"Overseas trips were often shopping trips. Travelers would return laden with booty which was too expensive to purchase in New Zealand. The main beneficiaries were foreign distributors and retailers. It was a very inefficient way of restricting consumption of luxury goods to the rich," says Michael Carter, a New Zealand academic economist. "Exchange and import controls spawned a variety of ingenious rackets. Under one scheme, those with access to foreign currency could go to the top of the queue for a new car, while ordinary people had to spend three or four years on a waiting list. Consequently, the favored few were enabled to buy a new car every year, and then sell it to the less fortunate for more than they paid for it."

In its zeal to protect manufacturers and their workers, New Zealand made it nearly impossible to import television sets. So a New Zealand businessman set up a firm that assembled televisions from imported parts, since none were produced domestically.

Here's how he described it:

"After much time and explanation and shaking of heads, the Japanese finally agreed to sell us the bits to assemble their sets in New Zealand. However, they explained that this was very costly. They were making tens of thousands of sets a day and we only wanted parts for a few thousand a year. At great cost they contracted outside people to come in, take assembled sets apart, sort out all the pieces we needed and put them in boxes. They got engineers to write out all the instructions in English for reassembly, and shipped them on their way. Naturally, someone has to pay for this, and, on average, they charged us for the parts, as a special favor, 110% of the price of the finished goods all boxed and ready to go to the retailer. We then opened a factory, imported much machinery, paid the highest wages in the neighborhood, employed the most intelligent engineers to decipher the instructions, used a great deal of electricity, and finally produced a TV set with negative New Zealand content at twice the imported price."

As part of the far-reaching 1984 economic reforms, many restrictions on imports were lifted. Around 90% of all imports now enter New Zealand without any tariffs, and tariffs on the remainder have been reduced. The result has been a surge in both imports and exports. In 1985, less than 8% of all consumer goods sold in New Zealand were imported. Ten years later, 20% were. The change was painful for New Zealand industry and for many New Zealand workers. Plants closed. Inefficient companies went under. Economic shock therapy like New Zealand's requires a painful period of transition that is more than some countries can tolerate. Unemployment peaked at 11% in 1991, but then fell as exports soared and the pace of economic growth quickened; it was at 6.8% in late 1997.

New Zealand consumers were big winners from the dismantling of trade barriers. Cars illustrate the point well. In 1986, New Zealand imported only 3,900 used cars from abroad, one-twentieth the number of new cars sold. When the government began to ease the restrictions on importing used cars in 1987, imports climbed. Thousands of New Zealanders who had been unable to afford new cars junked 15-year-old models for much newer cars from Japan.

The Japanese cars were still secondhand but were in far better shape than the clunkers the New Zealanders had been driving. Stringent auto inspection rules in Japan discourage the Japanese from holding onto their cars for more than three years. Many of the used Japanese cars sent to New Zealand had air-conditioning and automatic transmissions, features that were scarce on New Zealand-built models. To compete, New Zealand auto makers were forced to improve their products, just as Detroit companies were when Japanese imports began to grab market share. When auto import restrictions were removed altogether in 1989, New Zealanders imported 51,000 used cars. In 1995, imports of used cars were up to 81,000, exceeding the number of new cars built in New Zealand and of new-car imports.

Auto imports badly hurt companies that assemble cars. New Zealand plants assembled 95,400 passenger cars in 1981, but only 34,268 in 1995. General Motors and Toyota already have closed plants, and Ford and Mazda are following their lead. Employment in the auto assembly industry has declined, but new hiring elsewhere in the economy has more than offset those job losses.

New Zealand consumers are unquestionably enjoying the benefits of the changed policies. Between 1987 and 1990, the price of used cars fell by 13% and the price of new cars went down 18%, even as overall consumer prices rose 29%. Economists Liliana and Rainer Winkelmann found that the wholesale price of cars imported into New Zealand fell by 35% after the import restrictions were eased. And cars weren't an exception. Prices of photographic film dropped 42%, and the price of imported bourbon dropped 18%.

"Of course there has been a downside," quips economist Michael Carter. "Traffic congestion has also increased dramatically. But at least congestion is egalitarian. Vehicle ownership is widespread and not restricted to the rich and powerful."

Six thousand miles away, Argentina provides a different lesson, a cautionary tale of the harm that can come to an economy that tries to wall itself off from the rest of the world. Early in the twentieth century, Argentina was among the richest and fastest growing countries in the world. In its *Belle Epoque* just before World War I, it aspired, with considerable confidence, to match such similarly resource-rich and sparsely populated countries as Australia and Canada. Output per person in Argentina in 1913 exceeded that of Italy, Denmark, and France, and was only 10% below that of Canada. Today, despite recent successful economic reforms, Argentina's per-capita output is less than half that of Canada, Denmark, France, or Italy.

An early twentieth-century visitor to Buenos Aires "would have marveled at the splendors of the city: the impressive opera house, the graceful architecture, the sophisticated railway system," says Alan Taylor, a Northwestern University economist who has dissected Argentina's economic history. "Today, the city presents the same elegant facade, only frayed and decaying at the edges—and the visitor marvels that the city can function at all, given its dilapidated infrastructure. The satisfaction of living in one of the richest countries in the world is now a distant memory for the Argentines, who have struggled to come to terms with their sinking status."

A lot of things went wrong. Argentina's trade and finances were closely linked to Britain's on the eve of World War I. When Britain lost its economic footing, Argentina suffered.

The economic pain of World War I and the Great Depression convinced the Argentines they would be better off going their own way. Beginning in the 1930s, Argentina tried to turn an economy that was open to imports, foreign investment, and immigration into a self-sufficient economy—with terrible results. By 1980, Argentina's imports—and exports—represented a smaller share of its economy than was found in any of the other 100 countries for which the World Bank tallies the figures. Argentina's trade and other economic policies made life worse. Living standards steadily slipped behind the levels of developed countries. Argentina's per-capita income has never been closer to the developed-countries' average than it was before World War I.

With the election of Carlos Menem as president in 1989, Argentina opened a new chapter in its economic history. Menem's administration conquered inflation that was running at 5,000% a year, sold off billions of dollars' worth of government-owned businesses, and demolished restrictions on trade and investment. In the early 1990s, Argentina eliminated nearly all its rules discouraging imports, which had protected about one-third of all domestic production. Quotas were abolished. The average tariff on imports, 40%, was reduced to less than 10%. And Argentina agreed to eliminate trade barriers with its neighbors: Brazil, Uruguay, and Paraguay.

The changes paid off. An economy that had actually shrunk in the 1980s grew by 7% annually during the first four years of the 1990s—until a financial crisis in Mexico triggered an Argentine recession in 1995 from which the country is now recovering smartly. Economic growth and fewer restrictions on trade brought a flood of consumer imports that swept shoddy, expensive Argentine products off the shelves. Imports of all kinds, which had fallen by 8.6% a year in the 1980s, zoomed by 45.8% a year in the first half of the 1990s. Sales of imported autos and appliances, especially, soared. Argentina imported more cars in 1992 than in the previous ten-year period.

It took more than fifty years after the onset of the Great Depression for Argentina to reverse course and open its economy to foreign trade once again. Argentine living standards are beginning to improve, finally. But in those fifty years, trade helped Australia and Canada, once Argentina's peers, prosper, and made once-poor Asian countries rich. Argentina is half a century behind.

"The purpose of international trade, the reason why it is useful, is to import, not to export," economist Paul Krugman has written. The centuries-old mercantilist view, still echoing through Congress, chambers of commerce, and union offices, is that all exports are good because they bring in money and create jobs, but all imports are bad because they suck out money and destroy jobs. That's simply wrong. Americans get things they wouldn't otherwise have or couldn't otherwise afford by trading what they have for what others have. "The need to export," Krugman writes in a clever twist of conventional thinking on trade, "is a burden that a country must bear because its import suppliers are crass enough to demand payment."

15

Prospering Together

Why Americans and third-world workers will prosper together.

Information Management Resources runs a flourishing software factory. Teams of ten programmers, seated elbow-to-elbow in blue-paneled cubicles, churn out computer code on personal computers linked by networks. Some teams are updating computer software for the Discover credit card; others are fixing software problems for a Kentucky utility and a Connecticut insurance company. Information Management's executives say they must hire hundreds of new programmers each year to keep up with sales that reached $28 million in 1996 and were expected to more than double in 1997. This software factory could be anywhere in America. But it's not. Information Management is 8,000 miles away in a south Indian boomtown called Bangalore, where programmers are paid $5,000 a year to do the same kind of work as Americans who make $40,000.

Information Management has plenty of company in Bangalore. On the outskirts of town is Electronics City, a walled-in campus of computer software and hardware companies that includes local branches of Hewlett-Packard, Siemens, Motorola, and 3M. All are trying to cut labor costs by hiring cheap, talented Indian programmers. Nearby, construction cranes are erecting two skyscrapers—soaring high but improbably called Information Technology Park—which Singapore investors plan to fill with even more software firms working for Western companies. Mounted on top of buildings throughout Bangalore is the city's trademark: round microwave dishes that relay Indian software to American customers via satellite faster than it takes to say the word "nightmare."

Bangalore is one of the best places in the world to explore the threat and opportunity posed by low-wage competition. Americans fear that companies in low-wage nations like India will steal their jobs or undermine their wages—a fear that's likely to intensify as Asia's financial crisis leads to widespread salary cuts there. The rise of long-distance programming in Bangalore plays into that concern; it is globalization at its most terrifying. Bangalore's programmers are competing with Americans not for low-skilled jobs assembling plastic toys, but for the jobs of the future—and they're doing it by futuristic means.

If workers in the high-wage United States and in low-wage, high-tech Bangalore can coexist, then the United States can flourish against low-wage competition anywhere. Until a decade ago, distance would have kept Bangalore from competing with software workers in Boston and Silicon Valley. But with the advent of global computer networks, Bangalore shares a virtual border with the United States. Bangalore can perform high-value service jobs from abroad, just as Tijuana and other Mexican border towns can assemble seatbelts and engine parts once made in Detroit and Cleveland.

In the United States, the software industry already employs 620,000 workers. That number is predicted to climb to 1 million by 2005. Many doubt that projection because of the competition American software workers face from eager Indians willing to work for half the wages of McDonald's hamburger flippers. Won't trading with low-wage countries inevitably undermine wages and jobs in the United States? Won't opportunities for U.S. programmers and other well-paid service workers—lab technicians, architects, engineers, medical advisers—shrivel as employers turn to cheap professionals in other countries, who can work for U.S. companies via modem?

No, to both questions. Here's the bottom line: Trade with developing nations helps low-wage nations and high-wage nations alike. As third-world boomtowns and the United States become more tightly coupled, workers in both places benefit. When Bangalore prospers, so does the United States; the two places coexist more than they compete.

Critics of globalization focus on the wage gap between the United States and developing nations and figure that wages, like water, inevitably sink to the lowest level. But that view greatly exaggerates the lure of low-wage nations. It also underestimates the strengths of American workers, who remain the most productive in the world and are capable of competing with lower-paid foreign workers in many industries, though not certainly all. U.S. multinational companies employ nearly three times as many people at home as they do abroad—and they have done so since the Commerce Department began making such tallies in 1982. When wages plummet in developing nations, as they did when Mexico devalued its peso, U.S. firms are far more likely to take advantage by shifting jobs to Mexico from other developing nations, such as Malaysia, than by moving jobs from the United States. The reasons are two-fold: Low-wage nations often compete with each other for the same low-skill work—sewing shirts, for instance—so work shifts from one developing nation to the next, depending on where the wages are lowest; and U.S. companies tend to keep higher-skilled jobs here because this is where innovation is greatest. The leading competitors, leading financiers, and the leading suppliers reside in the United States.

The United States consistently tops the world in foreign investment, despite the high wages of its workers. All companies, domestic and foreign, within its borders create jobs in the United States. In their competition for talent, they push wages well above the minimum. Physicists talk about "critical mass," the moment when there is enough fissionable material to spark a nuclear chain reaction that produces vast amounts of power. That's what the U.S. economy has: critical mass, the world's densest concentration of the raw material for economic growth.

Foreign low-wage outposts will get only a small portion of the jobs created by U.S. economic growth. Searching for strategies to boost incomes in poor nations, the World Bank called long-distance services, such as computer programming and data inputting, "an area of special promise." But the Bank found the potential for third-world jobs far less than advertised. Although it is technically feasible for as much as 12% to 16% of service jobs in wealthy countries to be shifted offshore, at most only 1% to 5% of those jobs will actually go, the Bank concluded. "Companies demonstrate a natural reluctance to outsource activities that are strategically important and involve proprietary information," the World Bank reported. "This reluctance applies particularly to international outsourcing."

It's important to remember that low-wage countries aren't only competitors to the United States. They also represent opportunities for American companies as suppliers of needed services and of talented immigrants, and they offer markets for American exports. In each of those roles, they help American workers. In Bangalore, computer companies generally fix software problems that can cripple old-fashioned mainframe computers. There aren't enough Americans trained to do that work. At Information Management, for instance, new hires are immediately taught ancient mainframe codes like COBOL or assembly language. Bangalore's software houses are ensured a steady flow of contracts, but engineers there fear they are becoming "techno-coolies"— low-paid laborers hired to do dull, routine jobs that Americans can't be bothered with.

When foreigners pick up the slack, Americans are freed to concentrate on higher-paying, higher-value projects involving computer networks and advanced computer languages. In technology, America remains where the action is. That produces another salutary effect. Some of the best and the brightest residents of the world's low-wage countries come to the United States to work and to study, adding intellectual resources to the chain reaction that produces new industries, new jobs, and economic growth. Immigrant entrepreneurs run such Silicon Valley powerhouses as semiconductor maker Intel Corporation and network equipment maker 3Com Corporation. Thousands of Indian software engineers add their skills to high-tech operations around the country.

Workers in low-wage countries are consumers, too. As developing nations grow wealthier, partly through trade, wages will rise there, reducing the wage gap separating them from American workers. That already has happened in Japan and is being repeated in Taiwan, Hong Kong, Korea and other once-poor nations. Despite the fear of imports from low-wage countries, imports from countries whose wages are less than half America's are growing more slowly than imports to the United States from countries whose manufacturing wages match or exceed American levels.

The economic turmoil that engulfed Asia at the end of 1997 was an important reminder of the weaknesses developing nations have. Emerging economies are vulnerable to wild swings in investor confidences and to runs on their banking systems. But after the panics subside, growth resumes. The trajectory of growth may dip for a time in

Asia and Latin America, but over the next two decades economies there will grow more wealthy and will help lift the fortunes of Americans.

As they gain greater wealth, developing nations import more, and they often turn to U.S. suppliers and their workers for the airports, airplanes, telecommunications networks, computer systems, power generators, and other goods and services they lack. By the year 2000, estimates Jim Rohwer, who covered Asia for the *Economist* news magazine, "perhaps 400 million of those [Asian] consumers—three times as many as in the early 1990s—will have disposable incomes at least equal to the rich-world average today; they will be buying houses, cars, holidays, health care, and education. And if all this consumer spending is to take place, immense investments in capital equipment and infrastructure will be needed to make it possible."

Indians call Bangalore "the garden city," and not so long ago it used to be one. Bangalore was the kind of place that attracted retirees and honeymooners—a green, quiet city, located on a 3,000-foot-high plateau. As a young colonial soldier, Winston Churchill played polo on the fields of Bangalore. India's first prime minister, Jawaharlal Nehru, anointed Bangalore the "city of the future," and the Indian government set up sprawling research institutions there for science, space, and aeronautics. Bangalore is the home of three prestigious universities and more than a dozen lesser colleges.

Over the past ten years, that research infrastructure has attracted hundreds of Indian software companies and about forty multinationals to Bangalore. Software managers came for the same reasons that earlier waves of newcomers came to Bangalore: the skilled workforce, the weather, the easygoing attitude. But the software crowd came in such large numbers that they transformed the place. The population has nearly doubled to 5 million since 1980; the number of vehicles on the road has grown even faster, as have the slums, filled with India's poor in search of jobs. An antigrowth movement has arisen and has organized massive protests against global trade; an American seed company and a Kentucky Fried Chicken restaurant have been ransacked. A blue haze of auto exhaust hangs over the city, and scooters, cars, and buses play endless games of chicken along the congested streets.

Growth has overwhelmed Bangalore's infrastructure. Bangaloreans endure blackouts every day; indeed, the state utility ran newspaper ads to announce the surprising news that it *wouldn't* shut off power during Hindu New Year celebrations. Software companies must buy big Caterpillar generators and banks of heavy-duty batteries that click into action during power failures. Likewise, the city's water supply regularly runs dry. An elaborate water system built by British colonizers has been bulldozed or neglected; the remaining reservoirs have become breeding grounds for disease-carrying mosquitoes. Most homes now have water-storage tanks in the kitchen or on the roof. Angry old-timers have rechristened the garden city. They call it "the garbage city."

Still, there is a vibrancy to the place. Ever eager for comparisons with the United States, software companies say Bangalore is India's Silicon Valley, even though it sits on a plateau. Parts of the city have the feel of an American college town. Every Friday, after work, programmers in their twenties—nearly all of Bangalore's programmers are male—jump on their scooters and head to the pubs along Church Street to share $3 pitchers of Kingfisher beer and the latest gossip from work and the Internet. At the Guzzlers Inn, Venkat Raman is buying pitchers of beer to celebrate his imminent four-month assignment to work on a department store's mainframe computer in Acton, Massachusetts, northwest of Boston. He'll make about $3,200 a month, and if he is like many of his colleagues, he'll return to Bangalore loaded with appliances and computer gear.

Bangalore stumbled into the software business through a misguided protectionism that sharply contrasts to India's current eagerness to woo foreign investors. In 1977, the Indian government killed the local mainframe computer industry when it imposed steep tariffs on computers and software. International Business Machines Corporation chose to leave the country rather than accede to demands that the Indian government must become a majority partner in IBM's India ventures. Those decisions set India back years technologically, but had one unforeseen advantage. When personal computers began sweeping the global computer industry in the mid-1980s, Indian programmers could quickly learn the new technology because so few of them were employed in writing software for mainframes. Indians also were forced to learn how to write personal computer software concisely, to conserve computer memory—a big advantage over programming rivals—because Indian tariffs made personal computers so expensive. After the Indian government reversed course in 1991 and started opening its economy to foreign investors, the government actively began promoting software exports.

Ireland, Israel, and the Philippines also are popular sites for offshore programming. But Bangalore is the premier center because of its large number of educated, English-speaking programmers, and its low wages. With nearly a twelve-hour time difference between Bangalore and the U.S. West Coast, Indian programmers work on projects while their American counterparts sleep—a cyberspace version of a night shift.

As Bangalore's reputation for programming has spread, so have fears that its success will come at the expense of American software workers. Journalists William Wolman and Anne Colamosca warn, in *The Judas Economy:* "Bangalore has quietly put together all the ingredients of a broad frontal attack to American hegemony on the frontier of the information revolution, software." Foreign policy analyst John Stremlau fears a greater calamity. During a war involving the United States, "it is conceivable that Bangalore could be cast as a potential source of exotic high-tech weapons capable of disrupting U.S. systems of command, control, communication, and intelligence," he wrote in the journal *Foreign Policy.*

The reality is far less fearsome. Exports of Indian software and services are growing at 40% a year; even so, they totaled only $1 billion in 1997, or about 0.003% of the global market. Look at it this way: Microsoft records as much software revenue in a month as the entire Indian software industry exports in a year. And other developing nations lag behind India's software sales.

Most Indian software companies are stuck in a low-tech rut, as are other potential competitors from developing nations. The information technology industry has a glamorous image, but much of the computer work done abroad by low-wage workers involves typing information into computers or processing checks and airline tickets. About 60% of India's software exports come from sending its programmers abroad, a practice known locally as "body shopping" or "fleshware." American companies, short of software talent, recruit in Bangalore and elsewhere in India for young programmers to fill out a software team in the United States—and pay them United States wages. The back pages of India's leading computer magazine, *Computers Today,* are packed with ads offering jobs in the United States. One firm, called People.Com, asks Indians to e-mail resumes: "You've never heard of us. But then, we've never heard of you either," the full-page ad says.

Bangalore's specialty is fixing the mistakes of long-retired American and European programmers. Information Management, headquartered in Clearwater, Florida, is typical. The company bills itself as a specialist in "transitional outsourcing," a fancy name for using Bangalore programmers to update old American mainframe computer software, especially patching the machines so they can recognize the year 2000 without going haywire. At Information Management, about 400 employees prospect for work and design programs in the United States; another 600 programmers work in Bangalore.

Rather than steal business from the United States, this low-tech programming actually boosts the value of U.S. programmers. The less time Americans spend updating old technology, the more they can concentrate on newer, better paying software technologies, like networking. Designing new kinds of software requires constant conversations between software designers and potential users, to make sure the program works as promised. That kind of development is hard enough to do when people are sitting in the same room; trying to handle it from India would be disastrous.

In theory, the "Year 2000 problem" is straightforward. In the 1960s and 1970s, Western programmers tried to conserve expensive mainframe computer memory by using only two digits to represent the year in a date; the software assumed that all the dates were in the twentieth century. So, "67" represented 1967, "75" meant 1975, and, unfortunately, "00" meant 1900. By the year 2000, programmers figured, the computers would be long scrapped, and the software along with them. The surprise: Succeeding generations of engineers didn't replace software; they built on it. Now, with the year 2000 looming, all those parts of computer programs linked to dates must be located and fixed, so that computers can recognize the proper year. Otherwise, the machines will start to act weirdly and will reject credit card purchases because credit card payments seem to be a century in arrears.

Repairing these glitches is laborious, stultifying work for which there aren't enough programmers in the United States or elsewhere in the world. American companies have been paying once-retired programmers more than $100,000 a year to come back to work and fix the problems they inadvertently created. (One group of ex-retirees printed up T-shirts announcing: "The Dinosaurs Are Back.") India helps fill the demand for these programmers. Moreover, the work is routine enough that it can be handled from India and other locations abroad.

Software houses in Bangalore believe that Year 2000 projects will keep them busy writing, testing, and rewriting software through the first few years of the next century. Perhaps, but the work also will keep them far from the forefront of software technology—a conundrum faced by other developing nations trying to compete in global technology markets.

What's after Year 2000 projects? Bangalore's software managers are preparing for the advent of the common European currency. Fixing Europe's mainframes so they can recognize the euro will keep Bangalore software houses working overtime. N. R. Narayana Murthy, chairman of Infosys Technologies Ltd., a big Bangalore software firm, understands that most Indian firms are in a bind: They choose low-tech work because it's profitable, even though the work ensures that they'll remain second-class companies. "I'm tickled by the idea that we pose a threat to America," he says ironically. "The joke is that we're helping American programmers upgrade their knowledge. They can work on new technology while we're maintaining their old systems."

Writing in *The Times of India*, columnist Shabnam Minwalla warned that India's software industry was falling into a "bodyshopper trap." Indians specialize in software projects that amount to "routine drudgery which few in the West are willing to undertake," Minwalla complained. "Although such projects keep the money coming, they are utterly devoid of either creativity or beauty." To software managers who say that Indian firms are going through an evolution that will inevitably lead to higher-margin work, Minwalla replied: "Even after two decades of growth, the ugly duckling has shown few signs of metamorphosing into a software swan."

The most advanced software work in Bangalore is done at outposts of U.S. companies. Texas Instruments Inc.'s Bangalore office looks like offices in the United States. It's richly carpeted and provides individual workspaces for programmers. Its windows overlook one of Bangalore's few golf courses. Bangalore produces libraries of computer chip designs for the Dallas-based semiconductor maker. Electronics customers use those designs in the same way that home buyers consult catalogs of standardized architectural drawings and then add flourishes to the houses they want to build. Texas Instruments' engineers in Dallas work with customers to tailor the chips based on Bangalore's designs; then Texas Instruments makes the chips. Producing a full set of chip-design drawings used to take Dallas's overburdened engineers more than a year, says Srini Rajam, managing director of Texas Instruments' Bangalore center. With Bangalore sharing the work, turnaround has been cut to four to six weeks.

Workers in India and the United States benefit from the arrangement. Since Texas Instruments opened its Bangalore branch in 1985, the company has hired about 350 software engineers in Bangalore, added 400 engineers in Dallas and Houston, and is looking to hire another forty engineers in Texas. Indian wages of between $4,000 to $10,000 a year haven't undercut those in the United States, where demand for software talent has soared. Texas Instruments pays software engineers fresh from college $40,000 in Texas, and bumps their salaries to $60,000 in about four years.

Texas Instruments' Dallas and Bangalore centers collaborate regularly, which helps customers and boosts business for the company and its workers in both nations. "We stay in contact with India a couple of times a day," says Betty Baker, a Texas Instruments software engineer in Dallas. "If we want to make sure a problem is being worked on, we send it to India at the end of the day. We can get 16 or 17 hours of coverage that way."

Motorola Inc.'s Bangalore center is considered among the city's best. In 1993, the software team earned the U.S.-based Software Engineering Institute's top rating for quality, which the Bangalore group shares with a handful of U.S. software centers that write software for the space station. The top ranking means that programmers build software systematically, so the programs can be measured for accuracy and improved upon. After the *New York Times* reported that achievement, panic ensued in the U.S. computer industry. How could low-paid workers in India get the top mark? "It was like we were at the right hand of God," jokes Roger Fordham, the British-born managing director of the Bangalore software center.

The ranking is a major achievement, but it also highlights a weakness of many of Bangalore's programmers: They're methodical to a fault. Education in India, and elsewhere in Asia, emphasizes rote learning and test taking. That method produces graduates who generally follow instructions well but rarely challenge received wisdom. In the software field, where wild dreams and weird thoughts sometimes lead to hot-selling programs, that response can be a deadly disadvantage. "What Indians like to do is follow a process," says Fordham. "If you give them a good process, they'll follow it well. If you give them a bad process, they'll follow that too."

Motorola, headquartered in Schaumburg, Illinois, assigns its Bangalore programmers to work on some of the firm's most advanced satellite and communications projects. But that's far from the norm in Bangalore.

Those who view Bangalore and the Indian software industry as a threat to U.S. workers imagine the Indians as successors to the Japanese, whose consumer electronics and autos outperformed U.S. products and created new markets dominated by Tokyo. But India is not Japan and is unlikely to repeat Tokyo's success. Even during Japan's rebuilding years, after World War II, it had the essentials of a developed nation and was guided by efficient bureaucrats. India, on the other hand, is a desperately poor nation that is trying to modernize but is being held back by bureaucrats renowned for sloth and corruption.

Before Japanese firms tried to crack the U.S. market for stereos, televisions, and autos, they refined their products in ferocious competition at home. By contrast, Indian companies rarely produce new software for local consumers. India's domestic software market is tiny—with sales of about $1 billion—and is plagued by piracy. Bangalore is more an offshore factory for the United States than a Japanese-style competitor—and is likely to remain that way. American programmers who are slow or unable to upgrade their skills will lose their jobs to Indian software factories, but U.S. software professionals who keep up with the latest technology will flourish. In software, even the Japanese have been unable to wrest the lead from U.S. companies, apart from video-game cartridges designed for Nintendo or Sega game systems.

"It's inconceivable that a company in India could rise up like Netscape and come up with a new product that sets the tone for the industry," says Prabhakar Koushik, who returned home to Bangalore after studying and researching advanced computers at Virginia Tech for eleven years. (Netscape Communications Corporation's browser lets consumers easily search the Internet.)

India's great poverty also will keep it lagging the United States. Few Indians grow up in the computer culture that has taken hold in the United States; they don't breathe computers the way many American kids do. A college professor in India makes roughly $6,000 a year; a factory worker makes less than $1,500. On those kinds of salaries, very few families can afford to buy $2,000 computers for their homes. There are thirty-nine personal computers for every 100 people in the United States; for every 100 Indians there are about two. By early 1997, the United States had 40 million regular Internet users, and the number was mushrooming; India, with a population nearly four times as large, had 30,000, and the country's sole Internet access company was turning away customers because its phone lines were jammed. India's computer use will surely grow over the next few decades, but so will America's, making it extraordinarily difficult for India and other information-age laggards to catch up.

India's greatest advantage is price, but even that edge is starting to dull. To be competitive and to compensate U.S. firms for the hassle of dealing at long distance, Bangalore's companies must bid no more than two-thirds the price that U.S. firms bid for the same software projects. But costs are escalating in Bangalore. Salaries—$5,000 a year for starting programmers, and $12,000 a year for managers—are rising by 25% a year after inflation, a much steeper curve than in the United States. To recruit and keep employees, Indian firms must offer incentives that are unknown in the United States: subsidized or free lunches, free home telephones, subsidized loans for cars and homes, free bus transport to work, and steep bonuses for sticking with the same employer for several years.

Howard Rubin, chairman of Hunter College's computer science department, compared the costs of doing computer work in India and in the United States. After making adjustments for higher U.S. productivity, Rubin figured that Indian software writers now cost about one fourth of their U.S. counterparts, but will move to about one half in a few years. Meanwhile, the costs of doing business—including buying computers, telephones, and Internet connections, and training workers—are about 50% higher in India than in the United States.

If Bangalore's success is harming U.S. programmers, there should be clear signs by now—and there aren't any. Instead, a worldwide software boom has pushed demand ahead of supply around the world, lifting salaries everywhere. The greater demand has given Indian companies a chance to move up in the U.S. market. Instead, U.S. firms and the workers they employ have stayed ahead of foreign competitors through innovation and marketing. Information technology industries have learned, from the agonies of the automobile and consumer electronics industries, the price of lethargy.

The Information Technology Association of America estimates that there are at least 190,000 unfilled jobs for computer and software workers in the United States, and it sees little hope that those slots will be filled any time soon. "The scarcest resource U.S. companies face today is not oil, coal, or copper, but skilled people," the trade association reported. Unemployment among U.S. computer scientists dipped below 2% in 1994 and hasn't risen higher since then; in the last quarter of 1996, the unemployment rate actually fell below 1% and stayed around that level through the summer of 1997.

With job shortages, software wages are rising in the United States, sometimes in double-digit leaps, after years of stagnation. TRW Inc., the giant aerospace and automotive firm, says it often has to pay bonuses of $5,000 to $10,000 just to sign new programmers. Information Management, with offices in Bangalore and Clearwater, says it increased salaries in Florida by 15% at the end of 1996, and awarded another 10% early in 1997. "People I could hire for $35,000 in the early '90s, I now have to pay $50,000 for," says Satish Sanan, the company's Indian-born president. "There's a tremendous shortage of software engineers. It's a myth that jobs will go to India."

Indeed, to crack the U.S. market, the most farsighted of Bangalore's Indian-owned companies realize that they must set up operations in the United States, despite the higher wages here. Infosys Technologies, which is ranked among India's most innovative software companies, tried marketing software from afar. In early 1996, Infosys started using its Website to give away a suite of software tools, called Websetu (*setu* means bridge in Sanskrit), that companies can use to design Internet software linked to corporate mainframes. But only two or three users a week bothered to visit the site. "We are a long way from understanding the psyche of Net customers," says N. R. Narayana Murthy, the company's chairman. Infosys is planning to set up a software development center in the United States so that it can be physically closer to customers and can better understand the local market and technology. "We have to shift the center of gravity of our thinking from here in Bangalore to where our market is," says Murthy. "We need to attract top-quality talent in the United States."

But that's the opposite of saying that Bangalore and other third-world outposts are threats to U.S. workers. As Infosys and its competitors build operations in the United States, they will hire Americans to contact customers, figure out what they need, and write the requirements for the software—all well-paying jobs. The actual software code may be written in Bangalore, but the technology will remain American-designed, and most of the jobs will remain American-based.

That appraisal now is championed by technology guru Edward Yourdon, who started the handwringing over Bangalore and other developing nations with his 1992 book, *Decline & Fall of the American Programmer.* He argued that "international competition will put American programmers out of work, just as Japanese competition put American automobile workers out of work in the 1970s." He included an illustration of an extinct dodo bird labeled, "The American programmer, circa 1999." Now, he's changed his mind. "There's a whole new wave of technology that we can take advantage of even faster than Bangalore has," he says, citing especially the Internet and multimedia computers. He has even written a new book about the current opportunities: *Rise & Resurrection of the American Programmer.*

Each year, 80,000 Indian high school students take entrance exams for the Indian Institute of Technology (IIT), the nation's premier engineering school, which has campuses in five Indian cities. Only 2,000 are selected. And each year, 60% of the IIT graduates who majored in computer-related fields leave for the United States, either to study or to work. IIT alumni account for three-fourths of the PhD degrees in engineering awarded to Indians in the United States. American companies siphon off the best graduates from other Indian universities too. Of the 55,000 Indians who graduate each year with some training in computers, U.S. companies say they'll only consider the top 10,000 for jobs.

Venugopal Puvvada is one of the minority of IIT grads who remained in India. After earning a master's degree from the IIT in Madras, he took a job at Texas Instruments in Bangalore, which he says is the sole company in India where he could fully use his training. "The percentage of

IIT graduates going to the U.S. is increasing," says the 27-year-old software engineer. "One of the reasons is money, but also there are major opportunities for study."

Immigration benefits the United States and, surprisingly, India too. For America, immigration eases low-wage competition; software firms in Bangalore and elsewhere boost wages to keep even more of their star programmers from emigrating. Already, about 20% of Bangalore's programmers switch jobs every year. Immigration also adds to America's intellectual capital, which produces innovation and jobs.

For India, the gains are more long-term. Initially, the brain-drain hurts. Microland Ltd., which builds computer networks in India, sent one of its best software engineers to work in Atlanta so he could learn more about Internet technology and train his colleagues in India. He came back for two or three months, says Pradeep Kar, the company's chairman, but then left permanently for the United States, where he could command higher wages and could better use his training.

Eventually, some of the emigrées return to India—and that helps both India and America. The returnees act as role models for Indian industry. They have improved their technical skills abroad, and have learned lessons in finance and marketing that aren't taught at home. They often take prominent positions in lobbying groups that pressure the hidebound Indian government to open the economy to wider trade and imports from America. "The new paradigm in India is the capitalist paradigm," says Indi Rajasingham, an IIT graduate who emigrated to the United States and now is forming a venture-capital fund, InterStrat Inc., to invest in Indian technology companies. "The Indian middle class sees the lifestyle of the middle class in the United States and wants to emulate it."

As Bangalore and other Asian economies prosper, they become better markets for American goods and services. Given the cultural and economic ties between Bangalore's software professionals and the United States, American names and brands have cachet. One billboard advertises the *New York Times* crossword puzzle; another, Oracle software. Levi Strauss & Co., which imports its 501 Jeans from the United States and makes other brands in India, is making a big splash downtown. A third billboard responds with reverse snob-appeal: "Sunnex Jeans: Not Made in America. Thankfully." Even the Ford Escort is a status symbol in India.

In Bangalore, Pradeep Kar's office is a mixture of India and the United States. On his bookshelf are a biography of Warren Buffett and a book by Bill Gates. Underneath is a green stone carving of Ganesha, the multiarmed Hindu elephant god of creation that is especially popular with Bangalore's software crowd. Kar's company, Microland, is one of India's fastest growing firms. It designs and constructs computer networks for India's largest banks from equipment and software made by U.S. companies; essentially, Microland is an importer and propagator of American technology. "We introduced Compaq to India," Kar says, ticking off the names of his suppliers. "We launched Netscape. We launched Sun Microsystems. We used Intel for networking."

Despite its population of nearly 1 billion people, India still is a fairly small market for consumer goods. Perhaps 10 million to 15 million people can afford to buy the goods common in American middle-class homes. India classifies another 100 million or so people as "middle class" because they have $100 a month in disposable income—enough to buy soap, watches, and toothpaste, and still save up for a washing machine. The import market for consumer goods will grow slowly because of India's great poverty and because it has only recently begun to dismantle import barriers. But India's potential as a market for U.S. goods and services is immense. A generation ago, engineers' families in Bangalore didn't own a car, a television, or even a phone. Now they have all three and are in the market for computers, software, cellular telephone equipment, and other things made by American workers.

Other once-poor nations are turning into lucrative markets for the United States as well. If China continues its rapid growth through the year 2005, U.S. exports to China will grow 20% more than its imports from Beijing, Purdue's Center for Global Trade Analysis predicts, because China's needs for infrastructure equipment and other U.S. goods will escalate as it grows wealthier.

As more Indians make enough money to buy computers, they will often turn to American-made gear. While the United States was buying $6.2 billion worth of Indian textiles, apparel, and other goods in 1996, it exported $3.3 billion worth of U.S.-made products to India. Of that export total, $177.6 million was in computers and accessories, an increase of 29% from the previous year. Software exports are growing about as fast, but their level is harder to gauge. India's National Association of Software and Service Companies estimates that U.S. software companies exported $280 million to India in 1997—a much higher figure than the U.S. estimate.

One major American gain from trade with India and with much of the developing world comes from vast projects to rebuild crumbling infrastructure and modernize antiquated telecommunications systems. Along India's western coast, 100 miles from Bangalore, two U.S. companies have been selected to build power plants to boost Bangalore's electric supply. At one site, Cogentrix Energy Inc., of Charlotte, North Carolina, is planning a 1,000-megawatt power plant. At another site, Science and Engineering Applications Corporation, of Brookville, Maryland, a firm started by a former NASA scientist who was born in India, has signed a deal with the Indian government to build a smaller power plant on a barge docked off the coast. That project would use a General Electric gas turbine built in the United States.

Similarly, Raytheon Company has a contract to build a modern airport outside of town, with runways long enough for a Boeing 747, and air-traffic systems designed and made in the United States. Hughes Network Systems, a subsidiary of General Motors Corporation, has been chosen to build and operate a modern telephone system in Bangalore, using radio-telecommunications equipment that Hughes makes in Maryland. And Motorola will supply equipment to one of Bangalore's two cellular telephone licensees. The Bangalore equipment largely will be made at Motorola's European factories, but other Motorola telecommunications projects in India will use systems designed and produced in Illinois, Texas, and elsewhere in the United States.

All these projects require permits from the Indian bureaucracy, a labyrinth that was designed by the British and refined by the Indians. Enron Corporation of Houston, for instance, was forced to renegotiate a deal to build a multibillion-dollar power plant after a new political party was voted into state office, frightening foreign investors throughout India. But the needs of Indian companies are so great that the government is under relentless pressure to approve infrastructure projects and stick to the deals.

The development of General Electric's medical-equipment business in Bangalore shows that broader trade benefits both the United States and India. GE started operations with an Indian partner in a factory near Bangalore's software houses. At first, GE used cheap Indian manufacturing wages to reduce the cost of a $25,000 ultrasound scanner that was previously made in Japan. But GE managers realized that there was a market in India, and elsewhere in the developing world, for a cheaper portable scanner that doctors could cart from village to village. GE's Bangalore operations designed and manufactured a $12,000 ultrasound unit to be as compact as a sewing machine.

Ultrasound technology is controversial in India because it can be used to identify the sex of fetuses. Some parents then choose to abort pregnancies rather than give birth to girls. (For years, villagers in patriarchal India have let newborn girls die rather than raise them. Middle-class parents have aborted female fetuses after learning their sex through fetal tests.) GE says it's illegal to use ultrasound machines in India for gender selection, and GE employees are supposed to report customers suspected of acting illegally. Controversy aside, portable ultrasounds are used to diagnose problems of the heart, breasts, and kidneys, thus expanding health care for the two-thirds of India's population who live in villages, as well as creating jobs for those who build the machines and run them.

The portable ultrasounds help U.S. workers, too. Many of the machine's computer components are imported from the United States, as is the sturdy plastic casing. GE has used the portable units to broaden the Indian market for ultrasound technology. The company provides financing for rural diagnostic centers, and it services the machines through computer hookups. As Indian physicians see what the portables can do, they better understand the value of more elaborate, U.S.-made machines. For every seven portables that GE sells in India, GE figures it exports to India one advanced ultrasound machine that is made in a Milwaukee factory where workers earn around $45,000 a year.

There's a heated debate over whether trade worsens the wage gap between skilled and unskilled workers. Most academics say trade plays a secondary role, and they name technological change as the biggest culprit. Most Americans don't believe that. By a 40% to 17% margin, for instance, Americans believe that expanded trade lowers wages in the United States, according to a *Business Week*/Harris poll taken in September 1997.

The case for trade always seems naïve. But even the most careful researchers haven't been able to find evidence that trade does much to worsen the wage gap. Robert Z. Lawrence, a Harvard trade economist, hunts for clues of trade's impact with the persistence of a paleontologist examining fossils. He reasons that if trade with low-wage countries is depressing wages in the United States, that ought to be reflected in lower prices for imports made by low-skilled foreign labor. Specifically, the price of such imports ought to be dropping faster, or at least not rising as quickly, as the price of imports made by more highly skilled labor. Lawrence finds an opposite pattern. Prices of imports made by low-skilled labor aren't dropping as fast as prices of goods made by highly skilled workers. At most, he figures trade explains only 10% of the widening of the U.S. wage gap; other economists put the figure at 20% or 30%.

There have been losses from globalization. Increased imports cost about 1.2 million U.S. manufacturing jobs between 1978 and 1990 (about 6% of the factory job total), according to academic researchers, and many of those laid-off workers have had a difficult time finding new jobs that match their old salaries. And immigration pulls down wages among unskilled workers. Since 1980, immigration of both skilled and unskilled workers has soared. Immigrants are 25% more likely to have graduate school training than Americans are, and immigrants from India are among the better-educated immigrants. But immigrants are also two to three times as likely to have failed to finish high school.

Americans who lack high school diplomas suffer economically from competition with unskilled foreigners because the supply of poorly educated workers already exceeds the number of available jobs. Unskilled immigrants make the competition worse. A study by three Harvard economists estimates that immigration is responsible for as much as half the decline in wages of high school dropouts relative to persons with high school diplomas. But the effect is heavily concentrated at the bottom of the income scale. Competition from immigration has hardly any effect on the difference in wages between high school graduates and those who have gone on to college, the Harvard study finds.

Nearly all economists agree that technological change has a far greater impact on income inequality than trade or immigration. Think about the issue in the context of Bangalore. Trade with Bangalore and other third-world outposts has done little to depress wages for American software workers, but technology has brought immense change. Until the Year 2000 problem surfaced, U.S. mainframe programmers not only couldn't get raises, they were being offered early retirement or otherwise restructured out the door. Meanwhile, programmers who were skilled in new Internet technology—"Webmasters," in computer lingo—could command fat salaries. The income gap among programmers widened.

What's clear from Bangalore is what's clear from South Carolina. Trade produces winners and losers, often in the same places. Some U.S. workers will surely find it hard to get raises because their bosses can move work to Bangalore—or merely threaten to move it. Likewise, not everyone in Bangalore approves of the rise of the software industry because of the congestion it has brought to the city.

But if India and the United States turned away from trade, it would hurt both nations. The growth of the software industry has shown skeptical Indians, raised to equate foreign investment with imperial control, how trade can boost incomes. That's a lesson that's still being learned in Asia, Latin America, and the Middle East. Meanwhile, the rise of the Indian software industry has enriched America through immigration and through new markets for its bounty. As Bangalore and America grow closer, workers in both places will prosper.

16

The End of Work?

Where the jobs of the future will come from.

In Kurt Vonnegut's novel, *Player Piano,* machines do nearly all of the work that people used to do in Ilium, New York—and they do it a lot more efficiently. The government's Reconstruction and Reclamation Corps—"Reeks and Wrecks"—provides make-work for the dispossessed. This is the final victory of automation. First, machines replace muscle, then routine work, now brainwork. Ed Harrison, a disgruntled engineer, explains the score to a college student, named Buck Young.

> "What have you got against machines?" said Buck.
> "They're slaves."
> "Well, what the heck," said Buck. "I mean they aren't people. They don't suffer. They don't mind working."
> "No. But they compete with people."
> "That's a pretty good thing, isn't it—considering what a sloppy job most people do of anything?"
> "Anybody that competes with slaves becomes a slave," said Harrison thickly.

Vonnegut's 1952 novel was inspired by what he saw a few years earlier as a publicist at General Electric Company in Schenectady, New York, a few miles from Ilium's setting. At the time, GE was developing automated machine tools to cut rotor blades for gas turbines. GE managers and engineers "spoke frankly of unhappiness that would be caused by automation," Vonnegut later said. In *Player Piano's* foreword, he wrote: "This is not a book about what is, but a book about what could be."

Vonnegut's dark vision didn't come true. Over the next forty years, GE and other big defense contractors failed to get automated machine tools to work effectively. The machines turned out to be too expensive, too complex, and too rigid to replace large numbers of workers—even though the Air Force paid the bills for many of the machines. Failure didn't stop further predictions of doom. In 1983, Robert Jastrow, a respected NASA scientist, forecast that robots would replace 25% of U.S. factory workers by the late 1990s. Not even close. The U.S. robot industry is stumbling along, selling roughly 10,000 robots a year, and crowing because its sales reached almost $1 billion in 1996. That's about one-fourth of the amount Americans spend annually on bowling.

Vonnegut's fear has dogged society since the Industrial Revolution. In each generation, social critics prophesy that technology is growing so sophisticated that it will produce massive unemployment. At best, a cadre of supereducated managers will keep their jobs overseeing the wondrous technology, while the rest of humanity is jobless; at worst, all of humankind will be enslaved by machines. But the doomsayers have all been wrong—and they will continue to be wrong. Somehow, modern economies—the U.S. economy, in particular—produce far more jobs than they destroy, and they produce jobs at different skill levels.

In 1942, economist Joseph A. Schumpeter described the modern capitalist system as buffeted by "the perennial gale of creative destruction." By that, he meant that powerful technologies destroy outmoded organizations and the jobs associated with them, and create new ones. Without destruction, creation isn't possible. Switching to a metaphor from biology, he talked of "industrial mutation . . . that incessantly revolutionizes the economic structure *from within,* incessantly destroying the old one, incessantly creating a new one."

In terms of jobs, technological destruction begets creation. Between 1909 and 1919, carriage-making employment declined to 26,000 from 70,000, and auto industry jobs soared to 394,000 from 85,000. Likewise, telegraph industry employment, which peaked at 87,000 workers in 1929, declined to only 24,000 workers in 1970. By then, the telephone industry had created 536,000 new jobs.

More recently, the telephone industry has been pummeled. The Justice Department broke up AT&T in 1984, and ended Ma Bell's monopoly on telephone service. Since then, telephone industry employment has fallen by 132,000. But many new communications services have arisen; the cellular telephone industry alone has added 84,000 jobs. The communications industry, which includes telephones, mobile communications, cable TV, and satellite services, employs about 60,000 more workers now than it did when AT&T was broken apart. Employment is bound to continue to grow during the next few decades as projects to ring the world with low-cost computer and communications satellites loft into orbit.

Some broad employment trends are sure to continue. Thanks to technology and improved productivity, America will continue to devote fewer hours to growing food and making things, so manufacturing and agricultural jobs will continue to represent a smaller percentage of a growing workforce. That's a source of worry for defenders of the factory or the family farm, but, for Americans as a whole, it isn't a cause for alarm. America won't run out of jobs if there are relatively fewer farmers or assembly workers; rather, the jobs will be different from those we can envision today. Just as greater wealth allows the nation today to employ people in service jobs unimagined several decades ago—reading specialists, managers of video stores, intensive-care nurses, website designers, birth coaches, software reviewers—new service jobs will replace old factory jobs in the years ahead. Workers don't have to *make* something to get well-paying, productive jobs.

With the possible exception of science-fiction writers, no one foresaw today's job-creating technologies. (Jules Verne forecast submarines and moon landings; Arthur C. Clarke hatched the idea of global communications satellites.) And no one can accurately foretell tomorrow's opportunities. But the past teaches us to be optimistic. Consider the Internet, which grew out of a 1969 Pentagon research project to link scientists at different universities so they could share what were then expensive and scarce computers. For decades, only a few computer wizards owed their livelihood to the arcane network.

In the 1990s, after several inventions made it fairly easy for hobbyists to use, the Internet burst into the public consciousness. One of those inventions created the World Wide Web, which lets users jump from computer site to computer site by clicking on words highlighted in different colors. Then came web browsers, which allowed webheads to search the Internet by typing in phrases and clicking on different computer-screen boxes.

Nearly thirty years after the Internet's birth, net surfing has become an American home-entertainment craze. Thousands of companies have plugged their own computer networks, packed with information, into the Internet. All these activities have spawned jobs. The Global Internet Project, an offshoot of a computer trade group, estimates that the Internet created 760,000 jobs in the United States in 1996—an estimate that may be on the high side, but not outrageously so. Separate surveys in New York, Boston, and San Francisco have estimated that about 200,000 people in those metropolitan areas alone work in so-called new media companies, which design web pages and other software for the Internet.

The job estimates don't include jobs destroyed by the Internet—and there certainly will be many. As more people shop on the Internet, fewer salesclerks will be needed at suburban malls. As webheads spend time chatting with friends on the Net, they will watch less television and read fewer conventional magazines. That's bound to affect employment at traditional media. But big job losses won't occur overnight, so workers will have time to adjust. Just as it took the Internet decades before it started creating large numbers of jobs, so it will take a long time before the technology's destructive impact is clear. Old jobs have a way of hanging on. Since World War II, books have had to compete for the public's leisure time with radio, television, computers, and the Internet, but book-industry employment has more than doubled, to 121,000 workers since 1947.

In Silicon Valley, the home of many of the world's advances in personal computer technology, Cisco Systems Inc. is scrambling to keep up with the Internet's explosive growth. Founded in 1984 by two Stanford professors who figured out how to connect incompatible computers during the days when only professors cared about the Internet, Cisco now makes the specialized computer and communications equipment that underlies computer networks. Like pipes and valves carrying water across a city, Cisco makes the Internet's plumbing, which carries information across the globe. (Nevertheless, Cisco's rise has been so sudden that Cisco's marketers worry that the company is confused with Crisco, the shortening.)

Based in San Jose, California, Cisco is a job-producing machine. In 1991, Cisco employed 505; now it employs 10,700. Many of the jobs Cisco is filling—Internet appliance managers, corporate-data warehouse architects—didn't exist five years ago. Cisco isn't like Vonnegut's Ilium, where managers and engineers have the only decent jobs. Cisco engineers with a few years of experience make $55,000, but so do other employees who do much different work. As Cisco grows, it must fill sales, marketing, financial, manufacturing, and administrative jobs where common sense and business sense are valued as highly as computer sense.

Cisco's workers come from vastly different backgrounds. Mukund Mohan, a 24-year-old engineer, is a computer blueblood. He emigrated to the United States from Bangalore, India, where his father is a senior executive at one of India's largest computer firms, and his mother has an engineering degree. Ric Bednar, a 31-year-old engineer, is a blue-collar transplant. He hails from Ukiah, California, a small lumber town down on its luck. His father does maintenance work at the local hospital, where his mother once worked as a physical therapist. Mohan's parents expected him to become an engineer; Bednar drove beer trucks for three years after high school before deciding to go to college and study computing.

At Cisco, the two of them helped develop the electronic-commerce software that Cisco uses to do business over the Internet. Customers use the software to peruse Cisco products, order them, track their shipments, and figure out how to assemble them into a network. Mohan, the Bangalore native, writes software to encrypt communications, so Cisco's customers can feel safe ordering parts and discussing their plans over the Internet. Bednar, the Californian, designs the databases necessary to take orders and track shipments. The system has been so successful that Cisco figures about 30% of its sales now come over the Internet, and it hopes eventually to double that percentage.

The success of Cisco's electronic-commerce system creates other jobs—some technical, some not. David Evans, a 30-year-old information analyst with slicked-back hair, calls himself Cisco's "technological evangelist." He interviews hundreds of companies that want Cisco to buy their latest innovation. Now, he's hot on so-called push technology, which would let Cisco send information from its website to selected computer screens. Cisco salespeople and customers wouldn't have to read about Cisco's latest products in computer magazines; Cisco could electronically "push" press releases to them over the Internet instead.

Not far from Evans's office, Anupam Rastogi, another Indian expatriate, is figuring out how to comb through sales orders stored on Cisco's vast databases to uncover valuable marketing trends. Are sales surging in the Midwest? Are smaller companies more willing to buy over the Internet than larger firms? Rastogi can help Cisco's sales crew decide where to concentrate. "The challenge is: How do you pull out information that was entered into [Cisco's databases] for different purposes?" he says.

Many of the jobs created at Cisco don't require special computer skills. Secretaries, called "admins" at Cisco (short for administrative assistants), make between $35,000 and $50,000 a year. They do pretty much what secretaries have always done; they act as right hands for overburdened managers. Felicia Schulter, a tall, slim secretary to a Cisco senior vice president, answers his phones, gets him coffee, and sometimes even retrieves his car from the car wash.

But other parts of her job reflect the changes in technology over the past twenty years. She doesn't have to learn shorthand; instead, she must know how to handle software to make slide presentations. Before an important customer visits, she'll search the Internet for information on the customer's firm, to help her boss customize his presentation.

Cisco also hires generalists for jobs that sound technical, but really aren't. Sales engineers sketch how a network can be put together from Cisco products. But Cisco insiders say these jobs don't require real engineering expertise, any more than school janitors need engineering degrees to be called custodial engineers. Rather, sales engineers consult Cisco's electronic-commerce software to keep up on new products, see which ones work well together, and feed that information to salespeople who call on customers. Jim Grubb, a Cisco product manager, calls Cisco's products "nerd knobs," and says there are so many of them that "it's impossible for salesmen to keep up with them all."

Grubb, an ex-computer salesman with a hearty laugh, is overseeing development of a new Cisco Internet product. Only half the people on his development team are engineers; the rest are publicists, marketers, writers, and salespeople. As Cisco grows, so does its needs for diverse workers. Even the best software can't automate the different talents needed to turn an idea for a new product into a hit.

Figuring out precisely how technology will affect workers is a dauntingly complex task, and no one does it well. Karl Marx saw technology as a capitalist tool for eliminating rebellious employees. "It would be possible," he wrote in 1867, "to write a history of the inventions, made since 1830, for the sole purpose of supplying capital with weapons against the revolts of the working class." In some cases, Marx was right. British textile and apparel makers developed new cotton-spinning machines and textile-printing machines to lessen their dependence on skilled workers who were often unionized.

But technology isn't always an instrument of oppression; some new technologies bolster the role of workers. In the mid-1800s, faced with a civilian labor shortage, the U.S. Army perfected the so-called American system of manufacturing, which used interchangeable parts to manufacture guns. Other U.S. manufacturers copied the technique to make sewing machines, bicycles, and typewriters, and ultimately filled factories with workers. Other innovations spring from whimsy and imagination. Dedicated amateurs were among the first to realize the potential of radio to become a broadcast medium in the 1920s, and of personal computers to become business and entertainment tools in the 1980s. Both industries eventually created millions of jobs.

If any source should be able to accurately predict technology's effects on labor, it is the U.S. Bureau of Labor Statistics (BLS), the government's premier compiler of information about jobs and prices. The Bureau regularly makes predictions about employment prospects ten or fifteen years ahead— just a few seconds in the tick-tock of history. But it has done a woeful job, missing some of the most important social and economic changes of the past thirty-five years. The Bureau underestimated the rise of female participation in the workplace, the growth of older college students, and the broad increase in U.S. exports. Computer technology flummoxed the agency. It didn't foresee the explosive growth in demand for computer-trained workers, or the slide in demand for garment workers, who were replaced by labor-saving machinery.

With admirable candor, a 1992 Bureau report concluded: "BLS projections are too conservative. All occupations correctly projected to have the most rapid employment growth were underprojected in terms of the magnitude of that growth. Furthermore, those occupations correctly projected to decline or to have slow employment growth generally had greater declines or grew more slowly than projected."

How will technology affect jobs in the future? A number of social critics argue that computer technology will reverse the formula of creative-destruction. From now on, they say, technology will destroy more jobs than it creates. By their reading of history, IBM's chess-playing champion, Deep Blue, is just the latest symbol of the age of the thinking machine. As software is able to replicate human thought, the argument goes, there will be less work for people to do.

Technology critic Jeremy Rifkin predicts massive unemployment in his book, *The End of Work.* "The new computer-based technologies promise a replacement of the human mind itself," he says, "substituting thinking machines for human beings across the entire gamut of economic activity." Rifkin, a longtime foe of biotechnology research, is often derided in technology circles as a know-nothing, but his arguments resonate among some high-tech practitioners.

In a panel discussion sponsored by *IEEE Spectrum,* a magazine written for engineers, Rustum Roy, a Pennsylvania State University professor of materials science, argued that "with the computer revolution, you are not going to see some other new industry come up to use up whomever is put out of a job. There is no other new technology on the horizon that can conceivably absorb those people. So this time, the jobs that are lost are not coming back."

But nothing about the computer suggests that its effects will be different from those of other powerful technologies since the Industrial Revolution—steam power, railroads, electricity, automobiles—that produced more jobs than they destroyed. Computers don't actually replicate thinking. Essentially, computers are sorting and calculating machines; whatever minds are, they aren't that. Practitioners of a branch of computer science known as artificial intelligence have predicted thinking machines for fifty years and are still fifty years away from producing them.

Theodore Roszak, a critic of technology who shares Rifkin's concern about the effects of automation, dismisses the thinking-machine metaphor. The mind does far more than process data, he argues in *The Cult of Information.* "'Common sense' is a sprawling, lifelong blur of cumulative, largely ineffable personal experience that defies formal representation. A consensus may at last be forming that true intelligence embraces the entire bewildering pattern of learning and behavior called 'being human.'" It's the intuitive, commonsense part of human behavior that creates technologies like computers, and then figures out how to use those technologies in ways that create new opportunities for work.

America, more than any of its rivals, will be able to depend on innovation to produce jobs in the future, just as it has in the past. The United States is at the forefront of many of the technologies that are likely to produce the industries—and jobs—of the future, including the development of new materials, the miniaturization of motors and sensors, and the growth of wireless communications. Technology's job-producing potential is exemplified by the merging of two fields in which the United States has a broad lead over global competitors: information technology and biology.

At the moment, the juncture of biology and computers is astoundingly complex, dominated by scientists with postdoctoral degrees—roughly comparable to Internet technology twenty years ago. But if the technology pays off in new ways to diagnose and treat disease, and better ways to understand how the body functions, many jobs will be produced at many skill levels.

The merger of computers and biology is presently focused on decoding the 100,000 or so genes in the human body, which carry inherited traits. Scientists want to know the precise structure of those genes, what their functions are, and which genes are altered when diseases such as cancer spread through the body. Eric Lander, a senior researcher at the Whitehead Institute, a biotechnology research center in Cambridge, Massachusetts, compares the efforts to categorize genes to the formulation of the periodic table of elements in the nineteenth century—a scientific enterprise that spawned the chemical industry.

As one example, Lander foresees using genetic information to run regular cancer screenings, which would produce more work for lab technicians. "We'll be doing 1,000 times the number of assays [diagnostic tests]," he says. "Even if we increase the productivity of technicians by a factor of 20, we'll have an increasing number of jobs."

As biologists are learning more about genes, they are becoming overloaded with information. That's where computer technology comes in. "There's no way to follow the amounts and variations [in genes] on a piece of paper on a yellow pad," says Lander. "That's an information-technology problem. Information technology meets up with biology because, at heart, biology is driven by three billion letters of DNA, which specify 100,000 genes. We need to understand the relationships among those genes and the relationships [of genes] concerning their susceptibility toward disease." Only computers can handle such a vast number of gene combinations and comparisons.

In Silicon Valley, about a mile from Stanford University, Incyte Pharmaceuticals Inc. is a pioneer in the merging of biology and computers, which it calls bio-informatics. Every day, samples of human tissue, packed in dry ice, arrive at Incyte via FedEx. Technicians grind up the tissue and extract the genes by running the material through automated machines; then they analyze the results on color computer screens. If a tissue is from a prostate tumor, for instance, Incyte tries to determine which genes are active in the tumor and which aren't. In that way, scientists can eventually take a sample of a patient's genes and compare it against a prostate sample to see whether the patient is at risk for developing cancer. Incyte technicians then add the information to the company's vast database.

Many of Incyte's 450 employees have scientific or computing backgrounds. But, as the company grows, says Randy Scott, Incyte's president, the skills involved become more routine. Incyte is hiring dozens of biology majors at local colleges, at salaries of about $30,000 a year plus stock options, to sift through the company's databases and check that the data are accurate. Lab technicians running the gene-analysis lab's highly automated equipment don't need four-year degrees. "We're building an organization with entry-level talent for which we won't need biology degrees," Scott says. "We'd hire from two-year schools."

As Incyte develops its technology, it needs workers with skills that are far different from those of biologists and geneticists. Consider Ingrid Akerblom, the company's director of data analysis, who is using animation to make sense of the vast amount of information Incyte is collecting in its computers. As she scrolls through the company's "life sequence" database to look for information on prostate tumors, the computer screen shows her a list of all the tissue samples that might have relevant information; there are hundreds of genes listed. Even a dedicated and thorough scientist has trouble figuring out which genes to investigate first and how they're related to others.

So, instead of looking at the raw data, Akerblom is trying to figure out how to represent genes with computer graphics. One image presents genes as rows of colored boxes. Splash a treatment on the cells, and some of the boxes gently float upward—indicating that some of the genes are responding to the treatment—and some float downward. By visualizing the genes and representing them via animation, a researcher can make better sense of the data.

As bio-informatics grows, it will depend more and more on artistic talents and visual imagination. These aren't necessarily technical jobs; indeed, today's 12-year-olds hooked on Nintendo 64s may be the ones best suited for the visualization jobs of the future. "Graphics people are incredibly valuable in a world that's going from digital to visual," says Randy Scott, Incyte's president.

That's the case on the Internet as well; new-media companies spend much of their time trying to design compelling graphics and websites. Just as the printers of the eighteenth century defined the basic layout of newspapers through slugs of type and lead, new-media designers now are trying to define the news and entertainment formats of the twenty-first century. To the extent they succeed, the new technologies will gain a following and spawn new opportunities for employment. That's how the jobs of the future will be created, just as they were in the past.

17

What's to Be Done

How to ensure broadly shared prosperity.

T hroughout this book, we have described how changes in technology, education, and globalization are combining to produce prosperity for America's middle class. If we're right, the late 1990s will mark the beginning of an era of broadly shared prosperity. The rate of economic growth will accelerate from the sluggish pace that has plagued the United States since 1973. The added wealth will be more widely shared as the wage gap between more educated and less educated Americans diminishes. We're at an economic turning point.

We could be wrong, of course. A debilitating war could wreck the global trading system. The Federal Reserve could stumble. Financial markets around the world could crash, provoking a global economic crisis. China and India could transform themselves into threats to newly complacent American companies and workers, the way Japan Inc. threatened in the 1980s. Or, technology could boost the demand for skilled workers more rapidly than community colleges and other institutions can turn them out, worsening the economic divisions in America. In *Virtual Light,* written in 1993 by novelist William Gibson, the middle class vanishes by the year 2005; a rich, powerful techno-elite is served and protected by the rest of society. Bicycle messengers have jobs only because elites worry that hackers can intercept messages sent over computer networks.

We think Gibson, like Henry Adams, Kurt Vonnegut, and other pessimists who have stared into the future, is wrong about what lies ahead. We are profoundly encouraged by what we have seen. When an organization as hidebound as the U.S. Army takes the lead in modifying computers so average Americans can use them, the rest of society will follow. When a region as hostile to outsiders as upcountry South Carolina prospers because it opens itself to foreign trade and investment, that lesson will spread. When institutions as slighted as community colleges transform themselves into economic escalators for the middle class, more Americans will climb aboard to get the skills necessary to find better paying jobs. When companies as stodgy as Miller Brewing flourish because they trust their workers, other companies will take note.

Most of all, we are confident that the middle class will make the best use of the new opportunities. Larry Hanson did. The 54-year-old factory worker joined Allen-Bradley Company in Milwaukee straight out of high school, and worked at one mind-numbing job after another. Supervisors oversaw his every move as he bolted screws onto motor starters. "I vegetated for years," he says. "I'd do the same thing 3,000 times a day."

When Allen-Bradley decided to open its spiffy circuit board manufacturing center, which follows the Miller model of trusting workers, Hanson lobbied furiously for a job, even though it required more work. For three years, he took college courses at a Milwaukee engineering school during his off-hours, and he studied math with Allen-Bradley tutors during lunch. Now, Allen-Bradley demands more of him than of others in the factory. He and his coworkers learn different assembly skills and decide how to schedule production. But Hanson has thrived. His favorite task is the most challenging one. Using a microscope and electronic test equipment, he figures out why some circuit boards are defective and recommends how to fix them. Allen-Bradley benefits from higher productivity, and Hanson receives higher pay; he's now making $18 an hour, the factory's top rate.

What can be done to enhance the odds that the next chapter of American economic history will be a happy one for the American middle class? We offer some ways to ensure that the promising trends in technology, education, and globalization evolve as we predict. We aim our suggestions largely at the federal government because it is a major player in each of the economic forces we've examined, and because only the government, for all its faults, has a responsibility to improve the welfare of all citizens. For well over a century, from the land-grant colleges of the nineteenth century to the most progressive community colleges of today, government has provided, shaped, and financed education. For at least as long, government has also underwritten the development of some of the technologies that have most improved the lives of Americans—telegraphy, railroads, jet travel, inoculation against disease. In trade, governments make the rules, and only government can protect the victims—the people who cannot adapt as quickly as the economy changes.

Washington is usually divided between those who favor government activism and those who don't. We are on the activist side. We agree with political writer E. J. Dionne that government action can help resolve the irony that "a capitalist society depends on non-capitalist values in order to hold together and prosper." To lift the living standards of those in the middle of the middle class, the government must sometimes provide subsidies and intervene in the market.

We learned a lot about the direction in which government should move from an emissary from Vice President Dan Quayle, who was no fan of big government. In the early 1990s, Rand Kehl, an idealistic Air Force major assigned to Quayle's Council on Competitiveness, asked to meet us at *The Wall Street Journal*. The Competitiveness Council was a small White House agency that had a well-deserved reputation as toady for big business. Gucci-shoed lobbyists would enlist Quayle aides to secretly derail proposed environmental or safety regulations. President Clinton abolished the council shortly after he took office.

Kehl didn't want to talk about regulation. Instead, he said he wanted to "pick our brains" for an idea he had for a national crusade. During the Bush presidency, economic growth was so slack that it would have taken a century to double living standards. Why, Kehl wondered, weren't people outraged? Why did it have to take that long? Why couldn't living standards double in a single twenty-five-year generation, as they had during the Golden Age after World War II? Then he came to the reason for his visit: How would a White House initiative to double living standards be received by the press?

We politely told him that it wasn't our job to give such advice, and we didn't have much to give anyhow. But the memory of the meeting stayed with us. He was asking the right questions, though the Bush

Administration never sought to answer them. We propose a variation on the major's theme. Doubling living standards in a single generation of twenty-five years is implausible because it would require an unrealistically rapid increase in productivity; we don't expect a quick return to the Golden Age.

But the federal government can and should make doubling living standards the overarching goal of economic policy, and make sure that most Americans are included. The government ought to spend taxpayer money promoting policies that raise productivity and foster wage equality—and resist tax, trade, spending, and regulatory policies that don't advance those goals. It's a simple principle, but it has broad implications. Politicians pay lip service to it, but it rarely seems to guide their actions.

Better education—and more of it—is essential if the middle class is to prosper in the decades ahead. Education packs a double economic wallop. First, it helps the economy grow faster. By augmenting the skills and knowledge of the workforce, it quickens the pace at which productivity improves. Second, education counteracts the forces of inequality. By enlarging the supply of educated workers, who are most in demand, and reducing the supply of less educated workers, it narrows the wage gap.

Community colleges are, for many Americans, a bridge from yesterday's education to tomorrow's good jobs. The successful colleges work because they are closely attuned to the changing demands of the local labor markets; they add or drop courses as students' and employers' interests change. Through broad efforts in remedial education, community colleges also prepare students who have high school diplomas but aren't ready to do college-level work. This often-undervalued contribution has enormous payoffs to students and to society at large.

All this, of course, takes money. Community colleges should get more of it. Today, students pay about 20% of community college budgets. State and local governments pay about 60%, and various federal and private sources account for the remainder. Where taxpayers have a choice, as they do in referenda in Cleveland, they generally favor spending more on community colleges.

Some state governments foolishly are considering cutting back. Prodded by the governor, the head of the Alabama Commission on Higher Education proposed, in July 1997, to pare state funding for community colleges by $27.5 million (16%) and eliminate all funding for remedial education. A public outcry blocked the move. Massachusetts is considering a much wiser course. It is thinking about reducing or even eliminating tuition at community colleges in the hope of drawing more low-income students.

Government's role in financing and shaping education, particularly higher education, is long established. The Ordinance of 1785 set aside land for a school in every township in new territories west of Pennsylvania. On the eve of the Civil War, Congress authorized land grants to the states to establish colleges. More recently, nearly eight million returning veterans used the GI Bill to go to college after World War II.

Today's politicians, President Clinton in particular, are beginning to recognize the value of community colleges. The President appropriately sees the federal government's role primarily as a source of student aid. But the government should be smarter about how it spends its money. Despite a torrent of right-minded rhetoric, the President led the country astray in 1997 with his "HOPE scholarship," which the Republicans in Congress accepted, in order to get, in return, the tax cuts they so badly wanted.

Subsidizing college tuition bills for upper middle-class and affluent families may be successful politics, but it is lousy policy. The HOPE scholarship essentially is a tax credit that provides up to $1,500 a year toward tuition bills for the first two years of college, and a less generous credit for subsequent years of school. The new tax breaks give nothing to families with incomes so low that they don't pay any taxes, but will be offered to families with annual incomes as high as $110,000, many of whom would have sent their children to college anyhow. The result: The government is devoting $35 billion over five years to lift college attendance, but it isn't concentrating on the families where it would make the most difference—those with incomes below $40,000. Even worse, the design of the program could encourage colleges to raise their tuition charges, undoing much of the potential for luring more students.

Instead, the federal government should concentrate on making attendance easier for those who wouldn't otherwise go to college. Teenagers from the best-off 25% of American families are three times as likely to go to college as those in the worst-off 25%, and the gap has been widening since the late 1970s. The best way to increase college attendance among young people from the bottom half of American families is to expand and restructure the federal government's 35-year-old scholarship program, known since 1980 as Pell grants, and named for their advocate, Senator Claiborne Pell of Rhode Island. Despite some added funding in 1997, the maximum grant—now $3,000 a year—hasn't come close to matching the increase in college tuition, fees, room-and-board charges, and book prices since 1980.

Pell grants and other federal student-aid programs also need to be simplified so the average family can understand them. To apply for Pell grants today, students must fill out forms that look and feel like tax returns. Even after completing the form, students and their parents don't know how much money they're going to get from the government. That important bit of information comes only after the form is processed; it depends on a family's size, income, and assets, among other things, as well as the tuition at the targeted college.

Applicants must wrestle with language that would baffle a tax accountant. "The information you report is used in a formula, established by the U.S. Congress, that calculates your Expected Family Contribution, an amount you and your family are expected to contribute toward your education," the Education Department tells students. "If your Expected Family Contribution is below a certain amount, you'll be eligible for a Federal Pell Grant, assuming you meet all other eligibility requirements. Your financial aid administrator calculates your Cost of Attendance, and subtracts the amount. . . ." This is absurd. Americans can find out with a single phone call how large a mortgage they can get; surely the government can do the same for scholarships.

Giving students the money to pay for college education is the first step toward making the market in education work. But it isn't enough. Students also need help in weeding out the good community college programs from the bad. Everyone understands the value of a Yale Law School degree or a Harvard MBA, but what about the value of a pharmacist's assistant program at Cuyahoga Community College?

Issuing nationally accepted certificates of competence would help. In health care, the government or professional organizations run examinations that certify that recent graduates are qualified to practice dental hygiene and respiratory therapy. It's no coincidence that health care is one place where community colleges have met with enormous success; 65% of beginning nurses and allied health care professionals are trained by community colleges. Well-conceived and frequently updated standards and certification programs are a potent tool and could be expanded to almost any technical field, from auto mechanics to database management software.

Certificates establish a minimum standard that each program must meet. Community colleges should be required to provide a record of how many of their students pass certification tests. If applicants see that graduates are flunking the licensing exams, the programs won't survive. Certificates also give employers some assurance that a job applicant has achieved a certain level of competence, no matter how obscure the community college that he or she attended. In some fields and regions, community colleges will be forced to compete with other educational institutions or private companies offering courses designed to teach students what they need to get their certificates. That sort of competition will keep community colleges improving.

To prosper in today's labor market, many workers have to continue training and education later in life. The federal government annually spends $7.5 billion on various training programs, but it wastes a lot of that money because of cumbersome rules and needless duplication of services. In 1995, the General Accounting Office counted 163 separate federal training programs. In most of them, administrators and auditors spend a lot of time and money to make sure that training goes only to those for whom each program is intended. For example, one program is aimed at workers hurt by the Clean Air Act, another at those hurt by the North American Free Trade Agreement, and yet another for generically "dislocated workers."

The Clinton Administration had the right idea in 1996 when it proposed rolling seventy job-training programs into one, and giving unemployed and low-income workers "skill grants" or vouchers to buy training, just as the federal government gives Pell grants or scholarships so students can "buy" the college education they want. "The point is, it doesn't matter why you lost your job," former Labor Secretary Robert Reich said at the time. "If you lost your job, you should be able to get skills necessary for the next job." The proposal has languished in Congress; it should be passed.

Education is the long-run answer to the forces of inequality that have driven a wedge through American society. But it won't be enough to lift *every* American's living standards. Education takes a long time to pay off, and it can't rescue every worker left behind as the speed of technology and globalization makes some of us obsolete. Only the government can protect those who cannot adapt quickly, and it should. Among other things, that means making sure that the minimum wage isn't continually eroded by inflation as it was in the 1980s; protecting the right of workers to organize unions; and maintaining a tax code that takes more from the winners in the economy, the ones who can afford to pay more.

Dividing the economic spoils more evenly won't ensure a better life for the American middle class. A faster-growing economy that creates more wealth will be required. Technology, particularly computer technology, will be crucial. Prosperity depends on pushing even harder to discover and make use of new technology—not on giving way to fears that automation will destroy more jobs than it creates.

In many ways, the U.S. system of technological development works fine. America's research institutions are the envy of the world. Also unrivaled is America's venture capital system, which provides money and management to entrepreneurs who can exploit new technologies. New jobs and new industries are created regularly. The political message from Silicon Valley, Research Triangle, and the other clusters of technological creativity is: Leave us alone. (Except, of course, for the tax breaks high-tech industries regularly try to push through Congress.)

Some strengths of the U.S. system create conceits and mask problems. Federal support for research and development has helped create new industries, including satellite communications, nuclear energy, and biotechnology. Federal funding for R&D remains vast, at $70 billion a year, but the enterprise isn't as healthy as it seems. After accounting for inflation, federal spending isn't any greater today than it was in the mid-1960s, and most of the money is still earmarked for military projects, despite the demise of the Soviet Union. Compared to its main technological rivals, Germany and Japan, the United States now devotes a smaller percentage of its national income to civilian research and development, though civilian technology is generally more advanced.

A steady rise in industry spending on technology has somewhat ameliorated the problem. And the federal government wisely has boosted R&D funding for universities, which have a much better record than government laboratories for spawning useful technologies and transferring the knowledge and skills to industry. Federally funded university research has identified the functions of thousands of human genes and helped create the growing biotechnology industry. Gene research has already led to new ways to diagnose disease, as we have seen, and, over the next decade or two, may lead to cures.

Federal funding for research and development (R&D) should be increased. The best way to measure the effort that the government puts into R&D is to compare it to the size of the overall economy. Today, the federal government spends an amount equal to 0.4% of the gross domestic product on civilian R&D, the lowest percentage since 1960.

Equally important is how the money is spent. Since World War II, there has been a broad consensus that the federal government ought to fund basic research because there is little incentive for individual companies to search for answers to fundamental mysteries of science. Similarly, few dispute that the government ought to pay for research needed by the military.

But there has been a bitter debate about whether the government should pay for commercial research too. The Reagan and Bush White Houses and, more recently, the Republican-controlled Congress tried to limit such spending, arguing that private industry ought to be responsible for investing in anything that might have market appeal. They listed a series of boondoggles where the federal government invested billions of dollars to produce commercial breakthroughs, only to fail: the supersonic transport; the synthetic-fuels project, to squeeze oil substitutes from coal; the Clinch River nuclear plant, for using nuclear-weapons material to make electricity. All were losers that were kept alive by lawmakers who wanted to save jobs.

But government can be too frightened of failure. The federal government has a long history of technology investment that has produced great advances in living standards. In 1843, Congress appropriated $30,000—about $500,000 in today's dollars—to rig an experimental telegraph line from Baltimore to Washington. Not one to squander the opportunity, Samuel F. B. Morse made sure the system was ready for the presidential conventions, which were both held in Baltimore that year, and was able to report the nominations before anyone else.

Just as entrepreneurs take risks, so should the government. The arguments over the type of research the government should back frequently involve meaningless distinctions. At various times, the Internet has been considered basic research, military, or commercial—and sometimes all three. The ubiquitous computer network sprang from the mind of a research psychologist working for the Pentagon in the early 1960s, J.C.R. Licklider, who envisioned what he called, half-jokingly, an Intergalactic Computer Network. The Pentagon was interested, in part, because it wanted a communications system able to withstand nuclear attack; a decentralized computer network fit that requirement. Scientists also were intrigued by the idea of making telecommunications systems more efficient by breaking apart messages into "packets" of information that could be routed through different paths around the nation and reassembled by computer at the destination.

Although that technology had obvious commercial implications, the two leaders in computers and communications, AT&T and IBM, weren't interested in participating. IBM argued that computers weren't cheap enough to make such a network affordable.

Instead, the Pentagon's Advanced Research Projects Agency and the civilian National Science Foundation nurtured the Internet for more than twenty-five years. In 1994, enough companies finally saw the Internet's potential, and management of the system was turned over to commercial communications companies. The federal government continues to support research on higher-speed communications and software that could boost the Internet's efficiency. Meanwhile, thousands of companies are trying to use the Internet to sell goods, information, and entertainment, which will make life easier for many Americans as well as improve productivity and create new jobs—the very definition of rising living standards.

The federal government should act as a catalyst for advanced technologies that may have commercial application in future decades. Research projects should be kept small, whenever possible, so they don't become too hard to kill if the technology doesn't pan out. Commercial partners should be sought when there's a chance a project could lead to profitable products. And the government should focus on technologies that serve its special needs as well as broader goals. When the government acts as a customer, not simply as a dispenser of funds, it's usually a sharper buyer and is less swayed by pork-barrel politics. The federal government didn't develop jet engines simply because it was interested in aeronautical engineering, but because it needed faster fighter aircraft. Civilian jets followed quickly afterward.

The model pioneered by the Pentagon's Advanced Research Projects Agency should be followed: Create a community of researchers who meet to discuss their individual projects and critique each other's work. Information sharing is as important as funding; it was crucial in the agency's ability to develop the Internet, advanced computers, simulators, and other technologies that are now used widely in the civilian world.

Along with education and technology, globalization is the third major force that is critical for the betterment of the middle class. It is also the most politically precarious. Opposition is understandable; globalization relentlessly separates out economic winners from losers, sometimes creating prosperity and pain in the same place.

Fighting globalization almost always backfires. After Britain invented the modern textile factory in the 1770s, the government tried to block foreign competition by prohibiting artisan emigration until 1825 and forbidding most machinery exports until 1842. People and technology slipped out anyway. France set up its first cotton mill in 1778, the United States had one in 1791, and even India had one in 1817 when a British trading firm shipped a modern plant to Calcutta.

Pat Buchanan and Ross Perot would have the United States return to the policies of the Gilded Age at the end of the nineteenth century, when Congress erected high tariffs to block imports and to give U.S. manufacturers a protected market. Those tariffs boosted the growth of American firms that made cotton cloth and textile machinery. But J. Bradford DeLong, a University of California at Berkeley economist, notes that the tariffs also increased the cost of the machinery used to build railroads and factories, and probably reduced overall growth.

Since it became gospel that high tariffs deepened the Great Depression, American presidents have fought successfully in Congress for trade liberalization. But the battles have grown harsher over the past 15 years as a coalition of labor, environmental, and consumer groups has rallied opposition in the House of Representatives. Presidential victories have come at a steep price: the truth. To sell the North American Free Trade Agreement (NAFTA) with Mexico and Canada, and the world trade pact negotiated in Geneva, the Bush and Clinton Administrations greatly exaggerated the number of jobs that would be created in the United States. As the extent of their hyperbole became clear, public support for future trade expansion diminished further.

In the fall of 1997, for the first time since President Franklin D. Roosevelt started cutting tariffs in 1934, the White House failed to win

Congressional approval of a measure to liberalize trade significantly. Rather than suffer certain defeat in the House, President Clinton withdrew his request for authority to negotiate new trade initiatives, including the expansion of NAFTA to include other Latin American countries. Many lawmakers said they opposed the trade proposal because they had been deceived by grandiose White House claims during the fight over NAFTA.

The first principle of globalization must be candor. The U.S. economy is so vast that each trade pact adds only a little to growth; the benefits are cumulative. As markets for U.S. goods and services expand abroad, the companies that can feed those markets grow; but those that can't feed them wither. Overall, workers benefit because the stronger companies create more and better jobs than the weaker ones lose. And consumers benefit because they can buy imported VCRs, tomatoes, and silk dresses at lower prices. That may not be an easy argument to sell to a skeptical public, but it's a truthful one that may restore some credibility to free-trade proponents.

Labor unions and their allies in Congress, such as House Minority Leader Richard Gephardt, a Missouri Democrat, go too far when they propose a "social tariff" or other trade restrictions on countries that don't enforce environmental or labor standards. Such sanctions would increase the price of imported goods so steeply that U.S. consumers and industrializing nations would be hurt.

Instead, lawmakers ought to concentrate on passing laws to establish worker-retraining vouchers. That way, when workers in places like Iva, South Carolina lose their jobs because of low-cost imports, they can use retraining vouchers to pay for the education they will need to get jobs elsewhere in the economy, perhaps in the industries that are bolstered by trade liberalization.

The administration should also make labor issues a part of trade negotiations. One way, suggested by Syracuse University economist J. David Richardson: Classify labor unions as vital U.S. service businesses and add them to the trade agenda. When negotiators meet in Geneva to work out new market liberalization plans, U.S. trade negotiators should try to win for unions the same rights as American architectural and engineering firms to do business abroad. Union services can become a growing American export business, as American labor organizers set up subsidiaries in developing nations to work with local organizers and strengthen fledgling unions.

The United States can also stiffen the entrance requirements to join free-trade pacts with America. As part of the NAFTA agreement, the United States, Canada, and Mexico set up national labor boards to judge whether the NAFTA partners are living up to laws regulating occupational safety and child labor. Their procedures are so cumbersome that it's doubtful any NAFTA nation will ever be fined, and even if one is, the fine will be minuscule. Sanctions aren't the real problem, though. Any multilateral agreement in which the parties regularly fine each other will quickly fall apart in acrimony.

The most glaring problem is the failure to include the right to organize as a major area of concern. In 1995, the U.S.-based NAFTA labor board determined that, based on credible evidence, a Sony subsidiary in Nuevo Laredo and the Mexican government had intimidated workers to defeat an organizing drive. American and Mexican officials discussed the case, but nothing more was required. The NAFTA pact didn't empower the panel even to issue a report criticizing the objectionable activities.

With nations in Latin America and Asia clamoring to join the United States in expanded free-trade pacts, our negotiators can insist that labor boards be authorized under trade pacts to investigate and publicize cases where governments or companies systematically deprive workers of the right to organize. In Mexico and other developing nations, independent unionists are often battered by the government as well as by government-supported unions. In India, for instance, a tiny minority of unionized workers are protected by elaborate government rules, but the vast bulk of workers, who are unable to join government-sanctioned unions, live in penury. An adverse ruling by a labor board set up as part of a multilateral trade pact would highlight those abuses, give workers a better chance to organize, and challenge U.S. unions to expand overseas just as U.S. corporations do.

During America's Golden Age after World War II, unions helped promote a rising living standard for U.S. workers; the unions' weakness since 1973 has been one reason for the disappointing growth in living standards since then. With strengthened labor boards, unions might begin to see globalization as an ally instead of a blood enemy. Unions "have to change the terms of trade, not block trade," says Pharis Harvey, executive director of the union-backed International Labor Rights Fund.

Globalization affects workers in another way too: through immigration. As descendants of European immigrants, both of us value the contributions that immigrants make to the United States. Many of those benefits—the regeneration of American ideals, the mixing of diverse cultures, the lesson that hard work and sacrifice pay off—can't be quantified economically. But it's important that sentiment alone not rule the immigration debate. The United States today is a different nation than it was during the great wave of immigration in the late nineteenth and early twentieth centuries. Then, America's burgeoning factories and mines had unquenchable demands for the unskilled labor that steamed toward Ellis Island or San Francisco Bay.

Today, the supply of unskilled labor greatly outstrips the demand, and immigration only increases the oversupply. Memories of hard-working immigrant grandparents don't change the fact that today's immigrants are two to three times as likely as native-born Americans to lack high school diplomas, at a time when even a high school diploma isn't enough to make it in the labor market. The chances that American applicants will get better jobs and move ahead are bound to be diminished. At the peak of the Civil Rights movement in 1965, American idealism made reuniting families the top priority of immigration policy. As a result of this change and others, only about 10% of the 720,000 immigrants admitted each year win admission because they are skilled workers or hold advanced degrees.

Changes in that formula are necessary; the percentage of immigrants admitted because of skills should be increased. Those immigrants are far more likely to prosper, and to add to the nation's economic well-being, than those without much education. One possibility is adaptation of the point systems that Canada and Australia use for admitting immigrants: they give extra credit to those with skills and advanced education. Prospective immigrants to Australia need 115 points for entry. College grads get 70 points just for their education; high school dropouts get zero. Families could still bring relatives from abroad, although at a slower pace. But America would benefit more immediately from a greater influx of skilled, educated immigrants.

It's foolish to think that the current immigration system will remain intact when many Americans are hurting economically. To stave off a broad reaction against immigrants from all nations—the kind of reaction that shut the gates to America in the 1920s—change is necessary.

All of our suggestions have a simple goal in mind: To ensure that the broadly shared prosperity we foresee becomes a reality. After twenty years of disappointing growth and widening inequality, the forces shaping the economy are finally moving in the right direction for the American middle class. Ultimately, they represent the best hope for the poor as well. Only when the middle class feels secure in its economic status and hopeful about its future does America mobilize the political will to attack problems of poverty, especially the destitution of America's urban underclass.

Over the next twenty years, life should get better for many millions of Americans. Our journey from the flatlands of Iowa at the turn of the twentieth century to the software houses of India at the turn of the twenty-first century has convinced us that it will.

Notes

This book is based on hundreds of interviews, with experts and with ordinary people. We have not cited the interviews in these notes, but everyone we quote in the text is identified by his or her real name. Where we relied on work published by others, sources are noted herein. We have not, however, given specific citations for data published by the Census Bureau, Bureau of Labor Statistics, Bureau of Economic Analysis, or other U.S. government agencies.

Chapter I. Broadly Shared Prosperity

The specific examples in this chapter come from our reporting and are detailed in later chapters of the book.

page 5. In the Age of Anxiety: This figure (15%) like others in this book, is adjusted to remove the effects of inflation by using the government's Consumer Price Index. This measure probably overstates inflation and understates recent increases in income and wages, but not sufficiently to change the basic story of this book. Using an alternative and probably more accurate inflation measure, the Commerce Department's deflator for personal consumption expenditures, the inflation-adjusted median income of married couples rose by 109% between 1950 and 1973, and by only 18% between 1973 and 1996.

page 5. "We cannot . . .": Michael Elliott, *The Day Before Yesterday: Reconsidering American's Past, Rediscovering the Present.* New York: Simon & Schuster, 1996, p. 19.

page 9. "Productivity isn't . . .": Paul Krugman, *The Age of Diminished Expectations.* Cambridge, MA.: The MIT Press, 1990, p. 15.

page 9. "To a pretty close . . .": A. J. Vogl, "Drift, Diversion, and Snake Oil. An Interview with Economist Paul Krugman." *Across the Board,* May 1, 1994, p. 25.

page 9. From World War II: The official productivity statistics probably understate productivity gains, particularly in recent years. But there is no doubt that growth in productivity slowed significantly around 1973, and little proof in the official data that it has accelerated recently.

page 9. In 1800: Stanley Lebergott, *The Americans: An Economic Record.* New York: W. W. Norton & Co. Inc., 1984, p. 301.

page 9. The percentage: Stanley Lebergott, *Manpower in Economic Growth: The American Record Since 1800.* New York: McGraw-Hill Book Co., 1964, p. 510. U.S. Bureau of the Census, *Statistical Abstract of the United States: 1996,* Washington, DC, 1996, p. 410, Table 641.

page 9. "There is . . .": H. W. Brands, *Reckless Decade: America in the 1890s.* New York: St. Martin's Press, 1995, p. 177.

page 10. We consume: The typical American family spends about 14% of its income on food today; its counterpart in 1901 spent 43%. U.S. Bureau of the Census, *Historical Statistics of the United States: Colonial Times to 1970,* Washington, DC, 1975, p. 321. U.S. Bureau of Labor Statistics, "Consumer Expenditures in 1995," press release USDL-95-489, Dec. 1, 1995.

page 10. In 1950: Authors' calculation from Bureau of Labor Statistics and Bureau of Economic Analysis data.

page 10. Think about barbers: Charles Schultze of the Brookings Institution called our attention to this example, which is the basis for an exam question often given to graduate students in economics.

page 11. Add another: Authors' calculation; assumes the distribution of income is unchanged.

page 11. To middle-class: According to the National Association of Realtors, the monthly principal and interest payment on the median-priced existing home was $700 in April/May 1997.

page 11. If productivity: *Annual Report of the Board of Trustees of the Federal Old-Age and Survivors' Insurance and Disability Insurance Trust Funds 1996,* p. 137, Table II.G4. To reach financial stability so that promised benefits can be paid over the next 50 years, a payroll tax increase of 1.39 percentage points would be needed. If the economy grew a half-percentage point faster than projected, it would take a tax increase of 0.87 percentage point.

page 13. Americans who use: David H. Autor, Lawrence F. Katz, and Alan B. Kreuger, "Computing Inequality: How Computers Changed the Labor Market." Cambridge, MA: National Bureau of Economic Research (Working Paper No. 5956), May 1997.

page 16. In 1941, Simon Kuznets: Simon Kuznets, *Economic Change.* New York: Norton, 1953, p. 281, quoted in Angus Maddison, *Dynamic Forces in Capitalist Development.* Oxford, England: Oxford University Press, 1991, p. 72.

Chapter 2. Looking Back to Look Ahead

page 21. The International: Richard Mandell, *Paris 1900: The Great World's Fair.* Toronto: University of Toronto Press, 1967, pp. xi, 65, 68.

page 22. "It is . . .": Ernest Samuels, ed., *Henry Adams, Selected Letters.* Cambridge, MA: Harvard University Press, 1992, p. 395. Paul David called our attention to this passage.

page 22. On display: List is taken from the catalog of exhibitors, preserved on microfilm at the Smithsonian Institution.

page 22. "Everyone . . .": *Report of the Commissioner General for the United States for the International Universal Exhibition at Paris 1900.* Washington, DC: 1901. Vol. 3, p. 336.

page 22. So, in: *Report of the Commissioner General,* p. 369.

page 22. Somerville, Massachusetts: Reed Ueda, *Avenues to Adulthood: The Origins of High School and Social Mobility in an American Suburb.* Cambridge, England: Cambridge University Press, 1987, pp. 114, 226–228.

page 23. Around 1890: Angus Maddison, *Dynamic Forecasts in Capitalist Development.* Oxford, England: Oxford University Press, 1991, p. 40.

page 23. And the flow: Claudia Goldin, "The Political Economy of Immigration Restriction in the United States, 1890 to 1921," in Claudia Goldin and Gary D. Libecap, eds., *The Regulatory Economy: A Historical Approach to Political Economy.* Chicago: University of Chicago Press, 1994, pp. 228–229.

page 23. "I can already . . .": Samuels, p. 395.

page 23. "There are . . .": Upton Sinclair, *The Jungle.* New York: New American Library Inc., 1960, pp. 16–17. Originally published in 1906.

page 24. In 1900: Stanley Lebergott, *The American Economy.* Princeton, NJ: Princeton University Press, 1976, p. 287. Stanley Lebergott, *The Americans: An Economic Record,* New York: W. W. Norton & Co., Inc., 1984, p. 433.

page 24. The percentage of babies: U.S. Bureau of the Census, *Historical Statistics of the United States, Colonial Times to 1970, Bicentennial Edition, Part 2.* Washington, DC, 1995. "Death Rate, by Age and Sex: 1900 to 1970," Series B181-192, p. 60.

page 24. Baby boys: Robert W. Fogel, "Nutrition and the Decline in Mortality since 1700: Some Preliminary Findings," in Stanley L. Engerman and Robert E. Gallman, eds., *Long-Term Factors in American Economic Growth.* Chicago: University of Chicago Press, 1986, p. 511. The average male born in 1931 grew to about 69.1 inches, about 2.2 inches taller than a male born at the turn of the century.

page 24. But that: The phase "prosperity decade" comes from George Henry Soule, *Prosperity Decade: From War to Depression, 1917–1929.* New York: Rinehart, 1947.

page 25. In 1897: Larry Ray Hurto, ed., *A History of Newton, Iowa,* 1992, privately printed, p. 17.

Chapter 3. Plugged In

Researching the saga of Maytag Corporation in the early part of this century involved interviews with a half-dozen survivors of Maytag's early years, all of them men in their late 80s or early 90s, living in Newton, Iowa. Maytag also made available its corporate history, ledgers, and photo files. Especially useful: a painstakingly detailed chronology of events and articles that historian Orville B. Butler compiled for Maytag's centennial anniversary in 1993.

The chapter also relies heavily on the work of two academics. Stanford University economic historian Paul A. David has drawn intricate parallels between the electric age and the computer era, and has turned the history of the dynamo into a metaphor for contemporary times. University of Pennsylvania historian Thomas P. Hughes has written several superb histories of the electric age and the development of technology in the United States.

page 26. "What curiosities . . .": John Winthrop Hammond, *Men and Volts: The Story of General Electric.* Philadelphia: J. B. Lippincott Co., 1941, p. 5.

page 26. People were "plugged in": David E. Nye, *Electrifying America: Social Meanings of a New Technology.* Cambridge, MA: The MIT Press, 1995, p. 19.

page 27. Stock traders: Thomas P. Hughes, *Networks of Power: Electrification in Western Society, 1880–1930.* Baltimore: The Johns Hopkins University Press, 1983, p. 57.

page 27. In 1901: Nye, reproduction of the Sears, Roebuck & Co. catalog ad featuring the electric belt, p. 154.

page 27. Scads of inventors: George Basalla, *The Evolution of Technology,* New York: Cambridge University Press, 1996, p. 74. Originally published in 1988.

page 27. "The streets, . . .": Theodore Dreiser, *Sister Carrie.* New York: New American Library, 1961, p. 13. Originally published in 1900.

page 27. In 1900: Maytag is described throughout the book by its contemporary name, Maytag Corporation. Over the past century, though, the company has been called by different names. In 1900, it was known as Parsons Band Cutter & Self Feeder Co.; in 1909, it was renamed Maytag Company; in 1986, it became Maytag Corporation.

page 28. Paul David: "Telescopic vision" remark in Paul A. David, "Computer and Dynamo: The Modern Productivity Paradox in a Not-Too-Distant Mirror." Center for Economic Policy Research, Stanford University, Reprint No. 5, July 1995, p. 317. The monograph was originally published by the Organization for Economic Cooperation and Development in 1991.

page 28. In 1849: Richard B. DuBoff, "The Introduction of Electric Power in American Manufacturing," *Economic History Review,* Vol. 20, Dec. 1967, p. 518.

page 29. "Old habit of mind . . .": Mark Twain, *A Connecticut Yankee in King Arthur's Court.* New York: Bantam Books, 1981, p. 121. Originally published in 1889.

page 30. "The whole plant . . .": E. H. Mullin, "Electric Power in the Machine Shop," *Cassier's Magazine,* Jan. 1898, p. 244.

page 30. About two-thirds: Stanley Lebergott, *The Americans: An Economic Record.* New York: W. W. Norton & Co., Inc., 1984, p. 355.

page 30. "His is the only . . .": Hammond, p. 115.

page 30. "It has proven . . .": DuBoff, p. 511.

page 31. The Keating Wheel Company: Warren D. Devine, Jr., "From Shafts to Wires: Historical Perspective on Electrification," *The Journal of Economic History,* Vol. 43, No. 2, June 1983, p. 359.

page 31. In 1899: Statistics on factory usage of motor-driven machinery from David, p. 327.

page 31. "Suddenly gone . . .": *Harper's* magazine article cited in Thomas P. Hughes, *American Genesis: A Century of Invention and Technological Enthusiasm.* New York: Penguin Books, 1990, p. 91. The anecdote concerning the *New York Sun* is on p. 88.

page 32. In 1926, F. H. Penney: Devine, p. 368.

page 33. Thus was born: Hughes, *Networks of Power,* p. 108.

page 33. By 1900: Paul David argues that Edison soon realized the technical superiority of AC and continued fighting Westinghouse only until he could sell his investments in the DC electric-generating business. Edison's "propaganda campaign . . . made considerable economic sense in the context, however unscrupulous it may have been," David writes in "Heroes, Herds and Hysteresis in Technological History:

Thomas Edison and 'The Battle of the Systems' Reconsidered," *Industrial and Corporate Change,* Vol. 1, No. 1, 1992, p. 171.

page 33. "Greater London . . .": Hughes, *Networks of Power,* p. 227.

page 35. After winning the election: *Newton Daily News,* March 27, 1920.

page 35. A rival washer-maker: *Newton Daily News,* April 21, 1920.

page 35. Rich was a front man: *Newton Daily News,* April 29, 1920. The account of the later sale of the utility comes from "A Century of Progress," a centennial history published by Iowa Southern Utilities Co., p. 14.

page 36. In 1924, Maytag manufactured: All production records come from Maytag historical records.

Maytag Production

Year	Washers and Engines Produced	Factory Workers	Machines per Worker	Factory Salary (in 1914 dollars)
1920	69,627	369	189	$ 765
1921	17,542	172	102	$ 570
1922	36,687	288	127	$ 715
1923	68,298	459	149	$ 890
1924	112,345	733	153	$ 964
1925	204,021	1,192	171	$ 988
1926	359,152	1,625	221	$1,175

page 36. Rejected in Denver: A. B. Funk, *Fred L. Maytag: A Biography.* Cedar Rapids, Iowa: Torch Press, 1936, pp. 57–61.

page 36. One history of Maytag: Robert and John Hoover, *An American Quality Legend: How Maytag Saved Our Moms, Vexed the Competition, and Presaged America's Quality Revolution.* New York: McGraw-Hill, Inc., 1993, p. 113.

page 37. In May, the *Newton Daily News:* Description of Maytag's plans in *Newton Daily News,* May 1, 1925.

page 37. The *Newton Daily News:* "Automatic machines" described in *Newton Daily News,* Dec. 18, 1926.

page 38. Between 1922 and 1926: River Rouge description in Hughes, *American Genesis,* p. 208, and in interview with Hughes.

page 39. Taylor "never loafed": John Dos Passos, *The Big Money.* New York: New American Library, 1979, p. 45. Originally published in 1936.

page 39. In 1929: Eugene O'Neill, *Dynamo.* New York: Horace Liveright, Inc., 1929, p. 92.

page 40. "The full transformation . . .": David, p. 336.

page 40. After surveying: Erik Brynjolfsson and Lorin Hitt, "Paradox Lost? Firm-Level Evidence on the Returns to Information Systems Spending," *Management Science,* Vol. 42, No. 4, April 1996, pp. 541–558.

page 40. Economist Daniel E. Sichel: Daniel E. Sichel, *The Computer Revolution: An Economic Perspective.* Washington, DC: The Brookings Institution, 1997.

Sichel and others also argue that the United States will have to invest more in computer technology to produce a historic rise in productivity that rivals the contribution of railroads, for instance. Railroads accounted for roughly 12% of the national stock of plant and equipment at the end of the last century, Sichel estimates. Current investment in computer equipment amounts to only 2% or 3% of national capital stock. But Sichel's comparison shortchanges the computer era. It leaves out massive spending on software and telecommunications equipment, and the microprocessors that control cars, televisions, heating and cooling systems, and myriad other devices. Add it all up, and it accounts for 10% or so of the national capital stock, pretty close to the railroad era.

page 41. After World War II, the U.S. Air Force: The account of postwar machine tools comes from David F. Noble, *Forces of Production: A Social History of Industrial Automation.* New York: Oxford University Press, 1986.

page 42. Says Stanford University: Nathan Rosenberg, "Uncertainty and Technological Change," paper prepared for Federal Reserve Bank of Boston's Conference on Technology and Growth, June 5–7, 1996, in Chatham, MA.

Chapter 4. "A People's College"

This chapter benefits greatly from the published work and helpful suggestions of Claudia Goldin of Harvard University, who has documented the impact of high schools on American workers. Details about Newton High School are drawn from documents and memorabilia in the collection of the Jasper County (Iowa) Historical Society. Descriptions taken from those resources and from various editions of *Newtonia,* the Newton High School yearbook, are not cited separately.

page 43. In 1910: Claudia Goldin, "How America Graduated from High School: 1910 to 1960." Cambridge, MA: National Bureau of Economic Research (Working Paper No. 4762), June 1994, p. 10, supplemented with personal communication.

page 43. High school existed: Edward Krug, *The Shaping of the American High School, Volume 1, 1880–1920,* Madison: University of Wisconsin Press, 1969, p. 64.

page 44. By the early 1930s: Goldin, p. 10.

page 45. "Just what . . .": Joseph A. Woodrow, *Some Pretty Girl, Please Write.* Santa Barbara, CA: Don Jose Publications, 1967, p. 14.

page 45. One unenlightened: Krug, Volume 1, pp. 178–179.

page 45. In a turn-of-the-century: State of Iowa, Department of Public Instruction, Des Moines, *Biennial Report for 1898–1899.* This volume and others like it, which record the evolution of public school education in Iowa and other states, are in the collection of the Monroe C. Gutman Library at the Harvard University School of Education.

page 45. But in 1915: Based on *Newtonia* 1916 and an interview with Lawrence Hammerly.

page 46. In a view: State of Iowa, Department of Public Instruction, Des Moines, *Biennial Report for 1900–1901.*

page 46. A 1924: "Pasadena's Colorful Graduation Pageant," *American Educational Digest,* No. 44 (October 1924), quoted in Edward Krug, *The Shaping of the American High School, Volume 2, 1920–1941.* Madison: University of Wisconsin Press, 1972.

page 47. "To quote . . .":Krug, *Volume 1,* pp. 175–176.

page 47. In Providence: Joel Perlmann, *Ethnic Differences: Schooling and Social Structure Among the Irish, Italians, Jews & Blacks in an American City, 1880–1935.* Cambridge, England: Cambridge University Press, 1988, p. 24.

page 47. Roughly half: American Association of Community Colleges, Website: <www.aacc.nche.edu>.

page 47. The new high school: Myrna Guthrie, "History of the Newton Community Schools," in Larry Ray Hurto, ed., *A History of Newton, Iowa,* 1992, privately printed, p. 118.

page 47. The fountain: Lucy Hall, *History of the Schools of Jasper County,* circa 1959, privately printed, pp. 91–92. (In the collection of the Jasper County Historical Society.)

page 47. In the 1922: Sinclair Lewis, *Babbitt.* New York: New American Library Inc., 1961, p. 154. Originally published in 1922.

page 48. In his annual: Krug, *Volume 1,* p. 225.

page 49. In 1934: Robert L. Smith, *Student Soldier Statesman Servant: An Autobiography,* March 1992, privately printed, p. 27.

page 49. "Although this . . .": Krug, *Volume 2,* p. 19.

page 50. "High school graduates . . .": Claudia Goldin and Lawrence F. Katz, "The Origins of Technology–Skill Complementarity," Harvard University, May 7, 1996, photocopied, p. 19. A shorter version of this paper appeared in the *American Economic Review* (see next note).

page 50. Workers selling: Claudia Goldin and Lawrence F. Katz, "Technology, Skill, and the Wage Structure: Insights from the Past." *American Economic Review,* Vol. 86, No. 2 (May 1996), p. 253.

page 50. John Dewey: Quoted in Krug, *Volume 1,* p. 415.

page 51. In much: Goldin, p. 6.

page 51. Just as the assembly: Claudia Goldin and Lawrence F. Katz, "The Decline of Noncompeting Groups: Changes in the Premium to Education, 1890 to 1940." Cambridge, MA: National Bureau of Economic Research (Working Paper No. 5202), August 1995, p. 5.

page 51. In 1922: W. Bristol, *A Trade Survey of Newton, Iowa, 1922.* Iowa City: The State University of Iowa, 1922, p. 56.

page 51. The NEA: "Taking Stock of the Schools," *Research Bulletin of the National Education Association,* Vol. III, No. 3, May 1925, p. 94.

page 51. Today: American Association of Community Colleges, Website: <www.aacc.nche.edu>.

page 52. Economic historian: Goldin, p. 7.

page 52. The hero: Elmer Rice, "The Adding Machine," in *Three Plays.* New York: Hill and Wang, 1965.

page 53. The fraction: Goldin and Katz, August 1995, Table 10.

page 53. O. Henry's: O. Henry, "Springtime à la Carte," in *41 Stories.* New York: Penguin Books U.S.A. Inc., 1984. p. 49.

page 53. "The experience . . .": Perlmann, p. 37.

page 53. One of the two: From Somerville, Massachusetts, city directories.

page 53. "The high school . . .": Reed Ueda, *Avenues to Adulthood: The Origins of the High School and Social Mobility in an American Suburb.* Cambridge, England: Cambridge University Press, 1987, p. 114.

page 53. Among boys: Ueda, p. 220. Ueda's statistics, on page 180, show that between 1896 and 1905, 96% of the English High School graduates who were sons of Yankee white-collar workers, and 71% of the sons of Irish white-collar workers, ended up in white-collar jobs themselves.

page 54. This increase: This paragraph and the ones that follow are based on Goldin and Katz, August 1995.

page 55. But, even: Goldin and Katz, August 1995, p. 23.

page 55. Economist Jan Tinbergen: Quoted in Goldin and Katz, August 1995, p. 1.

Chapter 5. The Golden Age

Dennis and Ann Kerley and Jim and Ann Marie Blentlinger and their families were interviewed initially for a story that appeared in the *The Wall Street Journal* on March 29, 1995, and were interviewed several times subsequently, in person and by telephone, for this chapter and the following one. The collections of the Chattanooga public library and data published by RiverValley Partners, an economic development organization in Chattanooga, were especially useful. Data drawn from the 1950 and subsequent decennial censuses conducted by the U.S. Bureau of the Census or from the Census Bureau's treasure chest, *Historical Statistics of the United States: Colonial Times to 1970,* are not cited specifically in these notes.

page 61. For a quarter century: (toilets) U.S. Bureau of the Census, decennial censuses; (air conditioning) Raymond Arsenault, "The End of the Long Hot Summer: The Air Conditioner and Southern Culture," *Journal of Southern History,* Vol. L, No. 4, November 1984, p. 611; (televisions) U.S. Bureau of the Census, Historical Statistics of the United States, Washington, DC, p. 796, and U.S. Bureau of the Census, *Statistical Abstract of the United States: 1996,* Washington, DC, 1996, p. 561.

page 61. "Union decline . . .": *Chattanooga Times,* Oct. 31, 1994, p. C1.

page 63. Though no official: Sheldon Danziger and Peter Gottschalk, *America Unequal.* New York: Russell Sage Foundation, and Cambridge, MA: Harvard University Press, 1995, p. 57.

page 64. In 1949: Danziger and Gottschalk, p. 47.

page 64. The U.S. economy: Calculated from U.S. Department of Commerce, *Survey of Current Business,* May 1997, Table 2a; U.S. Bureau of the Census, *Statistical Abstract of the United States 1996,* Washington DC, 1996, Table 2, as updated by the Census Bureau at <www.census.gov>.

page 64. From 1870: Calculated from Angus Maddison, *Monitoring the World Economy, 1820–1992,* Paris: Organization for Economic Cooperation and Development, 1995, p. 249.

page 64. At the bottom: Claudia Goldin and Robert A. Margo, "The Great Compression: The Wage Structure in the United States at Mid-Century," *The Quarterly Journal of Economics,* Vol. CVII, Issue 1, February 1992, pp. 1–32.

page 66. As *New York Times:* David Halberstam, *The Fifties.* New York: Fawcett Columbine, 1994. p. 132.

page 66. A wealthy: Halberstam, pp. 173–179.

page 67. "Life . . .": Halberstam, p. 497.

page 67. Galbraith observed: John Kenneth Galbraith, *The Affluent Society.* Boston: Houghton Mifflin Co., 1958, p. 140.

page 67. A 1958: Halberstam, pp. 633–635.

page 68. Contrast: The ad was published, among other places, in *The American Enterprise*, November/December 1995, p. 21.

page 68. In 1955: From Marian Mistrik, librarian for the American Transportation Association.

page 68. In 1950: From the Bureau of Economic Analysis, U.S. Department of Commerce.

page 69. "As the big jet . . .": Stephen E. Ambrose, *Eisenhower: Soldier and President*. New York: Simon & Schuster Inc., 1990, p. 490.

page 69. Millions of Americans: Thomas Petzinger, *Hard Landing*. New York: Times Business, 1995, pp. 16, 33.

page 69. Frank Borman: quoted in T. A. Heppenheimer, *Turbulent Skies: The History of Commercial Aviation*. New York: John Wiley & Sons, 1995, p. 314.

page 69. "This was . . .": Danziger and Gottschalk, pp. 1, 2

page 69. "I don't . . .": Sloan Wilson, *The Man in the Gray Flannel Suit*. New York: Simon & Schuster, 1955, p. 5.

page 70. Legal barriers: Claudia Goldin, *Understanding the Gender Gap: An Economic History of American Women*. New York: Oxford University Press, 1990, p. 175, supplemented with Census Bureau data.

page 70. Friedan: Betty Friedan, *The Feminine Mystique*. New York: Bantam Doubleday Dell Publishing Group Inc., 1984, p. 15. Originally published in 1963.

page 70. The "Port Huron Statement": Quoted in Todd Gitlin, *The Sixties: Years of Hope, Days of Rage*. New York: Bantam Books, 1993, p. 27.

page 71. "There is . . .": Michael Harrington, *The Other America: Poverty in the United States*. New York: Collier Books, Macmillan Publishing Co., 1994, p. 1.

page 71. "The United States . . .": Quoted in Danzinger and Gottschalk, p. 41.

page 71. James Tobin: James Tobin, *Full Employment and Growth: Further Keynesian Essays on Policy*. Cheltenham, U.K.: Edward Elgar Publishing Co., 1996. p. 231.

page 71. Believing: Lindley H. Clark Jr., "Speaking of Business: The Business Cycle Once Again Is Alive and Well," *The Wall Street Journal*, March 27, 1984, p. 35.

page 71. *TIME*: quoted in Landon Y. Jones, *Great Expectations: America and the Baby Boom Generation*. New York: Coward, McCann & Geoghegan, 1980, p. 72.

page 71. *Fortune*: Paul Krugman, *Peddling Prosperity*. New York: W.W. Norton & Co., 1994, p. 57.

page 72. "He said . . .": John Wilkes, *Trying Out the Dream: A Year in the Life of An American Family*. Philadelphia: J. B. Lippincott Co., 1975, p. 264.

page 72. "I love . . .": Wilkes, p. 249.

Chapter 6. The Age of Anxiety

page 73. The gloomy portrait: See Donald L. Barlett and James B. Steele, *America: Who Stole the Dream?* Kansas City: Andrews and McMeel, 1996.

page 73. A third view: Robert J. Samuelson, *The Good Life and Its Discontents: The American Dream in the Age of Entitlement*. New York: Times Books, 1995. Michael Elliott, *The Day Before Yesterday: Reconsidering America's Past, Rediscovering the Present*. New York: Simon & Schuster, 1996.

page 74. Data shown is from 1973 and 1996, or the years closest for which data are available. *People:* Data on intercourse, births, abortions and breastfeeding are from the National Center for Health Statistics of the Centers for Disease Control and Prevention. Data on high school seniors are from the University of Michigan's *Monitoring the Future* survey. Data on income, poverty and living arrangements are from the Bureau of the Census. *Consumers:* Data on supermarkets are from the Food Marketing Institute. Data on international travel are from the Commerce Department's Bureau of Economic Analysis. Data on meat and poultry are from the Department of Agriculture's Economic Research Service. *Health:* All data are from the National Center for Health Statistics of the Centers for Disease Control and Prevention. *Environment:* Data on recycling are from the Aluminum Association. Data on emissions are from the Environmental Protection Agency's Office of Air Quality Planning and Standards. *Workplace:* Data are from the Labor Department's Bureau of Labor Statistics. *Education:* Data are from the Department of Education's National Center for Health Statistics. Pell grants are in 1995 dollars. Drawings are copyright Robert Pizzo, and are reprinted with his permission.

page 75. Prices for 1973 and 1996, or the closest years for which data are available, come from manufacturers, retailers, service providers, newspaper advertisements, trade magazines, trade associations, and government surveys. Hourly wages are calculated from Commerce Department estimates on total wages and salaries, and total hours worked in domestic industries, including the government. Weekly wages are based on Bureau of Labor Statistics data on the length of the average work week (37 hours in 1973 and 34.4 hours in 1996).

page 76. Despite a reasonably: Christine Dugas, "Going Broke: Bankruptcy Stigma Lessens," *USA Today,* June 10, 1997, p. 1A. Also, Michelle Singletary and Albert B. Crenshaw, "Credit Card Flood Leaves Sea of Debt," *Washington Post,* Nov. 24, 1996, pp. A1, A24.

page 80. In 1970: American Automobile Association, Washington, DC.

page 82. After adjusting: Sheldon Danziger and Peter Gottschalk, *America Unequal.* New York: Russell-Sage Foundation, and Cambridge, MA: Harvard University Press, 1995, p. 46; personal communication with Danziger.

page 83. Data compiled: Christopher J. Mayer and Gary V. Englehardt, "Gifts, Down Payments, and Housing Affordability," Boston: Federal Reserve Bank of Boston, (Working Paper 94-5), December 1994, Table 1.

page 84. In 1970: Lewis Mandell, *The Credit Card Industry: A History.* Boston: Twayne Publishers, 1990, p. 153.

page 84. And by 1992: Federal Reserve data in U.S. Bureau of the Census, *Statistical Abstract of the United States: 1996,* Washington, DC, 1996, p. 516, Table 792.

page 84. "Consumers seem . . .": Mandell, p. 153.

page 85. In 1973: U.S. Treasury Department, Office of Tax Analysis, "Average and Marginal Federal Income, Social Security and Medicare Taxes for Four-Person Families at the Same Relative Positions in the Income Distributions, 1955–1995," photocopied, April 18, 1995.

page 85. A more comprehensive: Committee on Ways and Means, U.S. House of Representatives, *1993 Green Book,* Washington, DC: July 7, 1993, p. 1497. The figures refer to the middle 20% of families. Congressional Budget Office analyses that include corporate tax and excise taxes, all of which raise the price of goods to consumers, go back only as far as 1977.

page 86. The shuttering: *A History of Air Pollution Control in Chattanooga and Hamilton County.* Chattanooga, TN: Air Pollution Control Bureau, 1996.

page 87. Signal Mountain: RiverValley Partners, *Chattanooga, Tennessee, Data Book,* October 1995, Table D-3. Median household income in 1990 was $25,015 in Red Bank and $49,821 on Signal Mountain.

page 87. In 1973: DuPont chief executive's salary comes from the company's proxy statements.

page 88. A wave: National Research Council, *The New Americans: Economic, Demographic and Fiscal Effects of Immigration,* Washington, DC, 1997, Figures 2.1, 2.2.

Chapter 7. The Computer Paradox

Two books were especially helpful for this chapter. Thomas K. Landauer's *The Trouble with Computers: Usefulness, Usability and Productivity* is the best overview of the productivity failures of computers. Paul Ingrassia and Joseph B. White's *Comeback: The Fall and Rise of the American Automobile Industry,* details the computer travails of U.S. automakers.

page 90. Since the invention: *Economic Report of the President,* Feb. 1997, Table B-16.

page 90. Productivity has been increasing: Bureau of Labor Statistics report on productivity, first quarter 1997.

page 91. "My skepticism . . .": Edward F. Denison, *Accounting for Slower Economic Growth: The United States in the 1970s,* Washington, DC: The Brookings Institution, 1979, p. 134.

page 91. "The trouble with software . . .": Stewart Alsop, "The Trouble with Software Is . . . It Sucks!" *Fortune,* June 10, 1996, p. 100.

page 91. "You can see the computer age . . .": Robert M. Solow, "We'd Better Watch Out," in *New York Times Book Review,* July 12, 1987, p. 35.

page 93. *TIME* named: *TIME,* Jan. 3, 1983.

page 93. Manufacturing productivity: Manufacturing productivity grew 4.6% between the third quarter of 1996 and the third quarter of 1997. Bureau of Labor Statistics, "Productivity and Costs," third quarter 1997, Dec. 4, 1997.

page 93. But productivity growth: Statistics on service-sector productivity from Sharon Kozicki, "The Productivity Growth Slowdown: Diverging Trends in the Manufacturing and Service Sectors, *Federal Reserve Bank of Kansas City Economic Review,* first quarter 1997, Vol. 82, No. 1, p. 34.

page 94. "Not a day goes by . . .": William M. Bulkeley, "Technology, Economics and Ego Conspire to Make Software Difficult to Use," *The Wall Street Journal,* May 20, 1991, p. R7.

page 94. Humorist Dave Barry: Dave Barry, "From Cave Walls to Windows 95," *USAir Magazine,* Dec. 1996, p. 73.

page 94. "I'm literally navigating . . .": Clifford Stoll, *Silicon Snake Oil: Second Thoughts on the Information Highway.* New York: Anchor Books, 1995, p. 62.

page 94. Call it the Frankenstein factor: For a winning and winsome look at technological ironies, see Edward Tenner, *Why Things Bite Back: Technology and the Revenge of Unintended Consequences.* New York: Alfred A. Knopf, 1996. He enumerates such "revenge effects" as when improved power-door locks quadruple the number of drivers locked out of their cars.

page 94. Reliance Insurance Co.: Reliance's tale of woe was chronicled in articles by Leonard Zehr, "The Paper Palace: The Computerized Office Churns Out More Paper—Not Less," *The Wall Street Journal,* Sept. 16, 1985, p. 40C, and Thomas

McCarroll, "What New Age? High-Tech Gizmos for Home and Office Are Readily Available But Underused," *TIME*, Aug. 12, 1991, p. 44. A senior Reliance computer manager updated the company's plans in an interview.

page 95. Searching for a way out: Information on the banking company's ATM problems comes from a special section in the *Economist*, "Turning Digits into Dollars," Oct. 26, 1996, p. 6, and from interviews with First Union.

page 97. "Organizing the *The Wall Street Journal's* . . .": Tim Lemmer, "The Story Behind DJ's Coverage of the Conventions," *DJ Bulletin*, Sept. 3, 1996, p. 1.

page 97. Across town, at Georgetown University Hospital: A spokeswoman for the hospital said she couldn't find any information on the hospital's computer snags. But she said many of the hospital's programmers were dismissed after the hospital turned to an outside firm to run its computer systems.

page 98. Programming attracts: Cited in Thomas K. Landauer, *The Trouble with Computers: Usefulness, Usability and Productivity*. Cambridge, MA: MIT Press, 1995, p. 170.

page 98. "Imagine choosing . . .": Alsop, p. 101.

page 98. "America does indeed . . .": Michael L. Dertrouzos, Richard K. Lester, and Robert M. Solow, *Made in America: Regaining the Productive Edge*. New York: HarperPerennial, 1990, p. 166. *Made in America* was originally published by the MIT Commission on Industrial Productivity in 1989.

page 99. "Automate away from those assholes": Paul Ingrassia and Joseph B. White, *Comeback: The Fall and Rise of the American Automobile Industry*. New York: Touchstone Books, 1995, p. 33.

page 99. "Poletown was . . .": Ingrassia and White, p. 79.

page 99. Panicked GM managers: Ingrassia and White, p. 111. They cite a *Wall Street Journal* article by Amal Kumar Naj, "Tricky Technology: Auto Makers Discover Factory of the Future Is Headache Just Now," May 13, 1986, p. A1.

page 99. "We have relied . . .": Ingrassia and White, p. 172.

page 101. Allstate Corporation: Lee Gomes, "Why Prepping Mainframes for 2000 Is So Tough," *The Wall Street Journal*, Dec. 9, 1996, p. B1.

page 101. Overall, U.S. companies canceled: "Chaos," a 1994 report by the Standish Group, and follow-up interviews with Standish's chairman, Jim Johnson.

page 101. There isn't a precise estimate: "Futzing" estimate in William M. Bulkeley, "Data Trap: How Using Your PC Can Be a Waste of Time, Money," *The Wall Street Journal*, Jan. 4, 1993, p. B5.

page 101. Nielsen Media Research: Joan Indiana Rigdon, "Curbing Digital Dillydallying on the Job," *The Wall Street Journal*, Nov. 25, 1996, p. B1.

page 101. After the Internal Revenue Service: Brian T. Pentland, "Use and Productivity in Personal Computing: An Empirical Test," *Proceedings of the Tenth International Conference on Information Systems*, Boston, Dec. 4–6, 1989, pp. 211–222.

page 102. Similarly, when twenty-six business school students: Jeffrey E. Kottemann, Fred D. Davis, and William E. Remus, "Computer-Assisted Decision Making: Performance, Beliefs, and the Illusion of Control" *Organizational Behavior and Human Decisions Processes*, No. 57, 1994, pp. 26–37.

page 102. Even word processing: Landauer, pp. 53–55.

Chapter 8. Forward to the Future

This chapter reflects reporting at Allen-Bradley Company in Milwaukee; Schneider National Corporation in Green Bay, Wisconsin, and Johnson & Higgins in New York

City. The work of Massachusetts Institute of Technology economist Erik Brynjolfsson, who has untangled the so-called productivity paradox, was especially useful.

page 105. "Computers are no strangers . . .": *Business Week* Special Report on Computers, Jan. 21, 1958, pp. 68–92.

page 105. Ever hopeful: Neil Gross, "Zap! Splat! Smarts? Why Video Games May Actually Help Your Children Learn," *Business Week*, Dec. 23, 1996, p. 64.

page 107. Studies by MIT economists: Erik Brynjolfsson and Lorin Hitt, "Paradox Lost? Firm-Level Evidence on the Returns to Information Systems Spending," *Management Science*, Vol. 42, No. 4, April 1996, pp. 541–558.

page 107. Columbia University economists: William Lehr and Frank R. Lichtenberg, "Computer Use and Productivity Growth in Federal Government Agencies, 1987–1992," Cambridge, MA: National Bureau of Economic Research (Working Paper No. 5616), June 1996.

page 108. After a decade of stagnation: Manufacturing productivity grew 4.6% between the third quarter of 1996 and the third quarter of 1997. Bureau of Labor Statistics.

page 108. There's evidence that: Service productivity estimate by Mark Zandi, chief economist at Regional Financial Associates in West Chester, PA.

page 109. An insomniac: Historical information about Allen-Bradley is from John Gurda, *The Bradley Legacy: Lynde and Harry Bradley, Their Company and Their Foundation*. Milwaukee: The Lynde and Harry Bradley Foundation, 1992.

page 111. A study of thirty-one circuit board factories: Fernando F. Suarez, Michael A. Cusumano, and Charles H. Fine, "An Empirical Study of Flexibility in Manufacturing," *Sloan Management Review*, Fall 1995, pp. 25–32. Brynjolfsson quote and study of MacroMed are in Erik Brynjolfsson, Amy Austin Renshaw, and Marshall van Alstyne, "The Matrix of Change," *Sloan Management Review*, Winter 1996, pp. 37–54.

page 114. After surveying 584 factories: Maryellen R. Kelley, "Productivity and Information Technology: The Elusive Connection," *Management Science*, Vol. 40, No. 11, Nov. 1994, pp. 1406–1425.

page 117. To escape detection: Todd Lappin, "Truckin'," *Wired*, Jan. 1995.

page 121. The Johnson & Higgins system: The history of the Internet's predecessors comes from Martin Campbell-Kelly and William Aspray, *Computer: A History of the Information Machine*. New York: Basic Books, 1996, Chapter 12.

page 121. Even when Wall Street: Johnson & Higgins history in Richard Blodgett, *Johnson & Higgins at 150 Years*. Lyme, CT: Greenwich Publishing Group Inc., 1995.

page 123. But getting good results: Wanda J. Orlikowski, "Learning from Notes: Organizational Issues in Groupware Implementation," *The Information Society*, Vol. 9, 1993, p. 246.

page 124. But networks haven't yet: H. Waverly Deutsch, George F. Colony, and Thomas B. Rhinelander, "Managing Unruly Desktops," *The Forrester Report*, Jan. 1995.

Chapter 9. The Secret: No Bosses

Reporting in this chapter is based on visits to Miller's Trenton, Ohio, plant and Xerox's district office in Columbus, Ohio, and subsequent interviews with employees at both sites.

page 127. In an earlier era: Frederick Winslow Taylor, *The Principles of Scientific Management*. New York: Harper & Brothers, 1911.

page 127. "In our scheme . . .": Quoted in Robert Kanigel, *The One Best Way: Frederick Winslow Taylor and the Enigma of Efficiency*. New York: Viking Penguin Books USA Inc., 1997, p. 169.

page 127. Taylorism fit: See Thomas P. Hughes, *American Genesis: A Century of Invention and Technological Enthusiasm*. New York: Penguin Books, 1990, pp. 184–204.

page 128. About half: Daniel J. Meckstroth, *Employer Training Programs*. Arlington, VA: Manufacturers Alliance, 1997, p. 1.

page 128. "For the first time . . .": Edward F. Lawler III, *From the Ground Up*. San Francisco: Jossey-Bass Inc., 1996, p. 5.

page 128. Examining a 1994: Sandra E. Black and Lisa M. Lynch, "How to Compete: The Impact of Workplace Practices and Information Technology on Productivity." Washington, DC: U.S. Department of Labor, September 1996, photocopied.

page 128. Three other: Casey Ichniowski, Kathryn Shaw, and Giovanna Prennushi, "The Effects of Human Resource Management Practices on Productivity," April 1995, photocopied. Also, "Executive Summary: Human Resource Management and Competitive Performance in the Steel Industry."

page 133. Shortly after: David T. Kearns and David A. Nadler, *Prophets in the Dark: How Xerox Reinvented Itself and Beat Back the Japanese*. New York: HarperCollins Publishers Inc., 1993, p. xiii.

page 133. "Ray realized . . .": Martha A. Gephardt and Mark E. Van Buren, "The Power of High-Performance Work Systems." Alexandria, VA: American Society for Training and Development, undated.

Chapter 10. Alan Greenspan, Optimist at the Top

Reporting in this chapter comes from several years of on- and off-the-record interviews with Federal Reserve officials, including Alan Greenspan, and from Greenspan's speeches and his testimony before Congress.

page 140. He says: Alan Greenspan, "Remarks at the 1997 Haskins Partners Dinner of the Stern School of Business," New York University, May 8, 1997, p. 10.

page 140. "I spend . . .": David Wessel, "Alan Greenspan's Language Engenders Great Interest But Is Tough to Decipher," *The Wall Street Journal*, June 23, 1995, p. A1.

page 140. "The rapid . . .": Alan Greenspan, "Remarks before the National Governors Association," Feb. 5, 1996, p. 1.

page 141. The Fed: Thibant de Saint Phalle, *The Federal Reserve: An Intentional Mystery*. New York: Praeger Publishers, 1985.

page 141. At the time, William: William Grieder, *Secrets of the Temple*. New York: Touchstone/Simon & Schuster Inc., 1987, p. 714.

page 142. Greenspan, although: Quoted in Steven K. Beckner, *Back from the Brink: The Greenspan Years*. New York: John Wiley & Sons Inc., 1996, p. 14.

page 142. Former Labor: Robert B. Reich, *Locked in the Cabinet*. New York: Alfred A. Knopf, 1997, p. 80.

page 143. Greenspan addressed: Author's interview with Alan Greenspan, Sept. 9, 1997.

page 144. The toughest: See Greenspan, May 8, 1997.

page 144. Greenspan reads: David Wessel, "Choosing a Course: In Setting Fed's Policy, Chairman Bets Heavily on His Own Judgment," *The Wall Street Journal,* Jan. 27, 1997, p. A1.

page 146. "Either we are spinning . . .": Alan Greenspan, "Testimony to the House Banking and Financial Services Committee," July 23, 1996.

page 146. "This pattern . . .": Greenspan, May 8, 1997.

page 147. After Blinder: Alan Blinder and Richard E. Quandt, "Waiting for Godot: Information Technology and the Productivity Miracle?" Princeton, NJ: Princeton University, May 1997. Unpublished.

page 147. Thomas Melzer: Thomas C. Melzer, "Stable Prices: A Recipe for Growth," Henderson State University, Arkadelphia, PA, Feb. 27, 1997.

page 148. Not even Gary Stern: Gary Stern, "Economic Growth: A Framework for Discussion," *The Region,* Minneapolis: Federal Reserve Bank of Minneapolis, Sept. 1996, p. 3.

page 149. He forced: See Greenspan, "Testimony to the House Banking and Financial Services Committee," July 22, 1997.

page 150. "The current . . .": Alan Greenspan, "Remarks at the Annual Conference of the Association of Private Enterprise Education," Arlington, VA, April 12, 1997.

Chapter 11. Dream Catchers

This chapter was inspired by a 1994 visit to Kirkwood Community College in Cedar Rapids, Iowa, and by conversations with Claudia Goldin, Lawrence Katz, and Thomas Kane, all of Harvard University. Reporting was done in Cleveland, at Cuyahoga Community College; in Catonsville, Maryland, at Catonsville Community College; and in telephone interviews with dozens of community college students, alumni, teachers, and administrators. Except as indicated, enrollment data come from sources available at the Department of Education's National Center for Education Statistics: its annual *Digest of Educational Statistics,* its Internet site, or its published tables. Earnings data, except as noted, come from the Census Bureau's Current Population Survey.

page 153. The story for women: In 1980, college-educated women earned 34% more than high school graduates; in 1997, they earned 61% more.

page 154. "Based on . . .": Quoted in Michael M. Phillips, "Wage Gap Based on Education Levels Off," *The Wall Street Journal,* July 22, 1996, p. A2.

page 155. The supply: The Canadian experience is discussed in Peter Gottschalk and Timothy Smeeding, "Cross-National Comparisons of Earnings and Income Inequality," *Journal of Economic Literature,* Vol. XXXV, No. 2 (June 1997), p. 655; and in David Card and Richard Freeman, "Small Differences That Matter," in Richard Freeman, ed., *Working Under Different Rules.* New York: Russell-Sage Foundation, 1994. See also "Wages, Skills and Technology in the United States and Canada" (Working Paper ECWP-98), Canadian Institute for Advanced Research, 1997 (in Elhanan Helpman, ed., *General Purpose Technologies,* Cambridge, MA: MIT Press, forthcoming).

page 156. Adults: Duane E. Leigh and Andrew M. Gill, "Labor Market Returns to Community Colleges: Evidence for Returning Adults," *Journal of Human Resources,* Vol. XXXII, No. 2, pp. 334–353.

page 156. Veteran steelworkers: Louis S. Jacobson, Robert J. LaLonde, and Daniel G. Sullivan, "The Returns from Classroom Training for Displaced Workers," Westat Inc., Oct. 1994. Unpublished.

page 156. Randy Kohrs: David Wessel, "By the Bootstraps: One Family's Rebound Shows the Possibilities in the Economy of the 90's," *The Wall Street Journal,* Aug. 12, 1994, p. A1.

page 158. In the most thorough: Thomas Kane and Cecilia Elena Rouse, "Labor-Market Returns to Two- and Four-Year Colleges," *American Economic Review,* Vol. 85, No. 3, June 1995, pp. 600–614.

page 158. Brian Surette: Brian Surette, "The Impact of Two-Year College on the Labor Market and Schooling Experiences of Young Men." Washington, DC: Federal Reserve Board (Finance and Economics Discussion Series 1997-44), June 1997, p. 13.

page 159. "It was . . .": Scott Stevens, "CCC Opened in 1963, Created to Serve Have-Nots," *The Plain Dealer,* Dec. 31, 1995, p. 1.

page 160. "I want . . .": Jodi Schwan, "Clinton Pitches for Education," *The Plain Dealer,* Nov. 4, 1996, p. 2E.

page 161. The community college: Steven Brint and Jerome Karabel, *The Diverted Dream: Community Colleges and the Promise of Educational Opportunity in America, 1900–1985.* New York: Oxford University Press, 1989, p. 25.

page 161. "It is very . . .": Brint and Karabel, p. 40.

page 162. In the late 1940s: Brint and Karabel, p. 69.

page 162. One third: About 7.5% of 25- to 34-year-olds have associate degrees, and 25% have bachelor's degrees or higher degrees. *Digest of Educational Statistics 1996,* p. 18, Table 9.

page 162. In 1948: Brint and Karabel, pp. 68–71.

page 162. By the end: Data from Arthur Cohen and Florence Brawer, *The American Community College.* San Francisco: Jossey-Bass, 1982, reprinted in Brint and Karabel, p. 117.

page 167. "Put off . . .": Robert Zemsky, *What Employers Want: Employer Perspectives on Youth, the Youth Labor Market, and Prospects for a National System of Youth Apprenticeships.* Philadelphia: Trustees of the University of Pennsylvania, 1994, p. 6.

Chapter 12. Making It Simple

This chapter involved reporting at Fort Knox, Kentucky, the home of the Army's tank command, and at two of the nation's high-tech areas: Silicon Valley, California, and Boston, Massachusetts.

page 173. In 1992, for instance: W. Wayt Gibbs, "Taking Computers to Task," *Scientific American,* July 1997, p. 88.

page 174. "We're taking guys . . .": Major General Jeanne Holm, *Women in the Military: An Unfinished Revolution.* Novato, CA: Presido Press, 1982, p. 385.

page 175. M1 category-4 crews: Orr Kelly, *King of the Killing Zone: The Story of the M-1, America's Super Tank.* New York: Berkley Books, 1990, pp. 248–249.

page 176. The Sergeant York: Tom Clancy, *Armored Cav: A Guided Tour of an Armored Cavalry Regiment.* New York: Berkley Books, 1994, p. 56.

page 177. But nearly: Kathleen A. Quinkert, "Crew Performance Associated with the Simulation of the Commander's Independent Thermal Viewer (CITV)," U.S. Army

Research Institute for the Behavioral and Social Sciences, Technical Report 900, July 1990, pp. 30–31.

page 179. The Americans destroyed: Accounts of the Battle of 73 Easting appear in Clancy, pp. 256–261; see also Department of Defense, *Conduct of the Persian Gulf War: Final Report to Congress.* Washington, DC: Department of Defense, April 1992, pp. 750–751.

page 180. A-Deuce commanders: Robert S. Du Bois and Paul G. Smith, "Simulation-Based Assessment of Automated Command, Control, and Communications Capabilities for Armor Crews and Platoons: The Intervehicular Information System," U.S. Army Research Institute for the Behavioral and Social Sciences, Technical Report 918, Jan. 1991, pp. 98–99.

page 181. *Wall Street Journal:* George Anders, "Telephone Triage: How Nurses Take Calls and Control the Care of Patients from Afar," *The Wall Street Journal,* Feb. 4, 1997, p. A1. See also George Anders, *Health Against Wealth: HMOs and the Breakdown of Medical Trust.* Boston: Houghton Mifflin Co., 1996.

Chapter 13. The Balance of Trade

Reporting in this chapter comes from visits and interviews in Greenville, Spartanburg, and Iva, South Carolina.

page 189. Writer William Greider: William Greider, *One World, Ready or Not: The Manic Logic of Global Capitalism.* New York: Simon & Schuster, 1997.

page 190. Since 1986: South Carolina's apparel workforce shrank to 29,000 workers in 1996 from 45,000 in 1986. Nationally the apparel workforce dropped to 864,000 workers in 1996 from 1.1 million in 1986, according to the Bureau of Labor Statistics.

page 190. Sewing-machine operators: June 1997 figures, from South Carolina Employment Security Commission.

page 190. Between 1988 and 1994: South Carolina job losses in textile and apparel firms are based on Bureau of Labor Statistics figures. Statistics on jobs added by foreign-owned firms are from Mahnaz Fahim-Nader and William J. Zeile, "Foreign Direct Investment in the United States," *Survey of Current Business,* July 1996, p. 116.

page 191. Since 1987, South Carolina's: South Carolina's merchandise exports roughly tripled, to $6.7 billion in 1996 from $2.3 billion in 1987. During that same time, U.S. merchandise exports expanded at a slower pace, from $250.2 billion in 1987 to $612.1 billion in 1996. All the figures are from the Commerce Department.

page 191. In plants that export: Wage figures for exporters are reported in J. David Richardson and Karin Rindal, *Why Exports Matter: More!* Washington DC: Institute for International Economics and The Manufacturing Institute, 1996, p. 10. Wage figures for foreign-owned firms in the United States come from Ned G. Howenstine and William J. Zeile, "Characteristics of Foreign-Owned U.S. Manufacturing Establishments," *Survey of Current Business,* Jan. 1994, pp. 45–46.

page 192. After analyzing the economies: Jeffrey D. Sachs and Andrew Warner, "Economic Reform and the Process of Global Integration," *Brookings Papers on Economic Activity,* No. 1, 1995, pp. 1–95.

page 192. Economists: Jeffrey A. Frankel and David Romer, "Trade and Growth: An Empirical Investigation," Cambridge, MA: National Bureau of Economic Research (Working Paper No. 5476), March 1996.

Prior to the cross-country studies by Sachs and Warner, Frankel and Romer, and others, a number of scholars analyzed the trade policies of semi-industrialized countries and established that freer trade is associated with greater economic efficiency and growth. The reasons varied. Among the most important changes wrought by trade: Economic bottlenecks eased because of liberalized imports; foreign technology and competition prodded domestic firms to reform; and economic activity shifted into more efficient sectors. We are indebted to Columbia University economist Jagdish Bhagwati, who conducted one of the studies with Stanford's Anne Krueger, for pointing out the earlier work.

page 192. Novelist Dorothy Allison: Descriptions of Greenville in Dorothy Allison, *Bastard Out of Carolina.* New York: Plume/Penguin Group, 1993, pp. 17, 178.

page 194. Overall, the United States received: United Nations Conference on Trade and Development, *World Investment Report 1997: Transnational Corporations, Market Structure and Competition Policy.* New York: United Nations, 1997, annex Table B.1.

page 195. Blue-collar pay: June 1997 figures from South Carolina Employment Security Commission.

page 195. On average, foreign-owned plants: Howenstine and Zeile, pp. 45–46.

page 195. In Greenville County: In 1985, Spartanburg's per-capita income was 81.2% of the national average; in 1997, it had climbed to 85.6%. Greenville also gained. Per-capita income there was 91% of the national average in 1985, and 96.7% in 1997. Figures from Woods & Poole Economics, Inc., in Washington, DC.

page 196. In the 1920s: W. J. Cash, *The Mind of the South.* New York: Vintage Books, 1991, p. 260. Originally published in 1941.

page 198. "The inhabitant . . .": John Maynard Keynes, *The Economic Consequences of Peace,* cited in Sachs and Warner.

page 198. By that measure: In 1913, Great Britain's merchandise exports equaled 17.7% of its gross domestic product (GDP). In 1996, U.S. merchandise exports accounted for 8% of GDP. British historical statistic from Angus Maddison, *Monitoring the World Economy, 1820–1992.* Paris: OECD, 1995, p. 38. United States 1996 figures from Commerce Department.

page 199. By 1901: Rhonda Zingraff, "Facing Extinction?" in Jeffrey Leiter, Michael D. Schulman, and Rhonda Zingraff, eds., *Hanging by a Thread: Social Change in Southern Textiles.* Ithaca, NY: ILR Press, 1991, p. 207.

page 199. According to a study: James M. MacDonald, "Does Import Competition Force Efficient Production?" *The Review of Economics and Statistics,* Vol. 76, Nov. 1994, pp. 721–727.

page 200. In 1993: Bruce Ingersoll and Asra Q. Nomani, "Hidden Force: As Perot Bashes Nafta, A Textile Titan Fights It Quietly With Money," *The Wall Street Journal,* Nov. 15, 1993, p. A1.

page 201. Draper's business: Zach Coleman, "Textile Conglomerate in Indonesia Buys Draper Corp. of Kernersville," *Winston-Salem Journal,* Aug. 21, 1996, p. C12.

page 201. Milliken is secretive: Milliken & Co. won't comment on changes in its employment level. But a review of seven years of newspaper articles about Milliken shows that the company regularly estimated its employment at 14,000. Milliken's website now lists its employment at "more than 15,000."

page 201. Upstate South Carolina residents: "Buy foreign . . .": cited in Dudley Clendinen, "Textile Mills Squeezed in Modernization Drive," *The New York Times,* Oct. 26, 1985, p. 8.

page 201. Textile employment: Textile industry employment was 625,000 in 1997, 710,000 in 1987, and 898,000 in 1977. Figures from Bureau of Labor Statistics.

page 201. Textile makers were: In 1997, U.S. textile mills produced about 34 square yards of broadwoven goods per loom-hour; in 1987, the mills produced 12.9 square yards per loom-hour. Statistics from the American Textile Manufacturers Institute's "Textile Highlights," issues of March 1997 and June 1997.

page 203. Those workers remain: Jon D. Haveman, "The Effects of Trade-Induced Displacement on Unemployment and Wages," manuscript cited in Richardson and Rindal.

page 204. *Bobbin,* the leading: Susan L. Smarr, "Iva's Flight to the Top," *Bobbin,* May 1988.

page 205. Since NAFTA: Apparel employment dropped to 807,000 workers in January 1997; it had been 957,000 workers in January 1994, when NAFTA took effect. Statistics from the Bureau of Labor Statistics.

page 206. Exports to Mexico: United States–Mexico textile and apparel trade has boomed under NAFTA. American exports to Mexico of apparel—primarily, cut pieces of garments that are sewn in Mexico and shipped back to the United States—and of textiles rose to $2.8 billion in 1996; they were $1.6 billion in 1993, the year before NAFTA took effect. Imports of apparel from Mexico rose to $3.56 billion from $1.1 billion during the same time period. Meanwhile, apparel imports to the United States from Asia rose slightly: $16.8 billion in 1996, compared to $15.6 billion in 1993. The result: Garment trade with the United States is shifting from Asia to Mexico. Statistics from the American Textile Manufacturers Institute.

page 206. By 2017: Correspondence with J. David Richardson and testimony by C. Fred Bergsten before the House Ways and Means Committee, "The Imperative and Urgency of New Fast-Track Legislation," March 18, 1997.

page 206. Eliminating clothing tariffs: Gary Clyde Hufbauer and Kimberly Ann Elliot, *Measuring the Costs of Protection in the United States.* Washington, DC: Institute for International Economics, 1994, p. 89.

page 206. The Congressional Budget Office: Congressional Budget Office, *Trade Restraints and the Competitive Status of the Textile, Apparel, and Nonrubber-Footwear Industries.* Washington, DC, December 1991, pp. xi–xii.

Chapter 14. Imports: The Consumer's Friend

In addition to our reporting on New Zealand, Argentina, and the United States, this chapter relies on reporting in Japan by *The Wall Street Journal's* David Hamilton.

page 208. Racks of imported: U.S. Department of Labor, *Consumer Expenditure Survey,* various years. In 1972–1973, a four-person household spent 7.1% on clothing; in 1995, it spent 4.5%.

page 208. So do: Data provided by Standard & Poor's/DRI, personal communication.

page 210. As early as: Quoted in Douglas Irwin, *Against the Tide: An Intellectual History of Free Trade.* Princeton, NJ: Princeton University Press, 1996, p. 53.

page 210. In just four years: From Japan Tariff Association and Japan Electronic Industry Development Association.

page 212. "Daily life . . .": Quoted in Patrick Massey, *New Zealand: Market Liberalization in a Developed Economy.* New York: St. Martin's Press, 1995, pp. 188–189.

page 213. Before the reforms: Massey, p. 110.

page 213. "Overseas trips . . .": Michael Carter, "Bringing Home the Cup," *Christchurch (N.Z.) Press,* Sept. 13–14, 1995.

page 213. "After much time . . .": Massey, p. 23.

page 214. In 1985: *OECD Economic Surveys: New Zealand 1994.* Paris: Organization for Economic Cooperation and Development, 1994, p. 85.

page 214. New Zealand consumers: Data on sales and imports of cars come from the Motor Vehicles Dealers Institute, Wellington, New Zealand.

page 215. Between 1987 and 1990: Data from Statistics New Zealand, private communication.

page 215. Economists Liliana: Liliana and Rainer Wilkelmann, "Tariffs, Quotes and Terms of Trade: The Case of New Zealand," Christchurch, New Zealand: University of Canterbury, May 1997. Unpublished.

page 215. "Of course . . .": Carter, 1995.

page 215. Output per person: Angus Maddison, *Monitoring the World Economy, 1820–1992.* Paris: Organization for Economic Cooperation and Development, 1995, pp. 194–195.

page 215. Today, despite: *World Development Indicators 1997.* Washington, DC: The World Bank, 1997, Table 1.1.

page 215. An early: Alan M. Taylor, "External Dependence, Demographic Burdens, and Argentina's Economic Decline after the Belle Époque," *Journal of Economic History,* Vol. 52, Dec. 1992, pp. 907–908.

page 216. By 1980: *World Development Indicators,* Table 4.12, pp. 174–176.

page 216. Argentina's trade: See Alan M. Taylor, *On the Costs of Inward Looking Development: Historical Perspectives on Price Distortions, Growth and Divergence in Latin America from the 1930s to the 1980s.* Cambridge, MA: National Bureau of Economic Research, (Working Paper 5432), Jan. 1996.

page 216. Argentina's per-capita: Taylor, 1992, p. 911.

page 216. The average tariff: "Argentina—Recent Economic Developments." Washington, DC: International Monetary Fund, November 1995, p. 40. Also, Jonathan Friedland, "As Argentine Economy Booms, Workers Fret They'll Be Left Behind," *The Wall Street Journal,* June 25, 1997, p. A1.

page 216. An economy: International Monetary Fund, p. 1.

page 216. Imports of all kinds: World Bank, Table 4.7, p. 154.

page 216. Sales of imported: International Monetary Fund, p. 61.

page 217. "The purpose . . .": Paul Krugman, *Peddling Prosperity.* New York: W. W. Norton & Co., 1994, pp. 259–260.

Chapter 15. Prospering Together

To profile Bangalore and the Indian software industry, we interviewed programmers and managers at a dozen software companies in Bangalore and Bombay, along with venture capitalists and financial analysts in the two cities. Pradeep Kar, chairman of Microland ltd., and N. R. Narayana Murthy, chairman of Infosys Technologies Ltd., both of Bangalore, were especially helpful in giving a broad overview of the Indian software efforts.

page 219. In the United States: The U.S. software industry employed 619,400 people in 1996, according to the Business Software Alliance, and the number will increase to 1,030,500 by 2005. Statistics from *Building an Information Economy.* Washington, DC: Business Software Alliance, June 1997, pp. 5–6.

page 220. U.S. multinational companies: In 1994, U.S. multinationals employed 18.9 million people in the United States and 7 million people abroad. In 1982, the numbers were almost the same. Multinationals based in the United States employed 18.7 million in the United States and 6.6 million abroad. Statistics from Raymond J. Mataloni Jr., and Mahnaz Fahim-Nader, "Operations of U.S. Multinational Companies: Preliminary Results from the 1994 Benchmark Survey," *Survey of Current Business,* Dec. 1996, p. 12.

page 220. When wages plummet: S. Lael Brainard and David A. Riker, "Are U.S. Multinationals Exporting U.S. Jobs?" Cambridge, MA: National Bureau of Economic Research (Working Paper No. 5958), March 1, 1997.

page 220. Searching for strategies: *Global Economic Prospects and the Developing Countries: 1995.* Washington, DC: World Bank, 1995, p. 51.

page 221. Despite the fear: Between 1975 and 1994, imports from countries with manufacturing wages that are less than half of those paid in the United States grew from 2.4% of gross domestic product (GDP) to 3.6% of GDP. During that same time period, imports from countries with manufacturing wages at least equal to those paid in the United States grew from 0.6% to 3% of GDP. Treasury and Commerce Department analyses.

page 222. By the year 2000: Jim Rohwer, *Asia Rising: Why America Will Prosper as Asia's Economies Boom.* New York: Simon & Schuster, 1995, p. 32.

page 222. Indians call Bangalore: Many of the details of Bangalore history come from an interview with India's prominent sociologist, M. N. Srinivas, at his home in Bangalore, and from his essay, "Reminiscences of a Bangalorean," published in Bangalore: *Scenes from an Indian City.* Bangalore: Gangarams Publications Private Ltd.

page 222. Bangaloreans endure: *Sunday Times of India,* Bangalore edition, April 6, 1997.

page 224. Journalists William Wolman: William Wolman and Anne Colamosca, *The Judas Economy.* Reading, MA: Addison-Wesley Publishing Co., 1997, p. 88.

page 224. Foreign policy analyst: John Stremlau, "Dateline Bangalore: Third World Technopolis," *Foreign Policy,* No. 102, Spring 1996, p. 166.

page 224. Exports of Indian: National Association of Software and Service Companies, *The Software Industry in India: 1996.* New Delhi: NASSCOM, 1996, pp. 40, 49.

page 224. About 60%: Sanjay Anand, "NASSCOM Refutes Govt's Software Export Figures," *The Economic Times,* Feb. 1, 1997.

page 224. One firm: *Computers Today* (New Delhi), Vol. 13, No. 145, March 1997, p. 200.

page 225. One group: Cited in John M. Broder and Laurence Zuckerman, "Computers Are the Future, but Remain Unready for It," *The New York Times,* April 7, 1997, p. A1.

page 226. Writing in the: Shabnam Minwalla, "Indian Software in Bodyshopper Trap," *The Times of India,* (Mumbai), April 3, 1997.

page 227. After the *New York Times:* Edward A. Gargan, "India Booming as a Leader in Software for Computers," *The New York Times,* Dec. 29, 1993, p. A1.

page 229. There are thirty-nine: Statistics on Indian ownership of personal computers from the *Statistical Outline of India, 1996–97,* Tata Services Ltd., Mumbai, p. 251.

page 229. By early 1997: India's Internet population is estimated in "India's Sole ISP Stops Taking New Subscribers," *AdAge Daily Online,* Feb. 19, 1997. The U.S. Internet Population is reported in a *Business Week*/Harris poll, "A Census in Cyberspace," *Business Week,* May 5, 1997, p. 84.

page 230. The Information Technology: *Help Wanted: The IT Workforce at the Dawn of a New Century.* Arlington, VA: ITAA, Feb. 1997, pp. 5, 10.

page 230. Unemployment among: Unemployment statistics compiled by the Institute of Electrical and Electronics Engineers, Washington, DC.

page 231. That appraisal: Edward Yourdon's remarkable turnaround can be seen by comparing his 1992 book, *Decline & Fall of the American Programmer,* p. 1, with his 1996 book, *Rise & Resurrection of the American Programmer.* Both are published by Prentice Hall PTR, Englewood Cliffs, NJ.

page 233. India's National Association: Software groups in the two countries differ over how to count exports of software that arrive by modem or that are copied legitimately from master disks shipped to India. American software analysts also privately argue that India's NASSCOM inflates its figures to boost the standing of the Indian industry. But there's no evidence that NASSCOM's figures are any less reliable than figures routinely published by U.S. market research companies.

page 235. By a 40% to 17% margin: Poll numbers from a *Business Week*/Harris poll, "Freer Trade Gets an Unfriendly Reception," *Business Week,* Sept. 22, 1997, p. 34.

page 236. At most, he figures: Among economists, the argument over whether trade with low-wage nations undermines wages in the United States is as nasty as a barroom brawl. Overwhelmingly, economists say that technology has played a much more important role in worsening the wage gap between skilled and unskilled labor than trade has. Two economists, Edward Leamer of UCLA and Adrian Wood of the University of Sussex in England, have gained a following for their arguments that trade is the main culprit.

However, both their arguments have deep flaws. Using detailed quantitative analyses, Leamer can demonstrate that cheap imports diminished wages among apparel workers in the 1970s. But his data don't show a similar result in the 1980s, even though imports continued to climb through the 1980s. Wood must literally multiply by four his negative findings on the effects of trade before he can show broad consequences. Given those problems, Leamer and Wood are distinctly in the minority among economists.

But common sense says that trade must have some effect on wages. In one of the more evenhanded reviews of the subject, *Has Globalization Gone Too Far?,* Harvard economist Dani Rodrik argues: "If one believes that expanded trade has been a source of many of the good things that advanced industrial economies have experienced in the last few decades, one is forced to presume that trade also had many of the negative consequences that its opponents have alleged." (Dani Rodrik, *Has Globalization Gone Too Far?* Washington, DC: Institute for International Economics, 1997, p. 12.)

Still, the question remains: What share of wage inequality results from trade with low-wage nations? The answer: Not much.

page 236. Increased imports cost: Jeffrey D. Sachs and Howard J. Shatz, "Trade and Jobs in U.S. Manufacturing," *Brookings Papers on Economic Activity,* No. 1, 1994, p. 7.

page 236. A study by three: George J. Borjas, Richard B. Freeman, and Lawrence F. Katz, "How Much Do Immigration and Trade Affect Labor Market Outcomes?" *Brookings Papers on Economic Activity,* No. 1, 1997, pp. 1–67.

Chapter 16. The End of Work?

Joseph Schumpeter's theory of creative destruction inspired this chapter, which was reported in Silicon Valley.

page 238. In Kurt Vonnegut's novel: Kurt Vonnegut, *Player Piano.* New York: Bantam Doubleday Dell Publishing Group Inc., 1988, p. 243. Originally published in 1952.

page 238. At the time: Vonnegut's comments about his work at General Electric are cited in David F. Noble, *Forces of Production: A Social History of Industrial Automation.* New York: Oxford University Press, 1986, pp. 359–360. Noble's book examines GE's failure to get automated machine tools to work efficiently in factories.

page 239. Failure didn't stop: Robert Jastrow, "The Robots Are Coming, The Robots Are Coming," *Peninsula Ties Tribune, Family Weekly,* Oct. 23, 1983.

page 239. The U.S. robot industry: According to the Robotics Industries Association, U.S.-based robotic companies sold 9,709 robots in 1996, worth $934.3 million—a record year for revenue. Overall, companies in the United States own 72,000 robots.

page 239. That's about one-fourth: A study by Harrison Price Company, of San Pedro, California, for Bowling Inc., an industry trade group, estimates that Americans spend $4.3 billion a year on bowling, including bowling-lane charges and sales of bowling equipment.

page 239. In 1942: Joseph A. Schumpeter, *Capitalism, Socialism and Democracy, Third Edition.* New York: Harper Colophon Books, 1975, pp. 81–87. The third edition was originally published in 1950.

page 239. In terms of jobs: Statistics from the Committee for Economic Development, *American Workers and Economic Change,* 1996, p. 16.

page 240. Since then, telephone industry: Statistics on communications employment from Bureau of Labor Statistics and Cellular Telecommunications Industry Association.

page 241. The Global Internet: Estimate by Takuma Amano and Robert Blohm for the Global Internet Project, a group created by the Information Technology Association of America, a computer industry trade group.

page 241. Separate surveys: New media companies employ 71,500 in the greater New York metropolitan area, according to "New York New Media Industry Survey," commissioned for Empire State Development, April 15, 1996. In the greater Boston area, new media employment is estimated at 86,000 in the "Economic Impact Study," published by the Massachusetts Interactive Media Council in 1996. San Francisco new media employment is 62,000, according to a report cited in Steve Lohr, "New York Area Is Forging Ahead in New Media," *The New York Times,* April 15, 1996, p. D1.

page 244. Karl Marx: George Basalla, *The Evolution of Technology.* New York: Cambridge University Press, 1996, pp. 110–112. Originally published in 1988.

page 244. In the mid-1800s: Basalla, pp. 118–119.

page 244. With admirable candor: Neal H. Rosenthal, "Evaluating the 1990 Projections of Occupational Employment," *Monthly Labor Review,* Aug. 1992, pp. 45–46.

page 245. Technology critic: Jeremy Rifkin, *The End of Work.* New York: G.P. Putnam's Sons, 1995, p. 5.

page 245. In a panel discussion: Trudy E. Bell, "Employment Roundtable: $urvival Calls for More Than Technical Fitness," *IEEE Spectrum,* March 1996, p. 22.

page 245. The mind does far more: Theodore Roszak, *The Cult of Information.* Berkeley, CA: University of California Press, 1994, p. xxiii.

Chapter 17. What's to Be Done

For recommendations about government policy, we turned for advice to a number of authorities who have long experience in either making policy or studying it. Especially helpful were: University of Maryland trade economist I. M. Destler; Stanford University economic historian Paul David; Harvard University immigration expert George Borjas; Harvard economic historian Claudia Goldin; Stanford economist Paul Romer; Harvard economist Thomas Kane; and former head of the Pentagon's Advanced Research Projects Agency, Craig Fields.

page 251. We agree with: E. J. Dionne Jr., *They Only Look Dead: Why Progressives Will Dominate the Next Political Era.* New York: Simon & Schuster, 1996, p. 297.

page 252. State and local governments: American Association of Community Colleges Website: <www.aacc.nche.edu>.

page 253. Massachusetts is considering: Richard Chacon and Kate Zernike, "Tuition-Free Community Colleges Eyed," *Boston Globe,* Aug. 1, 1997, p. 1.

page 253. Teenagers from the best-off: Data by Thomas Kane of Harvard University, cited in David Wessel, "The Outlook: Rising Cost of College Interests the Politicians," *The Wall Street Journal,* Dec. 30, 1996, p. A1.

page 254. It's no coincidence: Statistics about nurses from American Association of Community Colleges Website.

page 255. In 1995, the General Accounting Office: Budget of the United States Government, fiscal year 1996, p. 22.

page 255. "The point is . . .": Robert Reich press briefing at Carl Sandburg Community College, Galesburg, Illinois, Jan. 19, 1995, as cited in the White House Press Office transcript.

page 256. Compared to its main: Science and Engineering Indicators 1996. Washington, DC: National Science Foundation, appendix tables 4–33 and 4–34.

page 257. Today, the federal government spends: Budget of the United States Government, fiscal year 1998, historical tables, Table 9–7.

page 257. They listed a series of boondoggles: For an authoritative account of government technology failures, see Linda R. Cohen and Roger G. Noll, *The Technology Pork Barrel.* Washington, DC: The Brookings Institution, 1991.

page 257. In 1843, Congress appropriated: Brooke Hindle and Steven Lubar, *Engines of Change: The American Industrial Revolution 1790–1860.* Washington, DC: Smithsonian Institution Press, 1986, p. 86.

page 257. The ubiquitous computer network: Katie Hafner and Matthew Lyon, *Where Wizards Stay Up Late: The Origins of the Internet.* New York: Simon & Schuster, 1996, p. 38.

page 258. IBM argued: Hafner and Lyon, p. 80.

page 259. After Britain invented: Gregory Clark, "Why Isn't the Whole World Developed? Lessons from the Cotton Mills," *Journal of Economic History,* Vol. XLVII, No. 1, March 1987, p. 142.

page 259. Those tariffs: Paul David, personal correspondence.

page 259. But J. Bradford DeLong: J. Bradford DeLong, "Trade Policy and America's Standard of Living: An Historical Perspective," in Susan M. Collins, ed., *Imports, Exports and the American Worker.* Washington, DC: Brookings Institution, forthcoming.

page 261. The most glaring problem: Article 29 of the NAFTA Supplemental Agreement on Labor Cooperation says that arbitration boards may consider allegations of a "persistent pattern of failure by the Party complained against to effectively enforce its occupational safety and health, child labor or minimum wage technical standards." The right to organize is relegated to Annex 1, which enumerates "labor principles." Arbitration panels aren't authorized to consider violations of those principles.

page 262. As a result: National Research Council, *The New Americans: Economic, Demographic, and Fiscal Effects of Immigration.* Washington, DC: National Academy Press, 1997, Table 2.4, and estimates by George Borjas of Harvard University.

Selected Bibliography

Adams, Henry. *The Education of Henry Adams.* New York: Modern American Library, 1931. (Originally published in 1907.)

Allison, Dorothy. *Bastard Out of Carolina.* New York: Plume/Penguin Group, 1993.

Alsop, Stewart. "The Trouble with Software Is . . . It Sucks!" *Fortune,* June 10, 1996, pp. 100–101.

—. *American Workers and Economic Change.* Washington, DC: Committee for Economic Development, 1996.

Anders, George. "Telephone Triage: How Nurses Take Calls and Control the Care of Patients from Afar." *The Wall Street Journal,* February 4, 1997, p. A1.

Autor, David, Lawrence F. Katz, and Alan B. Krueger. *"Computing Inequality: Have Computers Changed the Labor Market?"* Cambridge, MA: National Bureau of Economic Research (Working Paper No. 5956), March 1997.

Baily, Martin Neil, and Alok K. Chakrabarti. *Innovation and the Productivity Crisis.* Washington, DC: Brookings Institution, 1988.

Barlett, Donald L., and James B. Steele. *America: Who Stole the Dream?* Kansas City: Andrews and McMeel, 1996.

Bartel, Ann P. "Training, Wage Growth, and Job Performance: Evidence from a Company Database." *Journal of Labor Economics,* Vol. 13, No. 3, 1995, pp. 401–425.

Bartel, Ann P., and Frank R. Lichtenberg. "The Comparative Advantage of Educated workers in Implementing New Technology." *The Review of Economics and Statistics,* Vol. LXIX, No. 1, February 1987, pp 1–11.

Basalla, George. *The Evolution of Technology.* New York: Cambridge University Press, 1996. (Originally published in 1988.)

Black, Sandra E., and Lisa M. Lynch. *How to Compete: The Impact of Workplace Practices and Information Technology on Productivity.* Washington, DC: U.S. Department of Labor, September 1996.

Blodgett, Richard. *Johnson & Higgins at 150 Years.* Lyme, CT: Greenwich Publishing Group Inc., 1995.

Borjas, George J., Richard B. Freeman, and Lawrence F. Katz. "How Much Do Immigration and Trade Affect Labor Market Outcomes?" *Brookings Papers on Economic Activity,* No. 1, 1997, pp. 1–67.

Brands, H. W. *Reckless Decade: America in the 1890s.* New York: St. Martin's Press, 1995.

Brint, Steven, and Jerome Karabel. *The Diverted Dream: Community Colleges and the Promise of Educational Opportunity in America, 1900–1985.* New York: Oxford University Press, 1989.

Bristol, W. *A Trade Survey of Newton, Iowa, 1922.* Iowa City: The State University of Iowa, 1922.

Brynjolfsson, Erik, Amy Austin Renshaw, and Marshall van Alstyne. "The Matrix of Change." *Sloan Management Review,* Winter 1997, pp. 37–54.

Brynjolfsson, Erik, and Lorin Hitt. "Paradox Lost? Firm-level Evidence on the Returns to Information Systems Spending." *Management Science,* Vol. 42, No. 4, April 1996, pp. 541–558.

"Business Week Reports to Readers on: Computers." *Business Week,* June 21, 1958, pp. 68–92.

Campbell-Kelly, Martin, and William Aspray. *Computer: A History of the Information Machine.* New York: Basic Books, 1996.

Carey, Max L., and Kevin Kasunic. "Evaluating the 1980 Projections of Occupational Employment." *Monthly Labor Review,* July 1982, pp. 22–30.

Cash, W. J. *The Mind of the South.* New York: Vintage Books/Random House, 1991. (Originally published in 1941.)

Clark, Gregory. "Why Isn't the Whole World Developed? Lessons from the Cotton Mills." *Journal of Economic History,* Vol. XLVII, No. 1, March 1987, pp. 141–173.

Danziger, Sheldon, and Peter Gottschalk. *America Unequal.* New York: Russell-Sage Foundation, and Cambridge, MA: Harvard University Press, 1995.

David, Paul A. "Computer and Dynamo: The Modern Productivity Paradox in a Not-Too-Distant Mirror." Center for Economic Policy Research, Stanford University, Reprint No. 5, July 1995, pp. 315–347. (Originally published by the Organization of Economic Cooperation and Development in 1991.)

Davis, Bob. "Painful Figures: Despite His Heritage, Prominent Economist Backs Immigration Cuts." *The Wall Street Journal,* April 26, 1996, p. A1.

Davis, Bob, and Lucinda Harper. "Reason for Hope: Middle Class's Fears About Coming Years Might Be Misguided." *The Wall Street Journal,* March 29, 1995, p. A1.

Denison, Edward F. *Accounting for Slower Economic Growth: The United States in the 1970s.* Washington, DC: Brookings Institution, 1979.

Denison, Edward F. *Trends in American Economic Growth, 1929–1982.* Washington, DC: Brookings Institution, 1985.

Dertrouzos, Michael L., Richard K. Lester, and Robert M. Solow. *Made in America: Regaining the Productive Edge.* New York: HarperPerennial, 1990. (Originally published by the MIT Commission on Industrial Productivity in 1989.)

Devine, Warren D., Jr. "From Shafts to Wires: Historical Perspective on Electrification." *The Journal of Economic History,* Vol. 43, No. 2, June 1983, pp. 347–372.

Dionne Jr., E. J. *They Only Look Dead: Why Progressives Will Dominate the Next Political Era.* New York: Simon & Schuster, 1996.

Dreiser, Theodore. *Sister Carrie.* New York: New American Library, 1961. (Originally published in 1900.)

Drucker, Peter. "Jobs in the New Economy." *Aspen Institute Quarterly,* Vol. 6, No. 1, Winter 1994, pp. 27–35.

DuBoff, Richard B. "The Introduction of Electric Power in American Manufacturing." *Economic History Review,* Vol. 20, December 1967, pp. 509–518.

Elliott, Michael. *The Day Before Yesterday: Reconsidering America's Past, Rediscovering the Present.* New York: Simon & Schuster, 1996.

Fahim-Nader, Mahnaz, and William J. Zeile. "Foreign Direct Investment in the United States." *Survey of Current Business,* July 1996, pp. 102–130.

Frankel, Jeffrey A., and David Romer. "Trade and Growth: An Empirical Investigation." Cambridge, MA: National Bureau of Economic Research (Working Paper No. 5476), March 1996.

Freeman, Richard B. *The Overeducated American.* New York: Academic Press, 1976.

Freeman, Richard B., and Lawrence F. Katz, eds. *Differences and Changes in Wage Structures.* Chicago: University of Chicago Press, 1995.

Friedan, Betty. *The Feminine Mystique.* New York: Bantam Doubleday Dell Publishing Group Inc., 1984. (Originally published in 1963.)

Funk, A. B. *Fred L. Maytag: A Biography.* Cedar Rapids, Iowa: Torch Press, 1936.

Galbraith, John Kenneth. *The Affluent Society.* Boston: Houghton Mifflin Co., 1958.

Gibson, William. *Virtual Light.* New York: Bantam Books, 1994.

Gitlin, Todd. *The Sixties: Years of Hope, Days of Rage.* New York: Bantam Books, 1993.

Goldin, Claudia. "How America Graduated from High School: 1910 to 1960." Cambridge, MA: National Bureau of Economic Research (Working Paper No. 4762), June 1994.

Goldin, Claudia. "The Political Economy of Immigration Restriction in the United States, 1890 to 1921." In Claudia Goldin and Gary D. Libecap, eds., *The Regulatory Economy: A Historical Approach to Political Economy.* Chicago: University of Chicago Press, 1994.

Goldin, Claudia, and Lawrence F. Katz. "The Decline of Noncompeting Groups: Changes in the Premium to Education, 1890 to 1940." Cambridge, MA: National Bureau of Economic Research (Working Paper No. 5202), August 1995.

Goldin, Claudia, and Lawrence F. Katz. "Technology, Skill, and the Wage Structure: Insights from the Past." *American Economic Review,* Vol. 86, No. 2, May 1996, pp. 252–257.

Goldin, Claudia, and Lawrence F. Katz. "Why the United States Led in Education: Lessons from Secondary School Expansion, 1910 to 1940." Cambridge, MA: National Bureau of Economic Research (Working Paper No. 6144), August 1997.

Goldin, Claudia, and Robert A. Margo. "The Great Compression: The Wage Structure in the United States at Mid-Century." *The Quarterly Journal of Economics,* Vol. CVII, Issue 1, February 1992, pp. 1–32.

Gottschalk, Peter, and Timothy M. Smeeding. "Cross-National Comparisons of Earnings and Income Inequality." *Journal of Economic Literature,* Vol. XXXV, No. 2, June 1997, pp. 633–687.

Greenwood, Jeremy, and Mehmet Yorukoglu. "1974." Rochester Center for Economic Research (Working Paper No. 429), September 1996.

Greider, William. *One World, Ready or Not: The Manic Logic of Global Capitalism.* New York: Simon & Schuster, 1997.

Grubb, Norton. *Learning to Work: The Case for Reintegrating Job Training and Education.* New York: Russell-Sage Foundation, 1996.

Grubb, W. Norton. "The Economic Benefits of Sub-Baccalaureate Education." September 1995, unpublished.

Gurda, John. *The Bradley Legacy: Lynde and Harry Bradley, Their Company and Their Foundation.* Milwaukee: The Lynde and Harry Bradley Foundation, 1992.

Hafner, Katie, and Matthew Lyon. *Where Wizards Stay Up Late: The Origins of the Internet.* New York: Simon & Schuster, 1996.

Halberstam, David. *The Fifties.* New York: Fawcett Columbine, 1994.

Hall, Lucy. *History of the Schools of Jasper County.* Circa 1959 (privately printed). (In the collection of the Jasper County Historical Society.)

Hamilton, David P. "New Imports: One Tokyo Family Loves Its Italian Shoes and American Broccoli." *The Wall Street Journal,* March 14, 1997, p. A14.

Hammond, John Winthrop. *Men and Volts: The Story of General Electric.* Philadelphia: J. B. Lippincott Co., 1941.

Handle, Brooke, and Steven Lumbar. *Engines of Change: The American Industrial Revolution 1790–1860.* Washington, DC: Smithsonian Institution Press, 1986.

Harrington, Michael. *The Other America: Poverty in the United States.* New York: Collier Books, Macmillan Publishing Co., 1994. (Originally published in 1962.)

Henry, O. "Springtime à la Carte." In *41 Stories.* New York: Penguin Books USA Inc., 1984.

Hoover, Robert, and Hoover, John. *An American Quality Legend: How Maytag Saved Our Moms, Vexed the Competition, and Presaged America's Quality Revolution.* New York: McGraw-Hill, Inc., 1993.

Howenstine, Ned G., and William J. Zeile. "Characteristics of Foreign-Owned U.S. Manufacturing Establishments." *Survey of Current Business,* January 1994. pp. 34–59.

Hufbauer, Gary Clyde, and Kimberly Ann Elliott. *Measuring the Costs of Protection in the United States.* Washington, DC: Institute for International Economics, 1994.

Hughes, Thomas P. *American Genesis: A Century of Invention and Technological Enthusiasm.* New York: Penguin Books, 1989 (paperback, 1990).

Hughes, Thomas P. *Networks of Power: Electrification in Western Society, 1880–1930.* Baltimore: The Johns Hopkins University Press, 1983.

Hurto, Larry Ray, ed. *A History of Newton, Iowa.* 1992 (privately printed).

Ichniowski, Casey, Kathryn Shaw, and Giovanna Prennushi. "The Effects of Human Resource Management Practices on Productivity: A Study of Steel Finishing Lines." *American Economic Review,* Vol. 86, No. 3, June 1997, pp. 291–313.

Ingersoll, Bruce, and Asra Q. Nomani. "Hidden Force: As Perot Bashes Nafta, A Textile Titan Fights It Quietly With Money." *The Wall Street Journal,* November 15, 1993. p. A1.

Ingrassia, Paul, and Joseph B. White. *Comback: The Fall and Rise of the American Automobile Industry.* New York: Touchstone Books, 1995.

Iowa Retired Teachers Association, ed. *The Fourth R: Readin', Ritin', Rithmetic and Reminisin'.* 1976 (privately printed).

Jacobson, Louis S., Robert J. LaLonde, and Daniel G. Sullivan. "The Returns from Classroom Training for Displaced Workers." Westat Inc., October 1994.

Jones, Landon Y. *Great Expectations: America and the Baby Boom Generation.* New York: Coward, McCann & Geoghegan, 1980.

Kane, Thomas K., and Cecilia Elena Rouse. "Labor Market Returns to Two- and Four-Year Colleges." *American Economic Review,* Vol. 85, No. 3, June 1995, pp. 600–614.

Kanigel, Robert. *The One Best Way: Frederick Winslow Taylor and the Enigma of Efficiency.* New York: Viking Penguin, Penguin Books USA Inc., 1997.

Kanter, Rosabeth Moss. *World Class: Thriving Locally in the Global Economy.* New York: Simon & Schuster, 1995.

Kearns, David T., and David A. Nadler. *Prophets in the Dark: How Xerox Reinvented Itself and Beat Back the Japanese.* New York: HarperCollins Publishers Inc., 1993.

Kelley, Maryellen R. "Productivity and Information Technology: The Elusive Connection." *Management Science,* Vol. 40, No. 11, November 1994, pp. 1406–1425.

Kruger, Alan. "How Computers Have Changed the Wage Structure: Evidence from Microdata, 1984–1989." *The Quarterly Journal of Economics,* Vol. 108, No. 1, February 1993, pp. 33–60.

Krug, Edward A. *The Shaping of the American High School 1880–1920.* Madison: University of Wisconsin Press, 1969.

Krug, Edward A. *The Shaping of the American High School, Volume 2, 1920–1941.* Madison: University of Wisconsin Press, 1972.

Krugman, Paul. *The Age of Diminished Expectations.* Cambridge, MA: MIT Press, 1990.

Krugman, Paul. *Peddling Prosperity.* New York: W. W. Norton & Co., 1994.

Landau, Ralph, Timothy Taylor, and Gavin Wright, eds. *The Mosaic of Economic Growth.* Stanford, CA: Stanford University Press, 1996.

Landauer, Thomas K. *The Trouble with Computers: Usefulness, Usability and Productivity.* Cambridge, MA: MIT Press, 1995.

Lawler, Edward E., III. *From the Ground Up.* San Francisco: Jossey-Bass Inc., 1996.

Lawrence, Robert Z. *Single World, Divided Nations? International Trade and OECD Labor Markets.* Washington, DC: Brookings Institution Press; Paris: OECD Development Center, 1996.

Lebergott, Stanley. *The American Economy.* Princeton, NJ: Princeton University Press, 1976.

Lebergott, Stanley. *The Americans: An Economic Record,* New York: W. W. Norton & Co. Inc., 1984.

Lebergott, Stanley. *Manpower in Economic Growth: The American Record Since 1800.* New York: McGraw-Hill Book Co., 1964.

Lebergott, Stanley. *Pursuing Happiness: American Consumers in the Twentieth Century.* Princeton, NJ: Princeton University Press, 1993.

Lehr, William, and Frank R. Lichtenberg. "Computer Use and Productivity Growth in Federal Government Agencies, 1987–1992." Cambridge, MA: National Bureau of Economic Research (Working Paper No. 5616), June 1996.

Leigh, Duane E., and Andrew M. Gill. "Labor Market Returns to Community Colleges: Evidence for Returning Adults." *Journal of Human Resources,* Vol. XXXII, No. 2, Spring 1997, pp. 334–353.

Leiter, Jeffrey, Michael D. Schulman, and Rhonda Zingraff, eds. *Hanging by a Thread: Social Change in Southern Textiles.* Ithaca, NY: ILR Press, 1991.

Levy, Frank, with Richard Murnane and Lijian Chen. "Education and Skills for the U.S. Work Force." *Aspen Institute Quarterly,* Vol. 6, No. 1, Winter 1994, pp. 42–61.

Lewis, Sinclair. *Babbitt.* New York: New American Library Inc., 1961. (Originally published in 1922.)

Lynch, Lisa M., ed. *Training and the Private Sector: International Comparisons.* Chicago: University of Chicago Press, 1994.

Lynch, Lisa M., and Sandra E. Black. "Beyond the Incidence of Training: Evidence from a National Employers Survey." Cambridge, MA: National Bureau of Economic Research (Working Paper No. 5231), August 1995.

MacDonald, James M. "Does Import Competition Force Efficient Production?" *The Review of Economics and Statistics,* Vol. 76, November 1994, pp. 721–727.

Maddison, Angus. *Dynamic Forecasts in Capitalist Development.* Oxford, England: Oxford University Press, 1991.

Maddison, Angus. *Monitoring the World Economy, 1820–1992.* Paris: OECD, 1995.

Madrick, Jeffrey. *The End of Affluence.* New York: Random House, 1995.

Mandell, Lewis. *The Credit Card Industry: A History.* Boston: Twayne Publishers, 1990.

Mandell, Richard D. *Paris 1900: The Great World's Fair.* Toronto: University of Toronto Press, 1967.

Mansfield, Edwin. *The Economics of Technological Change.* New York: W. W. Norton and Co. Inc., 1968.

Massey, Patrick. *New Zealand: Market Liberalization in a Developed Economy.* New York: St. Martin's Press Inc., 1995.

Mataloni Jr., Raymond J., and Mahnaz Fahim-Nader. "Operations of U.S. Multinational Companies: Preliminary Results from the 1994 Benchmark Survey." *Survey of Current Business,* December 1996, pp. 11–37.

Mincer, Jacob. "Investment in U.S. Education and Training." Cambridge, MA: National Bureau of Economic Research (Working Paper No. 4844), August 1994.

Minwalla, Shabnam. "Indian Software in Bodyshopper Trap." *The Times of India* (Mumbai), April 3, 1997.

Murnane, Richard J., Frank Levy, and John B. Willett. "The Growing Importance of Cognitive Skills in Wage Determination." Cambridge, MA: National Bureau of Economic Research (Working Paper 5076), March 1995.

Murphy, Kevin M., W. Craig Riddell, and Paul M. Romer. "Wages, Skills and Technology in the United States and Canada." Canadian Institute for Advanced Research (Working Paper ECWP-98), 1997. (In Elhanan Helpman, ed. *General-Purpose Technologies.* Cambridge, MA: MIT Press, forthcoming.)

National Association of Software and Service Companies. *The Software Industry in India: 1996.* New Delhi: NASSCOM, 1996.

National Research Council. *Information Technology in the Service Society: A Twenty-First-Century Lever.* Washington, DC: National Academy Press, 1994.

National Research Council. *The New Americans: Economic, Demographic and Fiscal Effects of Immigration.* Washington, DC: National Academy Press, 1997.

Noble, David F. *Forces of Production: A Social History of Industrial Automation.* New York: Oxford University Press, 1986.

Nocera, Joseph. *A Piece of the Action: How the Middle Class Joined the Money Class.* New York: Simon & Schuster, 1994.

Norwood, Janet, ed. *Widening Earnings Inequality: Why and Why Now.* Washington, DC: Urban Institute, 1994.

Nye, David E. *Electrifying America: Social Meanings of a New Technology.* Cambridge, MA: MIT Press, 1995.

O'Neill, Eugene. *Dynamo.* New York: Horace Liveright, Inc., 1929.

Orlikowski, Wanda J. "Learning from Notes: Organizational Issues in Groupware Implementation." *The Information Society,* Vol. 9, 1993, pp. 237–250.

Patterson, James T. *Grand Expectations.* New York: Oxford University Press, 1996.

Reich, Robert B. *Locked in the Cabinet.* New York: Alfred A. Knopf, 1997.

Rice, Elmer. "The Adding Machine." In *Three Plays.* New York: Hill and Wang, 1965. (First performed in 1923.)

Richardson, J. David, and Karin Rindal. *Why Exports Matter: More!* Washington, DC: Institute for International Economics, and The Manufacturing Institute, 1996.

Rifkin, Jeremy. *The End of Work.* New York: G. P. Putnam's Sons, 1995.

Rohwer, Jim. *Asia Rising: Why America Will Prosper as Asia's Economies Boom.* New York: Simon & Schuster, 1995.

Rosenberg, Nathan. "Factors Affecting the Diffusion of Technology." *Explorations in Economic History,* Vol. 10, Fall 1972, pp. 3–33.

Rosenberg, Nathan. "Uncertainty and Technological Change." Federal Bank of Boston's Conference on Technology and Growth, June 1996, Chatham, MA.

Rosenthal, Neal H. "Evaluating the 1990 Projections of Occupational Employment." *Monthly Labor Review,* August 1992, pp. 32–48.

Roszak, Theodore. *The Cult of Information.* Berkeley: University of California Press, 1994.

Roueche, John E., Lynn Sullivan Taber, and Suanne D. Roueche. *The Company We Keep: Collaboration in the Community College.* Washington, DC: American Association of Community Colleges, 1995.

Rubin, Howard A., and Heidi Albrecht Battaglia. "An Overview of the Results of the 1996 Worldwide Benchmark Project." Rubin Systems Inc., Pound Ridge, NY, 1997.

Sachs, Jeffrey D., and Andrew Warner. "Economic Reform and the Process of Global Integration." *Brookings Papers on Economic Activity,* No. 1, 1995, pp. 1–95.

Sachs, Jeffrey D., and Howard J. Shatz. "Trade and Jobs in U.S. Manufacturing." *Brookings Papers on Economic Activity,* No. 1, 1994, pp. 1–84.

Samuelson, Robert J. *The Good Life and Its Discontents: The American Dream in the Age of Entitlement.* New York: Times Books, 1995.

Sazanami, Yoko, Shujiro Urata, and Hiroki Kawai. *Measuring the Costs of Protection in Japan.* Washington, DC: Institute for International Economics, 1995.

Schumpeter, Joseph A. *Capitalism, Socialism and Democracy: Third Edition.* New York: Harper Colophon Books, 1975. (Originally published in 1942.)

Sichel, Daniel E. *The Computer Revolution: An Economic Perspective.* Washington, DC: The Brookings Institution, 1997.

Sinclair, Upton. *The Jungle.* New York: New American Library Inc., 1960. (Originally published in 1906.)

Smith, Robert L. *Student Soldier Statesman Servant: An Autobiography.* 1992 (privately printed).

Stoll, Clifford. *Silicon Snake Oil: Second Thoughts on the Information Highway.* New York: Anchor Books, 1995.

Stremlau, John. "Dateline Bangalore: Third World Technopolis." *Foreign Policy,* No. 102, Spring 1996, pp. 153–168.

Suarez, Fernando F., Michael A. Cusumano, and Charles H. Fine. "An Empirical Study of Flexibility in Manufacturing." *Sloan Management Review,* Fall 1995, pp. 25–32.

Surette, Brian. "The Impacts of Two-Year College on the Labor Market and Schooling Experiences of Young Men." Washington, DC: Federal Reserve Board (Financial and Economic Discussion Series 1997-44), June 1997.

Taylor, Alan M. "On the Costs of Inward-Looking Development: Historical Perspectives on Price Distortions, Growth and Divergence in Latin America from the 1930s to the 1980s." Cambridge, MA: National Bureau of Economic Research (Working Paper 5432), January 1996.

Taylor, Alan M. "External Dependence, Demographic Burdens, and Argentina's Economic Decline after the Belle Époque." *Journal of Economic History,* Vol. 52, December 1992, pp. 907–936.

Taylor, Alan M. "Three Phases of Argentine Economic Growth." Cambridge, MA: National Bureau of Economic Research (Historical Working Paper No. 60), October 1994.

Tenner, Edward. *Why Things Bite Back: Technology and the Revenge of Unintended Consequences.* New York: Alfred A. Knopf, 1996.

Twain, Mark. *A Connecticut Yankee in King Arthur's Court.* New York: Bantam Books, 1981. (Originally published in 1889.)

Tyack, David B. *The One Best System.* Cambridge, MA: Harvard University Press, 1974.

Tyler, John, Richard J. Murnane, and Frank Levy. "Are More College Graduates Really Taking 'High School' Jobs?" *Monthly Labor Review,* Vol. 118, No. 2, December 1995, pp. 18–27.

Ueda, Reed. *Avenues to Adulthood: The Origins of the High School and Social Mobility in an American Suburb.* Cambridge, England: Cambridge University Press, 1987.

United Nations Conference on Trade and Development. *World Investment Report 1997: Transnational Corporations, Market Structure and Competition Policy.* New York: United Nations, 1997.

U.S. Department of Education, National Center for Education Statistics. *Digest of Education Statistics 1996.* Washington, DC: U.S. Government Printing Office, 1996.

U.S. Department of Labor. *Report on the American Workforce.* Washington, DC: U.S. Government Printing Office, 1995.

Vonnegut, Kurt. *Player Piano.* New York: Bantam Doubleday Dell Publishing Group Inc., 1988. (Originally published in 1952.)

Weinberg, Daniel H. *A Brief Look at Postwar U.S. Income Inequality.* Washington, DC: U.S. Bureau of the Census, 1996.

Wessel, David. "By the Bootstraps: One Family's Rebound Shows the Possibilities in the Economy of the 90's." *The Wall Street Journal,* August 12, 1994, p. A1.

Wessel, David. "Reaching Back: Scanning the Future, Economic Historian Plumbs Distant Past." *The Wall Street Journal,* February 13, 1996, p. A1.

Wessel, David. "Up the Ladder: Low Unemployment Brings Lasting Gains to Town in Michigan." *The Wall Street Journal,* June 24, 1997, p. A1.

Wessel, David, and Bob Davis. "In the Middle of the Middle: Two Families' Stories." *The Wall Street Journal,* March 29, 1995, p. B1.

Wilkes, Paul. *Trying Out the Dream: A Year in the Life of an American Family.* Philadelphia: J. B. Lippincott Co., 1975.

Wolman, William, and Anne Colamosca. *The Judas Economy.* Reading, MA: Addison-Wesley Publishing Co., 1997.

Woodrow, Ivan F. *A Century of Industrial Progress in Newton.* Newton, IA: News Printing Inc., 1961.

Woodrow, Joseph A. *Some Pretty Girl, Please Write.* Santa Barbara, CA: Don Jose Publications, 1967.

World Bank. *Global Economic Prospects and the Developing Countries: 1995.* Washington, DC: World Bank, 1995.

Yourdon, Edward. *Decline & Fall of the American Programmer.* Englewood Cliffs, NJ: Prentice-Hall PTR/Simon & Schuster, 1992.

Yourdon, Edward. *Rise & Resurrection of the American Programmer.* Upper Saddle River, NJ: Prentice-Hall PTR/Simon & Schuster, 1996.

Zemsky, Robert. *What Employers Want: Employer Perspectives on Youth, the Youth Labor Market, and Prospects for a National System of Youth Apprenticeships.* Philadelphia: Trustees of the University of Pennsylvania, 1994.

Acknowledgments

A book requires help from many people. We've been especially fortunate.

Without doubt, *The Wall Street Journal's* Washington bureau is the best place to practice journalism in America. Alan Murray, the Washington bureau chief, helped conceive the *Journal* stories that led to this book, gave us time to work on the project, and helped us strengthen our argument. Paul Steiger, the managing editor, encouraged us and reminded us that few stories are as important as the future of the American standard of living.

Our agents, Wes Neff and Bill Leigh, suggested that the *Journal* articles were the basis of a book, found us a first-rate publisher, and negotiated brilliantly on our behalf. They gave us the best advice authors can receive: "Write the best book you can, and we'll worry about selling it."

Our friend and mentor, June Kronholz, read every word of the manuscript, some chapters several times, and made our writing more elegant and incisive—her hallmarks as a journalist. She helped us figure out the difference between a newspaper story and a book chapter, saved us from untold errors of grammar and logic, and helped blend the prose of two writers into one book. Most important, June reassured us that we could write a book.

Our editor at Times Books, John Mahaney, made timely suggestions about the organization of the book and helped us stitch seventeen chapters into a cohesive whole. Maryan Malone, a thorough and precise copy editor with Publications Development Company, made sure our sentences said what we intended.

A number of economists generously helped us think through our argument. We relied heavily on the writings of economic historians Paul David of Stanford University and Claudia Goldin of Harvard University, as well as on numerous phone and e-mail conversations with them. Their criticism sharpened the book and gave us a taste of the terror their students must feel. We also are grateful to professors Jagdish Bhagwati, Thomas Kane, Alan Krueger, Lawrence Katz, Paul Krugman, Thomas Landauer, Lisa Lynch, Frank Levy, Kevin Murphy, and Paul Romer, as well as to Craig Fields, head of the Pentagon's Defense Science Board. The conclusions and predictions in this book—as well as any errors—are ours, not theirs.

We are heavily indebted to people who opened their lives to us, especially Dennis and Ann Kerley, and Jim and Ann Marie Blentlinger, who were the subjects of one of the *Wall Street Journal* stories, and Randy and Nancy Kohrs. They were friendly, thoughtful, and honest— even when they were answering the impertinent questions journalists sometimes pose.

As we searched the country for the examples to illustrate our points, we received valuable assistance from Ron Krajnovich of Maytag Corporation, Hans and Darlene Brosig of the Jasper County (Iowa) Historical Society, Ted Hutton and Shawna Todd of Allen-Bradley Co., Bill Wilson and Al Modugno of Johnson & Higgins, Robin Bird of Schneider National Corporation, Graciela Figueroa of Cuyahoga Community College, Lon Maggart, formerly of Fort Knox, Bobby Hitt of BMW AG, Renetta Greene of Greenville, South Carolina, Anupam Khanna of the World Bank and his wife Alka, Indi Rajasingham and G. Anandalingam of InterStrat Inc., Pradeep Kar of Microland Ltd., N. R. Narayana Murthy of Infosys Technologies Inc., Dennis Puffer of Miller Brewing Company, John Holohan of Miller's United Auto Workers local, and Michael Tutko and his staff at Xerox Corporation.

At *The Wall Street Journal,* Cindy Harper and Chris Georges worked with us on the original stories. David Hamilton did reporting in Japan for the book. Tom Petzinger kept our spirits high, as only he can. George Anders, Bhushan Bahree, Helene Cooper, John Harwood, Walt Mossberg, Tom Ricks, Jerry Seib, and Joe White offered advice and encouragement. Mimi Kirk and Sarah McBride tracked down obscure articles and facts.

Our children, Daniel and Joanna Davis, and Julia and Benjamin Wessel, put up with our too-frequent absences and grumpiness. They are the brightest part of our future, and our stiffest critics. As one of them said, "Dad, in twenty years I'll tell you if you were right."

Above all, we're grateful to our wives, Debra Bruno, who adeptly helped edit the manuscript, and Naomi Karp. For two years, they picked up the slack at home, tolerated us when we were home physically but working on the book mentally, and encouraged us to do the best book we could. Without them, this book would have been impossible.

Index